BERLITZ®

for

By the staff of Berlitz Guides

How best to use this phrase book

● We suggest that you start with the **Guide to pronunciation** (pp. 6-9), then go on to **Some basic expressions** (pp. 10-15). This gives you not only a minimum vocabulary, but also helps you get used to pronouncing the language.

● Consult the **Contents** pages (3-5) for the section you need. In each chapter you'll find travel facts, hints and useful information. Simple phrases are followed by a list of words applicable to the situation.

● Separate, detailed contents lists are included at the beginning of the extensive **Eating out** and **Shopping guide** sections (Menus, p. 39, Shops and services, p. 97).

● If you want to find out how to say something in Greek, your fastest look-up is via the **Dictionary** section (pp. 161-189). This not only gives you the word, but is also cross-referenced to its use in a phrase on a specific page.

● If you wish to learn more about constructing sentences, check the **Basic grammar** (pp. 156-160).

● Note the **colour margins** are indexed in Greek and English to help both listener and speaker. And, in addition, there is also an **index in Greek** for the use of your listener.

● Throughout the book, this symbol 🞄☞ suggests phrases your listener can use to answer you. If you still can't understand, hand this phrase book to the Greek-speaker to encourage pointing to an appropriate answer.

Revised edition – 1st printing
Printed in Hong Kong

Contents

Acknowledgments

We are particularly grateful to Andreas Kyriacou and Pantelis Kotatis for their help in the preparation of this book, and to Dr. T.J.A. Bennett who devised the phonetic transcription.

Guide to pronunciation

The alphabet

Here are the characters which comprise the Greek alphabet. The left-hand columns show the printed capital and small letters, while written letters are shown in the centre columns. The column on the right gives you the Greek names of these letters.

Α	α	_A_	_a_	**ahl**fah
Β	β	_B_	_b_	**vee**tah
Γ	γ	_Γ_	_γ_	**ghah**mah
Δ	δ	_Δ_	_δ_	**dhehl**tah
Ε	ε	_Ε_	_ε_	**ehp**seelonn
Ζ	ζ	_Z_	_z_	**zee**tah
Η	η	_H_	_n_	**ee**tah
Θ	θ	_Θ_	_θ_	**thee**tah
Ι	ι	_I_	_ι_	**yee**otah
Κ	κ	_K_	_u_	**kah**pah
Λ	λ	_Λ_	_λ_	**lahm**dhah
Μ	μ	_M_	_μ_	mee
Ν	ν	_N_	_ν_	nee
Ξ	ξ	_Ξ_	_ξ_	ksee
Ο	ο	_O_	_o_	**omee**kron
Π	π	_Π_	_π_	pee
Ρ	ρ	_P_	_ρ_	ro
Σ	σ ς	_Σ_	_σ_ ς	**seegh**mah
Τ	τ	_T_	_τ_	tahf
Υ	υ	_Y_	_υ_	**eep**seelonn
Φ	φ	_φ_	_φ_	fee
Χ	χ	_X_	_χ_	khee
Ψ	ψ	_Ψ_	_ψ_	psee
Ω	ω	_Ω_	_ω_	**omeh**ghah

Just knowing the alphabet is not, of course, enough to pronounce Greek. We're offering you a helping hand by providing "imitated pronunciation" throughout this book. This chapter is intended to make you familiar with the transcription we have devised, and to help you get used to the sounds of Greek.

As a minimum vocabulary for your trip, we have selected a number of basic words and phrases under the title "Some basic expressions" (pages 10–15).

An outline of Greek sounds

The imitated pronunciation should be read as if it were English except for any special rules set out below. It is based on Standard British pronunciation, though we have tried to take account of General American pronunciation also. Of course, the sounds of any two languages are never exactly the same; but if you follow carefully the examples given here, you will have no difficulty in reading our transcriptions in such a way as to make yourself understood.

Letters shown in **bold** should be read with more stress (louder) than the others.

Vowels

Letter	Approximate pronunciation	Symbol	Example	
α	like the vowel in car, but pronounced farther forward in the mouth	ah	άρωμα	**ah**rommah
ε	like e in sell	eh	μέρα	**meh**rah
η, ι, υ	like ee in meet	ee	κύριος	**kee**reeoss
ο, ω	like o in got	o	παρακαλώ	pahrahkah**lo**

Consonants

β	like **v** in **v**ine	v	βιβλίο	**v**eevl**ee**o
γ	1) before α, o, ω, ου, and consonants, a voiced version of the **ch** sound in Scottish loch	gh	μεγάλος	meh**gh**ahloss
	2) before ε, αι, η, ι, υ, ει, οι, like **y** in **y**et	y	γεμάτος	**y**ehmahtoss
δ	like **th** in **th**is	dh	δεν	**dh**ehn
ζ	like **z** in **z**oo	z	ζεστός	**z**ehstoss
θ	like **th** in **th**ing	th	θα	**th**ah
κ	like **k** in **k**it	k	καλός	**k**ahloss
λ	like **l** in **l**emon	l	λάθος	**l**ahthoss
μ	like **m** in **m**an	m	μέσα	**m**ehssah
ν	like **n** in **n**ew	n	νέος	**n**ehoss
ξ	like **x** in si**x**	ks	έξω	eh**ks**o
π	like **p** in **p**ot	p	προς	**p**ross
ρ	like **r** in **r**ed	r	πριν	p**r**een
σ, ς	1) before voiced consonants (β, γ, δ, ζ, μ, ν, ρ) like **z** in **z**oo	z	κόσμος	ko**z**moss
	2) elsewhere, like **s** in **s**ee	s/ss	Πόσο στο	**posso** sto
τ	like **t** in **t**ea	t	τότε	**t**otteh
φ	like **f** in **f**ive	f	φέρτε	**f**ehrteh
χ	like **ch** in Scottish loch	kh	άσχημος	ahs**kh**eemoss
ψ	like **ps** in dro**ps**y	ps	διψώ	dhee**ps**o

Groups of letters

αι	like **e** in g**e**t	eh	είναι	**ee**neh
ει, οι	like **ee** in s**ee**	ee	πείτε	p**ee**teh

ου	like **oo** in r**oo**t	oo	μου	moo
αυ	1) before voiceless consonants (θ, κ, ξ, κ, σ, τ, φ, χ, ψ), like **uff** in p**uff**	ahf	αυτό	ahf**to**
	2) elsewhere, similar to **ave** in h**ave**	ahv	αυγό	ahv**gho**
ευ	1) before voiceless consonants, like **ef** in l**eft**	ehf	ευχή	ehf**khee**
	2) elsewhere, like **ev** in l**eve**l	ehv	ευμενής	ehv**meh**neess
γγ	like **ng** in li**ng**er	ngg	Αγγλία	ahn**gg**leeah
γκ	1) at the beginning of a word like **g** in **g**o	g	γκαμήλα	gahmeelah
	2) in the middle of a word, like **ng** in li**ng**er	ngg	άγκυρα	**ahng**geerah
γξ	like **nks** in li**nks**	ngks	φάλαγξ	fahlahngks
γχ	like **ng** followed by the **ch** of Scottish lo**ch**	ngkh	μελαγχολία	mehlahng-khol**lee**ah
μπ	1) at the beginning of a word, like **b** in **b**eer	b	μπορείτε	bor**ree**teh
	2) in the middle of a word, like **mb** in lu**mb**er	mb	Όλυμπος	olleemboss
ντ	1) at the beginning of a word, like **d** in **d**ear	d	ντομάτα	dommahtah
	2) in the middle of a word, like **nd** in u**nd**er	nd	κέντρο	**keh**ndro
τζ	like **ds** in see**ds**	dz	τζάκι	**dzah**kee

Accent marks

An accent (ά) above a vowel indicates the stressed syllable. A diaeresis (two dots) written over a letter means that the letter is pronounced separately from the previous one, e.g., **καιρός** is pronounced keh**ross**, but in **Κάϊρο**, the α and ι are pronounced separately, **kah**eero.

Some basic expressions

Yes.	Ναι.	neh
No.	Όχι.	okhee
Please.	Παρακαλώ.	pahrahkahlo
Thank you.	Ευχαριστώ.	ehfkhahreesto
Thank you very much.	Ευχαριστώ πολύ.	ehfkhahreesto pollee
That's all right/ You're welcome.	Εντάξει/ Ευχαρίστως.	ehndahksee/ ehfkhahreestoss

Greetings Χαιρετισμοί

Good morning.	Καλημέρα.	kahleemehrah
Good afternoon.	Καλησπέρα.	kahleespehrah
Good evening.	Καλησπέρα.	kahleespehrah
Good night.	Καληνύκτα.	kahleeneektah
Goodbye.	Αντίο.	ahndeeo
This is Mr./Mrs./ Miss...	Ο κύριος/Η κυρία/ Η δεσποινίδα...	o keereeoss/ee keereeah ee dhehspeeneedhah
How do you do? (Pleased to meet you.)	Τι κάνετε;	tee kahnehteh
How are you?	Πως είστε;	poss eesteh
Very well, thanks. And you?	Πολύ καλά, ευχαριστώ. Και εσείς;	pollee kahlah ehfkhahreesto. keh ehsseess
How's life?	Τι κάνετε;	tee kahnehteh
Fine.	Καλά.	kahlah
I beg your pardon.	Με συγχωρείτε.	meh seengkhorreeteh
Excuse me. (May I get past?)	Συγγνώμη.	seenghnommee
Sorry!	Συγγνώμη!	seenghnommee

Questions   *Ερωτήσεις*

Where?	Που;	poo
How?	Πως;	poss
When?	Πότε;	**pot**teh
What?	Τι;	tee
Why?	Γιατί;	yeeah**tee**
Who?	Ποιος;	pee**oss**
Which?	Ποιος/Ποια/Ποιο;	pee**oss**/**pee**ah/**pee**o
Where is/are...?	Που είναι...;	poo **ee**neh
Where can I find/get...?	Που μπορώ να βρω/έχω...;	poo **bor**ro nah vro/**ehk**ho
How far?	Πόσο μακρυά;	**pos**so mahk**ree**ah
How long?	Σε πόσο χρόνο;	seh **pos**so **khron**no
How much/How many?	Πόσο/Πόσα;	**pos**so/**pos**sah
How much does this cost?	Πόσο κοστίζει αυτό;	**pos**so kos**tee**zee ahf**to**
When does ... open/close?	Πότε ανοίγει/ κλείνει...;	**pot**teh ah**nee**yee/**klee**nee
What do you call this/that in Greek?	Πως το λένε αυτό/ εκείνο στα Ελληνικά;	poss to **leh**neh ahf**to**/ eh**kee**no stah ehleenee**kah**
What does this/ that mean?	Τι σημαίνει αυτό/ εκείνο;	tee see**meh**nee ahf**to**/ eh**kee**no

Do you speak...?   *Μιλάτε...;*

Do you speak English?	Μιλάτε Αγγλικά;	mee**lah**teh ahngglee**kah**
Does anyone here speak English?	Μιλά κανείς Αγγλικά εδώ;	mee**lah** kah**nees**s ahngglee**kah** eh**dho**
I don't speak (much) Greek.	Δεν μιλώ (καλά) Ελληνικά.	dhehn **mee**lo (kah**lah**) ehleenee**kah**
Could you speak more slowly?	Μπορείτε να μιλάτε πιο αργά;	bor**ree**teh nah mee**lah**teh **pee**o ahr**ghah**

Could you repeat that?	Μπορείτε να το επαναλάβετε;	borreeteh nah to ehpahnahlahvehteh
Could you spell it?	Μπορείτε να το συλλαβήσετε;	borreeteh nah to seelahveessehteh
Please write it down.	Γράψτε το, παρακαλώ.	ghrahpsteh to pahrahkahlo
Can you translate this for me/us?	Μπορείτε να μου/ μας το μεταφράσετε;	borreeteh nah moo/mahss to mehtahfrahssehteh
Please point to the... in the book.	Παρακαλώ, δείξτε ... στο βιβλίο.	pahrahkahlo dheeksteh ... sto veevleeo
word	την λέξη	teen lehksee
phrase	την φράση	teen frahssee
sentence	την πρόταση	teen protahssee
Just a moment. I'll see if I can find it in this book.	Μια στιγμή. Να κοιτάξω εάν μπορώ να το βρω σε αυτό το βιβλίο.	meeah steeghmee. nah keetahkso ehahn borro nah to vro seh ahfto to veevleeo
I understand.	Καταλαβαίνω.	kahtahlahvehno
I don't understand.	Δεν καταλαβαίνω.	dhehn kahtahlahvehno
Do you understand?	Καταλαβαίνετε;	kahtahlahvehnehteh

Can/May...? Μπορώ...;

Can I have...?	Μπορώ να έχω...;	borro nah ehkho
Can we have...?	Μπορούμε να έχουμε...;	borroomeh nah ehkhoomeh
Can you show me?	Μπορείτε να μου δείξετε;	borreeteh nah moo dheeksehteh
I can't.	Δεν μπορώ.	dhehn borro
Can you tell me...?	Μπορείτε να μου πείτε...;	borreeteh nah moo peeteh
Can you help me?	Μπορείτε να με βοηθήσετε;	borreeteh nah meh voeetheessehteh
Can I help you?	Μπορώ να σας βοηθήσω;	borro nah sahss voeetheesso
Can you direct me to...?	Μπορείτε να μου δείξετε...;	borreeteh nah moo dheeksehteh

Wanting... *Ζητώντας...*

I'd like...	Θα ήθελα...	thah **ee**thehlah
We'd like...	Θα θέλαμε...	thah **the**hlahmeh
What do you want?	Τι θέλετε;	tee **the**hlehteh
Give me...	Δώστε μου...	**dho**steh moo
Give it to me.	Δώστε μου το.	**dho**steh moo to
Bring me...	Φέρτε μου...	**fehr**teh moo
Bring it to me.	Φέρτε μου το.	**fehr**teh moo to
Show me...	Δείξτε μου...	**dheek**steh moo
Show it to me.	Δείξτε μου το.	**dheek**steh moo to
I'm looking for...	Ψάχνω...	**psahkh**no
I'm hungry.	Πεινώ.	pee**no**
I'm thirsty.	Διψώ.	dhee**pso**
I'm tired.	Είμαι κουρασμένος/-η.	**ee**meh koorahz**meh**-noss/-ee
I'm lost.	Χάθηκα.	**khah**theekah
It's important.	Είναι σοβαρό.	**ee**neh sov**vah**ro
It's urgent.	Είναι επείγον.	**ee**neh eh**pee**ghonn

It is/There is... *Είναι/Υπάρχει...*

It is...	Είναι...	**ee**neh
Is it...?	Είναι...;	**ee**neh
It isn't...	Δεν είναι...	dhehn **ee**neh
Here it is.	Εδώ είναι.	eh**dho ee**neh
Here they are.	Εδώ είναι.	eh**dho ee**neh
There it is.	Εκεί είναι.	eh**kee ee**neh
There they are.	Εκεί είναι.	eh**kee ee**neh
There is/There are...	Υπάρχει/Υπάρχουν...	ee**pahr**khee/eepahr**khoon**
Is there/Are there...?	Υπάρχει/Υπάρχουν...;	ee**pahr**khee/eepahr**khoon**
There isn't/aren't...	Δεν υπάρχει/ υπάρχουν...	dhehn eepahr**khee**/ eepahr**khoon**
There isn't/aren't any.	Δεν υπάρχει/υπάρχουν καθόλου.	dhehn eepahr**khee**/ eepahr**khoon** kah**tho**lloo

It's... *Είναι...*

big/small	μεγάλος/μικρός*	mehghahloss/meekross
quick/slow	γρήγορος/αργός	ghreeghorross/ahrghoss
hot/cold	ζεστός/κρύος	zehstoss/kreeoss
full/empty	γεμάτος/άδειος	yehmahtoss/ahdheeoss
easy/difficult	εύκολος/δύσκολος	ehfkolloss/dheeskolloss
heavy/light	βαρύς/ελαφρύς	vahreess/ehlahfreess
open/shut	ανοικτός/κλειστός	ahneektoss/kleestoss
right/wrong	σωστός/λανθασμένος	sostoss/lahnthahzmehnoss
old/new	παλιός/καινούργιος	pahleeoss/kehnooryeeoss
old/young	γέρος/νέος	yehross/nehoss
beautiful/ugly	ωραίος/άσχημος	orrehoss/ahskheemoss
free (vacant)/ occupied	ελεύθερος/κατειλημμένος	ehlehfthehross/ kahteeleemehnoss
good/bad	καλός/κακός	kahloss/kahkoss
better/worse	καλύτερος/χειρότερος	kahleetehross/ kheerottehross
early/late	νωρίς/αργά	norreess/ahrghah
cheap/expensive	φτηνός/ακριβός	fteenoss/ahkreevoss
here/there	εδώ/εκεί	ehdho/ehkee

Quantities *Ποσότητες*

a little/a lot	λίγα/πολλά	leeghah/pollah
few/a few	λίγα/μερικά	leegah/mehreekah
much/many	πολύ/πολλοί	pollee/pollee
more/less	περισσότερα/ λιγότερα	pehreessottehrah/ leeghottehrah
more than/less than	περισσότερα από/ λιγότερα από	pehreessottehrah ahpo/ leeghottehrah ahpo
enough/too	αρκετά/πάρα πολύ	ahrkehtah/pahrah pollee
some/any	μερικά/αρκετά	mehreekah/ahrkehtah

---

* The endings of adjectives change according to gender and number, see the grammar section for a more detailed explanation.

A few more useful words   Περισσότερες χρήσι λέξεις

at	στο	sto
on	επάνω	ehpahno
in	μέσα	mehssah
to	προς	pross
after	μετά	mehtah
before (time)	πριν	preen
before (place)	πριν	preen
for	για	yeeah
from	από	ahpo
with	με	meh
without	χωρίς	khorreess
through	δια μέσου	dheeah mehssoo
towards	προς	pross
until	μέχρι	mehkhree
during	κατά την διάρκεια	kahtah teen dheeahrkeeah
next to	δίπλα από	dheeplah ahpo
near	κοντά	kondah
behind	πίσω από	peesso ahpo
between	ανάμεσα	ahnahmehssah
since	από	ahpo
above	επάνω	ehpahno
below	κάτω	kahto
under	κάτω από	kahto ahpo
inside	μέσα	mehssah
outside	έξω	ehkso
up	επάνω	epahno
down	κάτω	kahto
and	και	keh
or	ή	ee
but	αλλά	ahlah
not	δεν	dhehn
never	ποτέ	potteh
nothing	τίποτα	teepottah
very	πολύ	pollee
too (also)	επίσης	ehpeesseess
yet	ακόμη	ahkommee
soon	σύντομα	seendommah
now	τώρα	torrah
then	τότε	totteh
perhaps	ίσως	eessoss
only	μόνο	monno

Arrival

Passport control   Έλεγχος διαβατήριου

Here's my passport.	Ορίστε το διαβατήριο μου.	orreesteh to dheeahvah-teereeo moo
I'll be staying...	Θα μείνω...	thah **mee**no
a few days	λίγες μέρες	**lee**yehss **meh**rehss
a week	μια βδομάδα	meeah vdhomma**hdhah**
two weeks	δύο βδομάδες	**dhee**o vdhomma**hdhehss**
a month	ένα μήνα	**eh**nah **mee**nah
I don't know yet.	Δεν ξέρω ακόμα.	dhehn **kseh**ro ah**kom**mah
I'm here...	Είμαι εδώ...	**ee**meh eh**dho**
on holiday	για διακοπές	yeeah dheeah**kopp**ehss
on business	για δουλειά	yeeah dhoo**lee**ah
on a sightseeing tour	για περιοδεία στα αξιοθέατα	yeeah pehreeo**dhee**ah stah ahkseeo**theh**ahtah
I'm just passing through.	Είμαι περαστικός/-ή.	**ee**meh pehrahstee**koss**/-ee
I'm sorry, I don't understand.	Συγνώμη δεν, καταλαβαίνω.	seenghnommee dhehn kahtahlah**veh**hno
Does anyone here speak English?	Μιλά κανείς Αγγλικά εδώ;	**mee**lah kah**neess** ahng**glee**kah eh**dho**

ΤΕΛΩΝΕΙΟΝ
CUSTOMS

After collecting your luggage at the airport (αεροδρόμιο–ahehro**dhro**mmeeo) you have a choice. Use the green exit if you have nothing to declare, or the red exit if you are carrying items in excess of the permitted limit. Check through the chart on the following page for duty-free allowances into Greece.

εμπορεύματα για δήλωση goods to declare	τίποτα για δήλωση nothing to declare

	Cigarettes		Cigars		Tobacco	Spirits (liquor)		Wine
1	200	or	50	or	250 g.	1 l.	or	2 l.
2	300	or	75	or	400 g.	1¼ l.	or	5 l.

Perfume: 1) 50 g.   Toilet water: 1) ¼ l.
         2) 75 g.   2) ³/8 l.

1) visitors entering from non-EEC countries*
2) visitors entering from EEC countries*

I've nothing to declare.	Δεν έχω να δηλώσω τίποτε.	dhehn ehkho nah dheelosso teepotteh
I've...	Έχω...	ehkho
a carton of cigarettes	μια κούτα τσιγάρα	meeah kootah tseeghahrah
a bottle of ...	ένα μπουκάλι ...	ehnah bookahlee
It's for my personal use.	Είναι για προσωπική χρήση.	eeneh yeeah prossoppeekee khreessee
This is a gift.	Αυτό είναι ένα δώρο.	ahfto eeneh ehnah dhorro

Το διαβατήριο σας, παρακαλώ.	Your passport, please.
Έχετε τίποτα να δηλώσετε;	Do you have anything to declare?
Παρακαλώ ανοίξτε αυτή την αποσκευή.	Please open this bag.
Θα πρέπει να πληρώσετε φόρο για αυτό.	You'll have to pay duty on this.
Έχετε και άλλες αποσκευές;	Do you have any more luggage?

Άφηξη

---

* All allowances are subject to change without notice.

Baggage – Porter   *Αποσκευές – Αχθοφόρος*

Porter!	**Αχθοφόρε!**	ahkhthofforreh
Please take this...	**Παρακαλώ πάρτε...**	pahrahkahlo **pahrteh**
bag	**την τσάντα**	teen **tsahn**dah
luggage	**τις αποσκευές**	teess ahposkeh**vehss**
suitcase	**την βαλίτσα**	teen vah**lee**tsah
travelling bag	**το σακβουαγιάζ**	to sahkvooahyee**ahz**
That's mine.	**Αυτή είναι δική μου.**	ahf**tee** **ee**neh dhee**kee** moo
That's not mine.	**Αυτή δεν είναι δική μου.**	ahf**tee** dhehn **ee**neh dhee**kee** moo
Take this luggage...	**Πάρτε αυτές τις αποσκευές ...**	**pahrteh** ahf**tehss** teess ahposkeh**vehss**
to the bus/train	**στο λεωφορείο/τραίνο**	sto lehoforree**o**/**treh**no
to the luggage lockers	**στο τμήμα αποσκευών**	sto **tmee**mah ahposkeh**vonn**
There's one piece missing.	**Λείπει μια αποσκευή.**	**lee**pee meeah ahposkeh**vee**
How much is that?	**Πόσο κάνει αυτό;**	**posso kahn**ee ahfto
Where are the luggage trolleys (carts)?	**Που είναι τα καροτσάκια αποσκευών;**	poo **ee**neh tah kahrotsahkeeah ahposkeh**vonn**

Changing money   *Συνάλλαγμα*

Where's the currency exchange office?	**Που είναι το γραφείο αλλαγής συναλλάγματος;**	poo **ee**neh to grah**feeo** ahlah**yeess** seenahlahgh**mahtoss**
Where can I change some traveller's cheques (checks)?	**Που μπορώ να αλλάξω μερικά τράβελερς τσεκς;**	poo borro nah ahlahkso mehree**kah** trahvehlehrs tsehks
I want to change some dollars/pounds.	**Θα ήθελα να αλλάξω μερικά δολλάρια/μερικές Αγγλικές λίρες.**	thah eethehlah nah ahlahkso mehree**kah** dhollah-reeah/mehree**kehss** ahngleekehss **lee**rehss
Can you change this into drachmas?	**Μπορείτε να αλλάξετε αυτό σε δραχμές;**	bor**ee**teh nah ahlahksehteh ahfto seh dhrahkh**mehss**
What's the exchange rate?	**Ποια είναι η τιμή συναλλάγματος;**	peeah **ee**neh ee tee**mee** seenahlahgh**mahtoss**

BANK – CURRENCY, see page 129

Where is...? Πού είναι...;

Where is the...?	Πού είναι το...;	poo **ee**neh to
car hire	γραφείο νοίκιασης αυτοκινήτων	ghrah**fee**o **nee**keeahsseess ahftokke**enee**tonn
duty free shop	κατάστημα αφορολογήτων	kah**tah**steemah ahforrollo**yee**tonn
newsstand	περίπτερο	peh**reep**tehro
restaurant	εστιατόριο	ehsteeah**tor**reeo
ticket office	γραφείο εισιτηρίων	ghrah**fee**o eesseetee**ree**onn
tourist office	γραφείο τουρισμού	ghrah**fee**o tooreez**moo**
How do I get to...?	Πως μπορώ να πάω στο...;	poss bor**ro** nah **pah**o sto
Is there a bus into town?	Υπάρχει λεωφορείο για την πόλη;	ee**pahr**khee lehoffor**ree**o yeeah teen **pol**lee
Where can I get a taxi?	Που μπορώ να βρω ένα ταξί;	poo bor**ro** nah vro **eh**nah tah**ksee**
Where can I hire (rent) a car?	Που μπορώ να νοικιάσω ένα αυτοκίνητο;	poo bor**ro** nah neekee**ahs**so **eh**nah ahftok**kee**neeto

Hotel reservation Κράτηση ξενοδοχείου

Do you have a hotel guide?	Έχετε οδηγό ξενοδοχείου;	**eh**khehteh odhee**gho** ksehnodho**khee**oo
Could you reserve a room for me?	Μπορείτε να μου κρατήσετε ένα δωμάτιο;	bor**ree**teh nah moo krah**tees**sehteh **eh**nah dhom**mah**teeo
in the centre	στο κέντρο της πόλης	sto **kehn**dro teess **pol**leess
near the railway station	κοντά στο σιδηροδρο-μικό σταθμό	kon**dah** sto seedheero-dhrom**mee**ko stahth**mo**
a single room	ένα μονό δωμάτιο	**eh**nah mon**no** dhom**mah**teeo
a double room	ένα διπλό δωμάτιο	**eh**nah dhee**plo** dhom**mah**teeo
not too expensive	όχι πολύ ακριβό	**o**khee pol**lee** ahkree**vo**
Where is the hotel/ boarding house?	Που είναι το ξενοδοχείο/πανσιόν;	poo **ee**neh to ksehnodho-**khee**o/pahnsee**onn**
Do you have a street map?	Έχετε οδηκό χάρτη;	**eh**khehteh odhee**ko khahr**tee

HOTEL/ACCOMMODATION, see page 22

Car hire (rental) Ενοικίαση αυτοκινήτου

Car hire is fairly expensive. In high season book early, and give advance warning of any special requirements (air conditioning, automatic transmission). In principle, most companies require an international driving licence (Britons excepted), but will normally accept any national licence if it is more than 1 year old. Third party insurance is usually included.

I'd like to hire (rent) a car.	Θα ήθελα να νοικιάσω ένα αυτοκίνητο.	thah **ee**thehlah nah neek**ee**ahsso **e**hnah ahftok**kee**neeto
small	μικρό	meek**ro**
medium-sized	μετρίου μεγέθους	mehtr**ee**oo mehy**eh**thooss
large	μεγάλο	meh**ghah**lo
automatic	αυτόματο	ahftom**mah**to
I'd like it for a day/a week.	Θα το ήθελα για μια μέρα/βδομάδα.	thah to **ee**thehlah yeeah meeah **meh**rah/ vdhom**mah**dhah
Are there any weekend arrangements?	Υπάρχουν διευκολύνσεις για το Σαββατοκύριακο;	eepahrk**hoon** dheeehf**ko**lleens**ee**ss yeeah to sahvahtok**kee**reeahko
Do you have any special rates?	Έχετε ειδικές τιμές;	**e**hkhehteh eedhee**kehss** teem**ehss**
What's the charge per day/week?	Ποια είναι η τιμή για μια μέρα/βδομάδα;	peeah **ee**neh ee teem**ee** yeeah meeah **meh**rah/ vdhom**mah**dhah
Is mileage included?	Συμπεριλαμβάνονται τα χιλιόμετρα;	seembehreelahm**vah**nondeh tah kheelee**om**mehtrah
What's the charge per kilometre?	Ποια είναι η τιμή για κάθε χιλιόμετρο;	peeah **ee**neh ee teem**ee** yeeah **kah**theh kheelee**om**mehtro
I want full insurance.	Θέλω μικτή ασφάλεια.	**the**hlo meek**tee** ahs**fah**leeah
I've a credit card.	Έχω μια πιστωτική κάρτα.	**e**hkho meeah peestotteek**kee kah**rtah
What's the deposit?	Πόση είναι η εγγύηση;	**posse ee**neh ee ehngg**ee**eessee
Here's my driving licence.	Ορίστε η άδεια οδηγήσεως μου.	orr**ee**steh ee **ah**dheeah odheey**ee**ssehoss moo

CAR, see page 75

Taxi *Ταξί*

Taxis are metered in cities and are reasonably cheap, but additional charges (for night travel, luggage, waiting or over special holidays) are not shown. In the country, taxis are not always metered, but fixed rates do exist. Negotiate the approximate fare before leaving.

Where can I get a taxi?	Που μπορώ να βρω ένα ταξί;	poo borro nah vro **eh**nah tah**ksee**
Please get me a taxi.	Βρέστε μου ένα ταξί, παρακαλώ.	**vreh**steh moo **eh**nah tah**ksee** pahrahkah**lo**
What's the fare to...?	Ποια είναι η τιμή για...;	peeah **ee**neh ee tee**mee** yeeah
How far is it to...?	Πόσο μακρυά είναι...;	**posso** mahkree**ah** **ee**neh
Take me to...	Να με πάτε...	nah meh **pah**teh
this address	σε αυτή την διεύθυνση	seh ahf**tee** teen dhee**ehf**theensee
the airport	στο αεροδρόμιο	sto ahehrodh**rom**meeo
the town centre	στο κέντρο της πόλης	sto **kehn**dro teess **polless**
the ... Hotel	στο ξενοδοχείο...	sto ksehnodho**khee**o
Turn left/right at the next corner.	Στρίψτε αριστερά/ δεξιά στην επόμενη γωνία.	**streep**steh ahreesteh**rah**/ dhehksee**ah** steen eh**pom**mehnee ghon**neeah**
Go straight ahead.	Πηγαίνετε ίσια.	pee**yeh**nehteh **ees**seeah
Please stop here.	Παρακαλώ σταματήστε εδώ.	pahrahkah**lo** stahmah**tee**steh eh**dho**
I'm in a hurry.	Είμαι βιαστικός/-ή.	**ee**meh veeahstee**koss**/-ee
Could you drive more slowly?	Μπορείτε να οδηγήτε πιο αργά;	bor**ree**teh nah odhee**yee**teh peeo ahr**ghah**
Could you help me carry my luggage?	Μπορείτε να με βοηθήσετε να μεταφέρω τις αποσκευές μου;	bor**ree**teh nah meh voee**thees**sehteh nah mehtah**feh**ro teess ahposskeh**vehss** moo
Could you wait for me?	Μπορείτε να με περιμένετε;	bor**ree**teh nah meh pehree**meh**nehteh
I'll be back in 10 minutes.	Θα επιστρέψω σε 10 λεπτά.	thah ehpee**streh**pso seh 10 leh**ptah**

TIPPING, see inside back-cover

Hotel – Other accommodation

Hotel reservations are essential during the high season. But if you arrive without one, go to the EOT (national tourist board). The local tourist police will also advise on accommodation throughout the area.

Ξενοδοχείο (ksehnodho**khee**o)	Hotel. There's a high proportion of new hotels in Greece. The government classifies them in six categories according to comfort offered. After luxury class, there are categories A to E. Most hotels can insist on half or full board.
Μοτέλ (mot**tehl**)	Motel. There are a few motels which have sprung up in the past years along principal highways.
Πανδοχείο (pahndho**khee**o)	Inn. These are found in small towns and offer simple but good accommodation.
Πανσιόν (pahnsee**onn**)	Boarding house. Located in cities, room and board is available at a modest price.
Ξενώνας νεότητος (ksehnonnahss nehotteetoss)	Youth hostel. These are sometimes known as ''youth hostels'' in English. They are cheap and clean, and accommodation is usually dormitory-style. Your stay may be limited to five days. You will need an international membership card.
Διαμερίσματα (dheeahmeh-**reez**mahtah)	Apartment, bungalow. These are plentiful, particularly on the islands and in coastal resorts. However, you should book well in advance for the high season.
Δωμάτια (dho**mmah**teeah)	Rooms. These are often advertised in English, mainly on the islands. Accommodation will be cheap and clean, usually with use of the family bathroom and kitchen.

Can you recommend a hotel/boarding house?	Μπορείτε να μου συστήσετε ένα ξενοδοχείο/πανσιόν;	bor**ree**teh nah moo seestee**ss**sehteh **eh**nah ksehnodho**khee**o/ pahnsee**onn**
Are there any flats (apartments) vacant?	Υπάρχουν άδεια διαμερίσματα;	eepahrkhoon **ah**dheeah dheeahmeh**reez**mahtah

Checking in — Reception   Στην ρεσεπσιόν

My name is...	Το όνομα μου είναι...	to **onno**mmah moo **ee**neh
I've a reservation.	Έχω κρατήσει δωμάτιο.	**eh**kho krah**tee**ssee dhom**mah**teeo
We've reserved two rooms.	Έχομε κρατήσει δύο δωμάτια.	**eh**kommeh krah**tee**ssee **dhee**o dhom**mah**teeah
Here's the confirmation.	Εδώ είναι η επιβεβαίωση.	**ehdho eeneh ee** ehpeevehveh**hoss**ee
Do you have any vacancies?	Έχετε ακόμη άδεια δωμάτια;	**eh**khehteh ah**kommee** **ah**dheeah dhom**mah**teeah
I'd like a ... room.	Θα ήθελα ένα... δωμάτιο.	thah **ee**thehlah **ehnah**... dhom**mah**teeo
single/double	μονό/διπλό	**monno**/dhee**plo**
I'd like a room with...	Θα ήθελα ένα δωμάτιο με...	thah **ee**thehlah **ehnah** dhom**mah**teeah meh
twin beds	δύο κρεββάτια	**dhee**o krev**vah**teeah
a double bed	ένα διπλό κρεββάτι	**ehnah** dhee**plo** krev**vah**tee
a bath	μπάνιο	**bah**neeo
a shower	ντους	dooss
a balcony	μπαλκόνι	bahl**konn**ee
a view	θέα	**theh**ah
We'd like a room...	Θα θέλαμε ένα δωμάτιο...	thah **theh**lahmeh **ehnah** dhom**mah**teeo
in the front	στη πρόσοψη	stee **pross**opsee
at the back	στο πίσω μέρος	sto **peess**o **mehross**
facing the lake/ the mountains/ the sea	προς την λίμνη/ τα βουνά/ την θάλασσα	pross teen **leem**nee/ tah voo**nah**/ teen **thah**lahssah
on the ground floor	στο ισόγειον	sto ee**sso**yeeonn
It must be quiet.	Πρέπει να είναι ήσυχο.	**preh**pee nah **ee**neh **ee**sseekho
Is there (a)...?	Υπάρχει...;	eepahr**kee**
air conditioning	κλιματισμός	kleemahtee**zmoss**
heating	θέρμανση	**thehr**mahnsee
hot water	ζεστό νερό	zeh**sto** neh**ro**
laundry service	πλυντήριο	pleen**dee**reeo
room service	σέρβις δωματίου	**sehr**veess dhom**mah**teeoo
private toilet	ιδιωτική τουαλέττα	eedheeottee**kee** tooah**leh**tah

CHECKING OUT, see page 31

Could you put... in the room?	Μπορείτε να βάλετε ... στο δωμάτιο;	borreeteh nah vahlehteh ... sto dhommahteeo
an extra bed	ένα επιπρόσθετο κρεββάτι	ehnah ehpeeprosthehto krehvahtee
a cot	ένα παιδικό κρεββάτι	ehnah pehdheeko krehvahtee

How much? *Πόσο;*

What's the price...?	Πόσο κοστίζει...;	posso kosteezee
per week	την βδομάδα	teen vdhommahdhah
per night	την νύκτα	teen neektah
for bed and breakfast	το δωμάτιο και το πρόγευμα	to dhommahteeo keh to proyehvmah
excluding meals	χωρίς τα γεύματα	khorreess tah yehvmahtah
for full board (A.P.)	με πλήρης διατροφή	meh pleereess dheeahtroffee
for half board (M.A.P.)	με ημιδιατροφή	meh eemeedheeahtroffee
Does that include...?	Η τιμή συμπεριλαμβάνει...;	ee teemee seembehreelahmvahnee
breakfast	το πρόγευμα	to proyehvmah
meals	τα γεύματα	tah yehvmahtah
service	το ποσοστό υπηρεσίας	to possosto eepeerehsseeahss
Is there any reduction for children?	Υπάρχει έκπτωση για τα παιδιά;	eepahrkhee ehkptossee yeeah tah pehdheeah
Do you charge for the baby?	Το μωρό πληρώνει;	to morro pleeronnee
That's too expensive.	Είναι πολύ ακριβά.	eeneh pollee ahkreevah
Do you have anything cheaper?	Έχετε άλλο πιο φτηνό;	ehkhehteh ahlo peeo fteeno

How long? *Πόσο καιρό;*

We'll be staying...	Θα μείνουμε...	thah meenoomeh
overnight only	μόνο μια νύκτα	monno meeah neektah
a few days	λίγες μέρες	leeyehss mehrehss
a week (at least)	μια βδομάδα (τουλάχιστον)	meeah vdhommahdhah (toolahkheestonn)
I don't know yet.	Δεν ξέρω ακόμα.	dhehn ksehro ahkommah

NUMBERS, see page 146

Decision *Απόφαση*

May I see the room?	Μπορώ να δω το δωμάτιο;	borro nah dho to dhommahteeo
That's fine. I'll take it.	Είναι εντάξει. Θα το πάρω.	eeneh ehndahksee. thah to pahro
No, I don't like it.	Όχι, δεν μου αρέσει.	okhee dhehn moo ahrehssee
It's too...	Είναι πολύ...	eeneh pollee
cold/hot	κρύο/ζεστό	kreeo/zehsto
dark/small	σκοτεινό/μικρό	skotteeno/meekro
It's too noisy.	Έχει πολύ θόρυβο.	ehkhee pollee thorreevo
I asked for a room with a bath.	Ζήτησα δωμάτιο με μπάνιο.	zeeteessah dhommahteeo meh bahneeo
Do you have anything...?	Έχετε κάτι...;	ehkhehteh kahtee
better	καλύτερο	kahleetehro
bigger	μεγαλύτερο	mehghahleetehro
cheaper	φτηνότερο	fteenottehro
quieter	πιο ήσυχο	peeo eesseekho
Do you have a room with a better view?	Έχετε δωμάτιο με καλύτερη θέα;	ehkhehteh dhommahteeo meh kahleetehree thehah

Registration *Καταγραφή*

Upon arrival at a hotel or boarding house you'll be asked to fill in a registration form (έντυπο–**ehn**deepo). The desk clerk may keep your passport overnight.

Επώνυμο/Όνομα	Name/First name
Διεύθυνση/Οδός/Αριθμός	Home address/Street/Number
Εθνικότητα/Επάγγελμα	Nationality/Profession
Τόπος/Ημερομηνία γεννήσεως	Place/Date of birth
Έρχεστε απο.../Προορισμός...	Coming from .../Going to...
Αριθμός διαβατηρίου	Passport number
Τόπος/Ημερομηνία	Place/Date
Υπογραφή	Signature

What does this mean?	Τι σημαίνει αυτό;	tee seemehnee ahfto

Μπορώ να δω το διαβατήριο σας;	May I see your passport?
Παρακαλώ, συμπληρώστε αυτό το έντυπο;	Would you mind filling in this registration form?
Υπογράψτε εδώ, παρακαλώ.	Sign here, please.
Πόσο καιρό θα μείνετε;	How long will you be staying?

What's my room number?	Ποιος είναι ο αριθμός του δωμάτιου μου;	peeoss eeneh o ahreeth-moss too dhommahteeoo moo
Will you have our luggage sent up?	Θα στείλετε τις αποσκευές μας επάνω;	thah steelehteh teess ahposskehvehss mahss ehpahno
Where can I park my car?	Που μπορώ να σταθμεύσω το αυτοκίνητο μου;	poo borro nah stahth-mehfso to ahfto-kkeeneeto moo
Does the hotel have a garage?	Μήπως έχει το ξενοδοχείο γκαράζ;	meeposs ehkhee to ksehnodhokheeo gahrahz
I'd like to leave this in your safe.	Θα ήθελα να αφήσω αυτό στο χρηματοκι-βώτιο σας.	thah eethehlah nah ahfeesso ahfto sto khree-mahtokkeevotteeo sahss
What time is the front door locked?	Τι ώρα κλείνει η εξώπορτα;	tee orrah kleenee ee ehksopportah

Hotel staff   Υπάλληλοι ξενοδοχείου

maid	η καμαριέρα	ee kahmahreeehrah
manager	ο διευθυντής	o dheeehftheendeess
porter	ο θυρωρός	o theerorross
receptionist	ο/η* υπάλληλος υποδοχής/ ρεσεπσιονίστ	o/ee eepahleeloss eepodhokheess/ rehsehpsionneest

When calling for service, the best thing to say is παρακαλώ (pahrahkahlo – please).

---

* If referring to a man say o (o), if to a woman use η (ee).

General requirements *Γενικές ανάγκες*

The key to room..., please.	Το κλειδί του δωμάτιου..., παρακαλώ.	to kleedhee too dhommah-teeoo... pahrahkahlo
Is there a bath on this floor?	Υπάρχει μπάνιο σε αυτόν τον όροφο;	eepahrkhee bahneeo seh ahftonn tonn orroffo
What's the voltage here?	Πόσα βολτ είναι το ρεύμα εδώ;	possah volt eeneh to rehvmah ehdho
Where's the socket (outlet) for the shaver?	Που είναι η υποδοχή πρίζας για την ξυριστική μηχανή;	poo eeneh ee eepodhokhee preezahss yeeah teen kseereesteekee meekhahnee
Can you find me a...?	Μπορείτε να μου βρείτε...;	borreeteh nah moo vreeteh
babysitter	μια μπέϊμπυ σίτερ	meeah "babysitter"
secretary	μια γραμματέα	meeah ghrahmahtehah
typewriter	μια γραφομηχανή	meeah ghrahfommee-khahnee
May I have a/an/some...?	Μπορώ να έχω...;	borro nah ehkho
ashtray	ένα σταχτοδοχείο	ehnah stahktodhokheeo
bath towel	μια πετσέτα του μπάνιου	meeah pehtsehtah too bahneeoo
(extra) blanket	μια κουβέρτα (επιπρόσθετο)	meeah koovehrtah (ehpeeprosthehto)
envelopes	μερικούς φακέλλους	mehreekooss fahkehlooss
(more) hangers	(περισσότερες) κρεμάστρες	(pehreessottehrehss) krehmahstrehss
hot-water bottle	μια θερμοφόρα	meeah thermofforrah
ice cubes	παγοτιέρα	pahghotteeehrah
needle and thread	βελόνι και κλωστή	vehlonnee keh klostee
pillow	μαξιλάρι	mahkseelahree
reading lamp	μια λάμπα για διάβασμα	meeah lahmbah yeeah dheeahvahzmah
soap	σαπούνι	sahpoonee
writing paper	χαρτί αλληλογραφίας	khahrtee ahleeloghrah-feeahss
Where's the...?	Που είναι...;	poo eeneh
bathroom	το μπάνιο	to bahneeo
dining room	η τραπεζαρία	ee trahpehzahreeah
emergency exit	η έξοδος κινδύνου	ee ehksodhoss keendheenoo
hairdresser's	το κομμωτήριο	to kommotteereeo
lift (elevator)	το ασανσέρ	to ahssahnsehr

NUMBERS, see page 146

Telephone – Post (mail) Τηλέφωνο – Ταχυδρομείο

Can you get me Athens 1234567?	Μπορείτε να καλέσετε Αθήνα 1234567;	borreeteh nah kahleh-sehteh ahtheenah 1234567
Do you have any stamps?	Έχετε γραμματόσημα;	ehkehteh ghrahmah-tosseemah
Would you post (mail) this for me, please?	Μπορείτε να μου ταχυδρομήσετε αυτό σας, παρακαλώ;	borreeteh nah moo tahkheedhrommeessehteh ahfto sahss pahrahkahlo
Are there any letters for me?	Υπάρχουν γράμματα για μένα;	eepahrkhoon ghrah-mahtah yeeah mehnah
Are there any messages for me?	Υπάρχει καμμιά παραγγελία για μένα;	eepahrkhee kahmeeah pahrahnggehleeah yeeah mehnah
How much are my telephone charges?	Πόσος είναι ο λογαριασμός του τηλεφώνου μου;	possoss eeneh o loghahreeahzmoss too teelehfonnoo moo

Difficulties Δυσκολίες

The... doesn't work.	... δεν λειτουργεί.	... dehn leetooryee
air conditioner	Το σύστημα κλιματισμού	to seesteemah kleemahteezmoo
light	Το φως	to foss
radio	Το ράδιο	to rahdheeo
television	Η τηλεόραση	ee teelehorrahssee
The tap (faucet) is dripping.	Η βρύση στάζει.	ee vreessee stahzee
There's no hot water.	Δεν υπάρχει ζεστό νερό.	dhehn eepahrkhee zehsto nehro
The washbasin is blocked.	Ο νιπτήρας είναι βουλωμένος.	o neepteerahss eeneh voolommehnoss
The window is jammed.	Το παράθυρο δεν ανοίγη.	to pahrahtheero dhehn ahneeyee
The curtains are stuck.	Οι κουρτίνες είναι σκαλωμένες.	ee koorteenehss eeneh skahlommehnehss
The bulb is burned out.	Ο λαμπτήρας κάηκε.	o lahmbteerahss kaheeke
My room has not been made up.	Το δωμάτιο μου δεν ετοιμάστηκε.	to dhommahteeo moo dhehn ehteemahsteekeh

POST OFFICE AND TELEPHONE, see page 132

The... is broken.	... έσπασε.	... ehspahsseh
blind	Το ρολό	to rollo
lamp	Η λάμπα	ee lahmbah
plug	Η πρίζα	ee preezah
shutter	Το εξώφυλλο	to ehksoffeelo
switch	Ο διακόπτης	o dheeahkopteess
Can you get it repaired?	Μπορείτε να το διορθώσετε;	borreeteh nah to dheeorthossehteh

Laundry – Dry cleaner's *Πλυντήριο – Στεγνοκαθριστήριο*

I want these clothes...	Θα ήθελα να δώσω αυτά τα ρούχα για...	thah eethehlah nah dhosso ahftah tah rookhah yeeah
cleaned	καθάρισμα	kahthahreezmah
ironed/pressed	σιδέρωμα	seedehrommah
washed	πλύσιμο	pleesseemo
When will they be ready?	Πότε θα είναι έτοιμα;	potteh thah eeneh ehteemah
I need them...	Τα χρειάζομαι...	tah khreeahzommeh
today	σήμερα	seemehrah
tomorrow	αύριο	ahvreeo
before Friday	πριν την Παρασκευή	preen teen pahrahskehvee
Can you ... this?	Μπορείτε να... αυτό;	borreeteh nah... ahfto
mend	διορθώσετε	dheeorthossehteh
patch	μπαλώσετε	bahlossehteh
stitch	ράψετε	rahpsehteh
Can you sew on this button?	Μπορείτε να ράψετε αυτό το κουμπί;	borreeteh nah rahpsehteh ahfto to koombee
Can you get this stain out?	Μπορείτε να καθαρίσετε αυτόν τον λεκέ;	borreeteh nah kahthah-reessehteh ahftonn tonn lehkeh
Is my laundry ready?	Είναι έτοιμα τα ρούχα μου;	eeneh ehteemah tah rookhah moo
This isn't mine.	Αυτό δεν είναι δικό μου.	ahfto dhehn eeneh dheeko moo
There's something missing.	Κάτι λείπει.	kahtee leepee
There's a hole in this.	Υπάρχει μια τρύπα σε αυτό.	eepahrkhee meeah treepah seh ahfto
It's shrunk.	Μάζεψε.	mahzehpseh

Hairdresser – Barber   Κομμωτήριο – Κουρείο

Is there a hairdresser/ beauty salon in the hotel?	Υπάρχει κομμωτήριο/ ινστιτούτο καλλονής στο ξενοδοχείο;	eepahrkhee kommo- teereeo/eensteetooto kahlonneess sto ksehnodhokheeo
Can I make an appointment for ...?	Μπορώ να κλείσω ραντεβού για την ...;	borro nah kleesso rahndehvoo yeeah teen
I'd like it cut and shaped.	Θα ήθελα κόψιμο και φορμάρισμα.	thah eethehlah kopseemo keh formahreezmah
I want a haircut, please.	Θέλω να με κουρέψετε, παρακαλώ.	thehlo nah meh koorehpsehteh pahrahkahlo
bleach	ξέβαμμα	ksehvahmah
blow-dry	στέγνωμα	stehghnommah
colour rinse	ένα ρενσάζ	ehnah rehnsahz
dye	μια βαφή	meeah vahfee
face pack	μια μάσκα για το πρόσωπο	meeah mahskah yeeah to prossoppo
manicure	μανικιούρ	mahneekeeoor
permanent wave	μια περμανάντ	meeah pehrmahnahnd
setting lotion	αφρό-λακ	ahfro-lahk
shampoo and set	σαμπουάν και μιζ αν πλι	sahmbooahn keh meez ahn plee
with a fringe (bangs)	με φράντζα	meh frahndzah
I'd like a shampoo for ... hair.	Θα ήθελα ένα σαμπουάν για ... μαλλιά.	thah eethehlah ehnah sahmbooahn yeeah ... mahleeah
normal/dry/greasy (oily)	κανονικά/ξηρά/ λιπαρά	kahnonneekah/kseerah/ leepahrah
Do you have a colour chart?	Έχετε ένα δειγματολόγιο;	ehkhehteh ehnah dheeghmahtolloyeeo
Don't cut it too short.	Μη τα κόψετε πολύ κοντά.	mee tah kopsehteh pollee kondah
A little more off the...	Να τα κόψετε λίγο ακόμη...	nah tah kopsehteh leegho ahkhommee
back	πίσω	peesso
neck	στο σβέρκο	sto svehrko
sides	στα πλάγια	stah plahyeeah
top	επάνω	ehpahno
I don't want any hairspray.	Δεν θέλω λακ.	dhehn thehlo lahk
I'd like a shave.	Ξύρισμα, παρακαλώ.	kseereezmah pahrahkahlo

DAYS OF THE WEEK, see page 150

Would you trim my..., please?	Παρακαλώ, μου κόβετε λίγο...	pahrahkahlo moo kovvehteh leegho
beard	τα γένεια	tah yehneeah
moustache	το μουστάκι	to moostahkee
sideboards (sideburns)	τις φαβορίτες	teess fahvorreetehss

Checking out Αναχώρηση

May I have my bill, please?	Μπορώ να έχω τον λογαριασμό, παρακαλώ;	borro nah ehkho tonn loghahreeahzmo pahrahkahlo
I'm leaving early in the morning.	Φεύγω αύριο νωρίς το πρωί.	fehvgho ahvreeo norreess to proee
Please have my bill ready.	Μπορείτε να μου ετοιμάσετε τον λογαριασμό, παρακαλώ.	borreeteh nah moo ehteemahssehteh tonn loghahreeahzmo pahrahkahlo
We'll be checking out around noon.	Θα φύγουμε κατά το μεσημέρι.	thah feeghoomeh kahtah to mehsseemehree
I must leave at once.	Πρέπει να φύγω αμέσως.	prehpee nah feegho ahmehssoss
Is everything included?	Συμπεριλαμβάνονται τα πάντα;	seembehreelahmvahnondeh tah pahndah
Can I pay by credit card?	Μπορώ να πληρώσω με πιστωτική κάρτα;	borro nah pleerosso meh peestotteekee kahrtah
I think there's a mistake in this bill.	Νομίζω κάνατε λάθος στο λογαριασμό.	nommeezo kahnahteh lahthoss sto loghahreeahzmo
Can you get us a taxi?	Μπορείτε να μας βρείτε ένα ταξί;	borreeteh nah mahss vreeteh ehnah tahksee
Would you send someone to bring down our baggage?	Θα μπορούσατε να στείλετε κάποιον να κατεβάσει τις αποσκευές μας;	thah borroossahteh nah steelehteh kahpeeonn nah kahtehvahssee teess ahposkehvehss mahss
Here's the forwarding address.	Αυτή είναι η επόμενη μου διεύθυνση.	ahftee eeneh ee ehpommehnee moo dheeehftheensee
You have my home address.	Έχετε τη διεύθυνση κατοικίας μου.	ehkhehteh tee dheeehftheensee kahteekeeahss moo
It's been a very enjoyable stay.	Η διαμονή ήταν πολύ ευχάριστη.	ee dheeahmonnee eetahn pollee ehfkhahreestee

TIPPING, see inside back-cover

Camping Κατασκήνωση (Κάμπινγκ)

There are camp sites all over Greece (except on Rhodes), and
it is illegal to camp anywhere else. They are usually clean and
imaginatively planned, with good facilities.

Is there a camp site near here?	Υπάρχει ένα μέρος για κάμπινγκ εδώ κοντά;	eepahrkhee ehnah mehross yeeah ''camping'' ehdho kondah
Can we camp here?	Μπορούμε να κατασκηνώσουμε εδώ;	borroomeh nah kahtahskeenossoomeh ehdho
Do you have room for a tent/caravan (trailer)?	Έχετε μέρος για την σκηνή/τροχόσπιτο;	ehkhehteh mehross yeeah teen skeenee/trokhospeeto
What's the charge...?	Πόσο κοστίζει...;	posso kosteezee
per day	την μέρα	teen mehrah
per person	το άτομο	to ahtommo
for a car	ένα αυτοκίνητο	ehnah ahftokkeeneeto
for a tent	μια σκηνή	meeah skeenee
for a caravan (trailer)	ένα τροχόσπιτο	ehnah trokhospeeto
Is the tourist tax included?	Συμπεριλαμβάνετε και ο τουριστικός φόρος;	seembehreelahmvahnehteh keh o tooreesteekoss forross
Is there/Are there (a)...?	Υπάρχει/ Υπάρχουν...;	eepahrkhee/ eepahrkhoon
drinking water	πόσιμο νερό	posseemo nehro
electricity	ρεύμα	rehvmah
playground	γήπεδο	gheepehdho
restaurant	εστιατόριο	ehsteeahtorreeo
shopping facilities	ευκολίες για ψώνια	ehfkolleeehss yeeah psonneeah
swimming pool	πισίνα	peesseenah
Where are the showers/toilets?	Που είναι τα ντους/οι τουαλέττες;	poo eeneh tah dooss/ee tooahlehtehss
Where can I get butane gas?	Που μπορώ να βρω υγραέριο;	poo borro nah vro eeghraehreeo

ΑΠΑΓΟΡΕΥΕΤΑΙ ΤΟ ΚΑΜΠΙΝΓΚ	ΑΠΑΓΟΡΕΥΟΝΤΑΙ ΤΑ ΤΡΟΧΟΣΠΙΤΑ
CAMPING PROHIBITED	NO CARAVANS (TRAILERS)

CAMPING EQUIPMENT, see page 106

Κατασκήνωση

Eating out

There are many types of places where you can eat and drink in Greece.

Γαλακτοπωλείο (ghahlahktopo**lleeo**)	This is a shop selling milk, butter, and yoghurt; you can also buy pastries and ice-cream.
Εστιατόριο (ehsteeah**torreeo**)	This is the general, collective word for restaurants.
Ζαχαροπλαστείο (zahkhahroplah**steeo**)	A tea-room, where you can also buy sweets.
Καφενείο (kafehn**eeo**)	A coffee house.
Ουζερί (oozeh**ree**)	A bar. The name is inspired by the typically Greek aperitif, *ouzo*.
Σνακ-μπαρ ("snack bar")	A snack-bar. The Greeks have taken over the word.
Ταβέρνα (tah**vehr**nah)	This is the sign to look for if you want to try some real Greek dishes.
Χασαποταβέρνα (khahssahpottah-**vehr**nah)	A grill-room attached to a butcher's shop.
Ψαροταβέρνα (psahrottah**vehr**nah)	This is a *taverna* specializing in seafood.
Ψησταριά (pseestah**reeah**)	Again, a kind of *taverna*, but specializing in charcoal-grilled food.

Greek cuisine *Ελληνική κουζίνα*

Although Greek cuisine cannot be compared to that of France, nevertheless it has a long and honorable tradition, going back to Plato and even further. In terms of simply-prepared dishes made from the freshest ingredients, it cannot be beaten.

Many Greek dishes have Turkish names and indeed are also found in Turkey. Both countries claim the existing cuisine as their own, but it seems more likely that it was evolved by the Greeks and taken on by the Turks during the many years that they occupied Greece. The Greeks were great travellers and exchanged culinary knowledge with many of the countries they passed through.

The principal elements of Greek cuisine are vegetables such as artichokes and aubergines, tomatoes and olives, olive oil, and seasonings like lemon juice, garlic, basil, oregano and rosemary.

Although meat dishes are limited (mutton and poultry are the most common), vegetables are fresh and inventively combined. Fish and seafood are excellent, the former possibly best when grilled and served with lemon wedges, but prices can go very high.

Care must be taken when having an aperitif before a meal not to eat too many hors d'oeuvres. These are very tempting ranging from whitebait to tiny parcels of stuffed vine leaves, numerous dips and canapés.

And when the heat of the afternoon sun has abated, what better way of waking from a siesta than with a strong black coffee and a very, very sweet pastry like *baclava*.

Meal times   Ώρες φαγητού

The Greeks like to eat quite late, it's not unusual to start dinner at 10 p.m. However, in most restaurants you can usually get a meal as early as you would at home.

Breakfast (το πρόγευμα – to **pro**yehvmah) is generally served between 7 and 10 a.m.

Lunch (το γεύμα – to **yehv**mah) is from about 12.30 to 3 p.m.

Dinner (ο δείπνος – o **dhee**pnoss) is from around 7 until midnight or 1 a.m. In nightclubs you can usually get served even later.

Τι θα πάρετε;	What would you like?
Σας συστήνω αυτό	I recommend this.
Τι θα πιείτε;	What would you like to drink?
Δεν έχουμε...	We haven't got...
Θέλετε...;	Do you want...?

Hungry? *Πεινασμένος;*

I'm hungry.	**Πεινώ.**	peeno
I'm thirsty.	**Διψώ.**	dheepso
Can you recommend a good restaurant?	**Μπορείτε να μου συστήσετε ένα καλό εστιατόριο;**	borreeteh nah moo seesteessehteh ehnah kahlo ehsteeahtorreeo
Where can I get a typical Greek meal?	**Που μπορώ να βρω Ελληνικό φαγητό;**	poo borro nah vro ehleeneeko fahyeeto
Are there any inexpensive restaurants around here?	**Υπάρχουν φθηνά εστιατόρια εδώ κοντά;**	eepahrkhoon ftheenah ehsteeahtorreeah ehdho kondah
Where can I get a snack?	**Που μπορώ να έχω ένα σνακ;**	poo borro nah ehkho ehnah ''snack''

If you want to be sure of getting a table in well-known restaurants, it may be better to telephone in advance.

I'd like to reserve a table for 4.	**Θα ήθελα να κρατήσω ένα τραπέζι για 4.**	thah eethehlah nah krahteesso ehnah trahpehzee yeeah 4
I'd like to reserve a table for...	**Θα ήθελα να κρατήσω ένα τραπέζι για...**	thah eethehlah nah krahteesso ehnah trahpehzee yeeah
this evening	**απόψε**	ahpopseh
for tomorrow	**αύριο**	ahvreeo
for lunch	**γεύμα**	yehvmah
We'll come at 8.	**Θα έλθουμε στις 8.**	thah ehlthoomeh steess 8
My name is...	**Το όνομα μου είναι...**	to onommah moo eeneh

Could we have a table...?	Μπορούμε να έχουμε ένα τραπέζι...;	borroomeh nah ehkhoomeh ehnah trahpehzee
in the corner	στη γωνία	stee ghonneeah
by the window	στο παράθυρο	sto pahrahtheero
outside	έξω	ehkso
on the terrace	στη ταράτσα	stee tahrahtsah
in a non-smoking area	στη περιοχή των μη καπνιστών	stee pehreeokhee tonn mee kahpneestonn

Asking and ordering   Ερωτώ και παραγγέλω

Waiter/Waitress!	Σερβιτόρε/Σερβιτόρα!	sehrveetorreh/ serveetorrah
I'd like something to eat/drink.	Θα ήθελα κάτι να φάω/πίνω.	thah eethehlah kahtee nah faho/peeno
May I have the menu, please?	Μπορώ να έχω την κάρτα με τα μενού, παρακαλώ;	borro nah ehkho teen kahrtah meh tah mehnoo pahrahkahlo
Do you have a set menu/local dishes?	Έχετε έτοιμο μενού/ ντόπια φαγητά;	ehkhehteh ehteemo mehnoo/doppeeah fahyeetah
What do you recommend?	Τι μας συστήνετε;	tee mahss seesteenehteh
Do you have anything ready quickly?	Έχετε κάτι που να γίνεται γρήγορα;	ehkhehteh kahtee poo nah yeenehteh ghreeghorrah
I'm in a hurry.	Είμαι βιαστικός/-ή.	eemeh veeahsteekoss/-ee
Could we have a/an... please?	Θα μπορούσαμε να έχουμε... παρακαλώ;	thah borroossahmeh nah ehkhoomeh... pahrahkahlo

ashtray	ένα σταχτοδοχείο	ehnah stahkhtodhohkheeo
cup	ένα φλιτζάνι	ehnah fleedzahnee
fork	ένα πηρούνι	ehnah peeroonee
glass	ένα ποτήρι	ehnah potteeree
knife	ένα μαχαίρι	ehnah mahkhehree
napkin (serviette)	μια πετσέτα	meeah pehtsehtah
plate	ένα πιάτο	ehnah peeahto
spoon	ένα κουτάλι	ehnah kootahlee
May I have some...?	Μπορώ να έχω...;	borro nah ehkho
bread	ψωμί	psommee
butter	βούτυρο	vooteero

NUMBERS, see page 146

lemon	λεμόνι	lehmonnee
oil	λάδι	lahdhee
pepper	πιπέρι	peepehree
seasonings	καρύκευματα	kahreekehvmahtah
vinegar	ξύδι	kseedhee

Some useful expressions for dieters and special requirements:

I'm on a diet.	Κάνω δίαιτα.	kahno dheeehtah
I don't drink alcohol.	Δεν πίνω αλκοόλ.	dhehn peeno ahlko-ol
I mustn't eat food containing...	Δεν πρέπει να τρώγω φαγητά που περιέχουν...	dhehn prehpee nah trogho fahyeetah poo pehreeehkhoon
flour/fat	αλεύρι/λίπος	ahlehvree/leeposs
salt/sugar	αλάτι/ζάχαρη	ahlahtee/zahkhahree
Do you have... for diabetics?	Έχετε... για διαβητικούς;	ehkhehteh... yeeah dheeahveeteekooss
cakes	κέικς	"cakes"
fruit juice	χυμούς φρούτων	kheemooss frootonn
a special menu	ειδικά μενού	eedheekah mehnoo
Do you have vegetarian dishes?	Έχετε πιάτα για χορτοφάγους;	ehkhehteh peeahtah yeeah khortofahghooss
Could I have... instead of dessert?	Μπορώ να έχω... αντί του επιδορπίου;	borro nah ehkho... ahndee too ehpeedhorpeeoo
Can I have an artificial sweetener?	Μπορώ να έχω ζαχαρίνη;	borro nah ehkho zahkhahreenee

And...

I'd like some more.	Θα ήθελα λίγο ακόμη.	thah eethehlah leegho ahkommee
Can I have more... , please?	Μπορώ να έχω περισσότερα... , παρακαλώ;	borro nah ehkho pehreessottehrah... pahrahkahlo
Just a small portion.	Μόνο μια μικρή μερίδα.	monno meeah meekree mehreedhah
Nothing more, thanks.	Τίποτε άλλο, ευχαριστώ.	teepotteh ahlo ehfkhahreesto
Where are the toilets?	Που είναι οι τουαλέττες;	poo eeneh ee tooahlehtehss

Breakfast Πρόγευμα

For Greeks the first meal of the day is the least important. It usually comprises a few cups of strong, black coffee and maybe some sweet rolls or cakes. However, visitors are normally given a continental breakfast, and some hotels will even provide an English breakfast with bacon and eggs.

I'd like breakfast, please.	Θέλω να προγευματίσω, παρακαλώ.	**theh**lo nah proyehvmah-**tee**sso pahrahkahlo
I'll have a/an/ some...	Θέλω...	**theh**lo
bacon and eggs	αυγά με μπέικον	ahv**ghah** meh "bacon"
boiled egg	ένα βραστό αυγό	**eh**nah vrahsto ahv**gho**
soft/hard	μελάτα/σφικτά	mehlahtah/sfeektah
eggs	αυγά	ahv**ghah**
fried eggs	τηγανιτά αυγά	teeghahneetah ahv**ghah**
scrambled eggs	χτυπητά αυγά	khteepeetah ahv**ghah**
fruit juice	ένα χυμό φρούτων	**eh**nah kheemo **froo**tonn
grapefruit	κρέιπφρουτ	"grapefruit"
orange	πορτοκάλι	porto**kah**lee
ham and eggs	αυγά με ζαμπόν	ahv**ghah** meh zahm**bonn**
jam	μαρμελάδα	mahrmehlahdhah
marmalade	μια μαρμελάδα πορτοκάλι	meeah mahrmehlahdhah porto**kah**lee
toast	ένα τοστ	**eh**nah tost
yoghurt	γιαούρτι	yeeahoortee
May I have some...?	Μπορώ να έχω...;	borro nah **eh**kho
bread	ψωμί	psommee
butter	βούτυρο	**voo**teero
(hot) chocolate	(ζεστή) σοκολάτα	(zehstee) sokko**llah**tah
coffee	καφέ	kahfeh
decaffeinated	χωρίς καφεΐνη	khorr**eess** kahfeheenee
black/ with milk	μαύρο/με γάλα	**mahv**ro/meh **ghah**lah
honey	μέλι	mehlee
milk	γάλα	**ghah**lah
cold/hot	κρύο/ζεστό	**kreeo**/zehsto
pepper	πιπέρι	peepehree
rolls	ψωμάκια	psommahkeeah
salt	αλάτι	ahlahtee
tea	τσάι	**tsah**ee
with milk	με γάλα	meh **ghah**lah
with lemon	με λεμόνι	meh lehmonnee
(hot) water	(ζεστό) νερό	(zehsto) nehro

What's on the menu?   Τι περιέχει η κόρτα με τα μενού;

When ordering, one of the possibilities is to stroll into the kitchen and have a look at what's cooking in the various pots and pans. This is acceptable and even encouraged in some restaurants.

However, if you don't want to do that, under the headings below you'll find alphabetical lists of food and dishes that might be offered on a Greek menu with their English equivalent. You can simply show the book to the waiter. If you want some fruit, for instance, let him point to what's available on the appropriate list. Use pages 36 and 37 for ordering in general.

Reading the menu   Διαβάζοντας το μενού

Επιπλέον...	... extra
Κατά παραγγελία	Made to order
Κατά προτίμηση	Of your choice
Κρύα πιάτα	Cold dishes
Μενού της μέρας	Set menu of the day
Ο μάγειρας σας συστήνει...	The chef recommends...
Πιάτο της μέρας	Dish of the day
Σπεσιαλιτέ	Specialities
Σπιτίσιο	Home made
Συστήνομε...	We recommend...
Το σπεσιαλιτέ του καταστήματος	Speciality of the house
Σπεσιαλιτέ της περιοχής	Local specialities

αναψυκτικό	ahnahpseekteeko	soft drink
αστρακοειδή	ahstrahkoeedhee	shellfish
επιδόρπια	ehpeedhorpeeah	desserts
θαλασσινά	thahlahseenah	seafood
κυνήγι	keeneeyee	game
κρασί	krahssee	wine
κρέας	krehahss	meat
κρέας στη σχάρα	krehahss stee skhahrah	grilled meat
λαχανικά	lahkhahneekah	vegetables
ομελέττες	ommehlehtehss	omelets
παγωτό	pahghotto	ice cream
πάστες	pahstehss	pastries
παστίτσιο	pahsteetseeo	pasta
πατάτες	pahtahtehss	potatoes
πατάτες τηγανιτές	pahtahtehss teeghahneetehss	chips (french fries)
πουλερικά	poolehreekah	poultry
ποτά	pottah	drinks
πρώτο πιάτο	protto peeahto	first course
ψάρι	psahree	fish
ρίζι	reezee	rice
σαλάτες	sahlahtehss	salads
σούπες	soopehss	soups
τυρί	teeree	cheese
φρούτα	frootah	fruit

Starters (Appetizers) Ορεκτικά

I'd like an appetizer.	Θα ήθελα ένα ορεκτικό.	thah **ee**thehlah **eh**nah orrehktee**ko**
What do you recommend?	Τι μας συστήνετε;	tee mahss see**stee**nehteh
αβοκάδο	ahvo**kkah**dho	avocado
αγγινάρες	ahnggee**nah**rehss	artichokes
αντζούγιες	ahn**dzoo**yee-ehss	anchovies
αυγά (με μαγιονέζα)	ahv**ghah** (meh mahyee**onneh**zah)	eggs (with mayonnaise)
γαρίδες	ghah**ree**dhehss	prawns (shrimp)
γαρίδες κοκταίηλ	ghah**ree**dhehss kok**teh**eel	prawn cocktail
ελιές (γεμιστές)	ehlee**ehss** (yehmee**stehss**)	(stuffed) olives
ζαμπόν (βραστό/ καπνιστό)	zahm**bonn** (vrah**sto**/ kahp**nee**sto)	ham (boiled/ smoked)
καβούρι	kah**voo**ree	crab
καραβίδα	kahrah**vee**dhah	crawfish
κρύο κρέας	**kree**o **kreh**hahss	cold meat
μανιτάρια	mahnee**tah**reeah	mushrooms
σκουμπρί	skoom**bree**	mackerel
πατέ	pah**teh**	pâté
πεπόνι	peh**ponn**ee	melon
ποικιλία ορεκτικών	peekee**lee**ah orrehktee**konn**	assorted appetizers
ραπανάκια	rahpah**nah**keeah	radishes
ρέγγα (καπνιστή)	**rehng**gah (kahp**nee**stee)	(smoked) herring
σαλάμι	sah**lah**mee	salami
σαλάτα	sah**lah**tah	salad
σαρδέλλες	sahr**dheh**lehss	sardines
σολομός (καπνιστός)	sollo**moss** (kahp**nee**stoss)	(smoked) salmon
σπαράγγια	spah**rahng**geeah	asparagus
στρείδια	**stree**dheeah	oysters
τόννος	**tonn**oss	tuna (tunny)
χαβιάρι	khahvee**ah**ree	caviar
χέλι (καπνιστό)	**kheh**lee (kahp**nee**sto)	(smoked) eel
χυμός φρούτου	khee**moss** **froo**too	fruit juice

ντολμαδάκια (dolmahd**hah**keeah)	vine leaves stuffed with rice and onions and flavoured with herbs.
ταραμοσαλάτα (tahrahmossah**lah**tah)	paté made from fish roe blended with bread, olive oil and onions.
κολοκύθια τηγανιτά (kolo**kee**theeah teeghahnee**tah**)	courgettes sliced into rounds, dipped into batter and fried.

Salads Σαλάτες

Salads are plentiful and very varied. Many are a meal in themselves, while others are more like dips than salads, served with flat bread or raw vegetables.

What salads do you have?	Τι σαλάτες έχετε;	tee sahlahtehss ehkhehteh
σαλάτα	sahlahtah	salad
αγγινάρες	ahnggeenahrehss	artichoke
κοκκινογούλια	kokkeenoghooleeah	beetroot
ντομάτες και	dommahtehss keh	tomato and
αγγούρια	ahnggooreeah	cucumber
μαρούλι	mahroolee	lettuce
μελιτζάνες	mehleedzahnehss	aubergine

γαριδοσαλάτα (ghahreedhossahlahtah)	shrimp in oil and lemon sauce
τζατζίκι (dzahdzeekee)	a salad made of yoghurt, cucumber, garlic, olive oil and mint
σκορδαλιά (skordhahleeah)	chopped garlic and potatoes in olive oil
χόρτα σαλάτα (khortah sahlahtah)	''herb salad''; boiled herbs with olive oil and lemon sauce, especially as a dressing for fish
χωριάτικη σαλάτα (khorreeahteekee sahlahtah)	a typically Greek salad made of olives, tomatoes, cucumber, onions, parsley, green peppers and *feta* (white goat cheese)
χούμους (khoomooss)	chick peas blended with tahini (sesame seed paste), oil, lemon and garlic

Egg dishes – Omelets Πιάτα αυγών – Ομελέττες

I'd like an omelet.	Θα ήθελα μια ομελέττα.	thah eethehlah meeah ommehlehtah
αυγά	ahvghah	eggs
μελάτα	mehlahtah	soft-boiled
σφικτά	sfeektah	hard-boiled
τηγανιτά (μάτια)	teeghahneetah (mahteeah)	fried
ποσσέ	posseh	poached
ομελέττα με αγκινάρες	ommehlehtah meh ahnggeenahrehss	artichoke omelet
ομελέττα με ζαμπόν	ommehlehtah meh zahmbonn	ham omelet

ομελέττα με λουκάνικα	ommeh**leh**tah meh loo**kah**neekah	sausage omelet
ομελέττα με ντομάτα	ommeh**leh**tah meh dom**mah**tah	tomato omelet
ομελέττα με πατάτες	ommeh**leh**tah meh pah**tah**tehss	potato omelet
ομελέττα με συκωτάκια πουλιών	ommeh**leh**tah meh seekot**tah**keeah poolee**onn**	chicken liver omelet
ομελέττα με τυρί	ommeh**leh**tah meh teer**ee**	cheese omelet

Soups *Σούπες*

You can find very tasty fish soups made either with tomato sauce or with eggs and lemon sauce.

I'd like some soup.	Θα ήθελα μια σούπα.	thah **ee**thehlah mee**ah soo**pah
What do you recommend?	Τι μου συστήνετε;	tee moo see**steen**ehteh
κοτόσουπα	kot**tos**soopah	clear chicken soup
κρεατόσουπα	kreh**ah**tos**soo**pah	clear meat soup
μαγειρίτσα	mahyeer**ee**tsah	typical Easter soup made of minced lamb entrails
ρεβύθια	reh**vee**theeah	chick-pea soup
σούπα αυγολέμονο	**soo**pah ahv**ghol**leh**mon**no	soup with rice, eggs and lemon juice
σούπα πατσάς	**soo**pah pah**tsahss**	tripe soup
σούπα τραχανάς	**soo**pah trahkhah**nahss**	semolina soup
σούπα φακές	**soo**pah fah**kehss**	lentil soup
σούπα χυλοπίττες	**soo**pah kheeloh**pee**tehss	noodle soup
τοματόσουπα	tommah**tos**soopah	tomato soup
ταχινόσουπα	tahkheen**os**soopah	"tahini" (sesame seed) soup
φασολάδα	fahssol**lah**dhah	kidney bean soup with tomatoes
χορτόσουπα	khort**os**soopah	vegetable soup

Particularly on the coast and the islands, fish soup and stew are favourite dishes. Try one of these:

| κακαβιά | kahkahvee**ah** | spicy fish stew |
| ψαρόσουπα | psahr**os**soopah | fish soup |

Fish and seafood Ψάρι και θαλασσινά

Aegean and Ionian waters supply coastal towns with a wealth of fish and seafood, while freshwater fish is available inland in lakeside areas. Fish is usually grilled or fried, basted with oil and served with lemon juice.

Certain fish dishes can turn out very expensive so make sure you know what you're ordering.

I'd like some fish.	Θα ήθελα λίγο ψάρι.	thah **ee**thehlah **lee**gho **psah**ree
What kinds of seafood do you have?	Τι είδη θαλασσινών έχετε;	tee **ee**dhee thahlahsseenonn **eh**khehteh
αντζούγιες	ahn**dzoo**yee-ehss	anchovies
αστακός	ahstah**koss**	lobster
αχινός	ahkhee**noss**	sea urchin
γαλέος	ghah**leh**oss	lamprey
γαρίδες	ghah**ree**dhehss	prawns (shrimp)
γλώσσα	**ghlos**sah	sole
γόπα	**ghop**pah	large sardine
καβούρι	kah**voo**ree	crab
καλαμάρι	kahlah**mah**ree	squid
καραβίδα	kahrah**vee**dhah	crawfish
κέφαλος	**keh**fahloss	mullet
λακέρδα	lah**kehr**dhah	salted tuna (tunny)
λιθρίνι	lee**three**nee	grey mullet
μπακαλιάρος	bahkahlee**ah**ross	fresh cod
μπακαλιάρος παστός	bahkahlee**ah**ross pah**stoss**	cured cod
μπαρμπούνι	bahr**boo**nee	red mullet
μύδια	**mee**dheeah	mussels
πέρκα	**pehr**kah	perch
πέστροφα	**peh**stroffah	trout
ρέγγα	**rehng**gah	herring
σαρδέλλα	sahr**dehl**lah	sardine
σκουμπρί	skoom**bree**	mackerel
σουπιά	soo**pee**ah	cuttlefish
στρείδια	**stree**dheeah	oysters
συναγρίδα	seenah**ghree**dhah	sea bream
σφυρίδα	sfee**ree**dhah	whiting
τόννος	**ton**noss	tuna (tunny)
τσιπούρα	tsee**poo**rah	gifthead fish
χελιδονόψαρο	khehleedhon**non**psahro	flying fish
χέλι	**kheh**lee	eel
χταπόδι	khtah**po**dhee	octopus

baked	του φούρνου	too **foornoo**
cured	παστός	pah**stoss**
deep fried	τηγανισμένος σε πολύ λάδι	teeghahneez**meh**noss seh po**llee lahd**hee
fried	τηγανιτός	teeghahnee**toss**
grilled	της σχάρας	teess **skhah**rahss
marinated	μαρινάτος	mahree**nah**toss
poached	ποσέ	po**sseh**
smoked	καπνιστός	kahpnee**stoss**
steamed	του ατμό	too **aht**mo
stewed	βραστός	vrah**stoss**

αστακός
(ahstah**koss**)
crawfish often served with oil and lemon sauce or garlic mayonnaise, expensive

γαρίδες με φέτα
(gah**reed**hehss meh **feh**tah)
sautéed onions, tomatoes and seasonings baked with shrimp and topped with *feta* cheese.

μαρίδες
(mah**reed**hehss)
fried smelt

ξιφίας
(ksee**fee**ahss)
swordfish, sometimes flavoured with oregano and grilled on a skewer

σουπιές με σπανάκι
(soopee**ehss** meh spah**nah**kee)
cuttlefish with spinach

σουφλέ από θαλασσινά
(soo**fleh** ah**po** thahlahssee**nah**)
shellfish soufflé

χταπόδι κρασάτο
(khtah**pod**hee krah**ssah**to)
octopus stewed in wine sauce

ψάρι μαγιονέζα Αθηναϊκή
(**psah**ree mahyeeon**neh**zah atheenahee**kee**)
flaked fish mixed with mayonnaise

ψάρι μαρινάτο
(**psah**ree mahree**nah**to)
mullet, sole or mackerel, fried and served with a piquant sauce of wine, tomato juice, vinegar and herbs

ψάρι στα κάρβουνα
(**psah**ree stah **kahr**voonah)
fish baked in coals

Meat   Κρέας

Even the simplest restaurant can do an honourable job with veal, lamb or pork chops. Pieces of meat are delicious when skewered and grilled over charcoal.

What kind of meat do you have?	Τι είδη κρέατα έχετε;	tee **ee**dhee kr**e**hahtah **eh**khehteh
I'd like some...	Θα ήθελα...	thah **ee**thehlah
beef	βοδινό	vodh**ee**no
pork	χοιρινό	kheer**ee**no
veal	μοσχάρι	moskh**ah**ree
lamb	αρνί	ahrn**ee**
αρνάκι του γάλακτος	ahrn**ah**kee too **gh**ahlahktoss	baby lamb
αρνίσιες μπριζόλες	ahrn**ee**ssee-ehss breez**o**llehss	lamb chops
γλώσσα	**gh**lossah	tongue
εντρεκότ	ehndreh**kott**	rib or rib-eye steak
εσκαλόπ	ehskah**lopp**	cutlet (scallop)
ζαμπόν	zahm**bonn**	ham
καρδιά	kahrdh**ee**ah	heart
καρρέ	kahr**reh**	rack
κεφάλι	keh**fah**lee	head
κιμάς	keem**ahss**	minced meat
κοτολέττες	kott**o**llehtehss	cutlets
λαρδί	lahrdh**ee**	bacon
λουκάνικα	look**ah**neekah	sausages
μοσχαρίσιες μπριζόλες	moskhahr**ee**ssee-ehss breez**o**llehss	veal chops
μπιφτέκι	beeft**eh**kee	beef steak
μπριζόλα	breez**o**llah	chop
μυαλό	mee**ah**hlo	brains
νεφρά	neh**frah**	kidneys
νεφραμιά	neh**frah**mee**ah**	sirloin
ουρά βοδινή	oor**ah** vodh**ee**nee	oxtail
παϊδάκια	paheedh**ah**keeah	cutlets
πλάτη	**plah**tee	shoulder
ροσμπίφ	roz**beef**	roast beef
σατωμπριάν	sahtobree**ahn**	thick fillet
σέλλα	**seh**lah	saddle
στήθος	**stee**thoss	breast
συκώτι	see**kott**ee	liver
φιλέτο	feel**eh**to	fillet
χοιρινές μπριζόλες	kheereen**ehss** breez**o**llehss	pork chops

baked	του φούρνου	too **foor**noo
barbecued	της σχάρας	teess **skhah**rahss
boiled	βραστός	vrah**stoss**
braised	μαγειρευμένος στη	mahyeerahv**meh**noss
	σάλτσα του	stee **sahl**tsah too
broiled	της σχάρας	teess **skhah**rahss
en casserole	της κατσαρόλας	teess kahtsah**rol**lahss
fried	τηγανιτός	teeghahnee**toss**
grilled	της σχάρας	teess **skhah**rahss
roasted	ψητός	psee**toss**
stewed	βραστός	vrah**stoss**
stuffed	γεμιστός	yehmees**toss**
rare	λιγοψημένος	leeghopsee**meh**noss
medium	μισοψημένος	meessopsee**meh**noss
well-done	καλοψημένος	kahlopsee**meh**noss

Meat dishes   Κρέατα

αρνάκι εξοχικό
(ahr**nah**kee ehkso-
kheeko)
spiced lamb baked in a parchment envelope

γιουβέτσι
(yeeoo**veh**tsee)
meat with Greek noodles or macaroni baked in
the oven

κοκορέτσι
(kokko**reh**tsee)
kidneys, tripe and liver roasted on a spit

μουσακάς (moossah-
kahss)
layers of sliced aubergine and minced meat,
oven-browned with a creamy cheese mixture

ντολμάδες
(dol**mah**dhehss)
minced meat and rice wrapped in vine or
cabbage leaves with white sauce

ντομάτες γεμιστές
(do**mmah**tehss
yehmees**tehss**)
tomatoes stuffed with rice and parsley or with
minced meat

παπουτσάκια
(pahpoot**sah**keeah)
vegetable marrow (zucchini) stuffed with rice
and/or meat, onions and white sauce and then
baked

σουβλάκι
(soov**lah**kee)
chunks of meat marinated in olive oil and lemon
juice, and grilled on a skewer

σουτζουκάκια
(soodzoo**kah**keeah)
minced-meat balls with cumin in tomato sauce

Game and poultry *Κυνήγι και πουλερικά*

While chicken is found throughout the year and prepared in a variety of different ways, birds such as quail and woodcock only start to appear regularly on the menu in September.

I'd like some game.	Θα ήθελα κυνήγι.	thah **ee**thehlah **kee**ne**ee**yee
γαλοπούλα	ghahlo**poo**lah	turkey
καπόνι	kah**pon**nee	capon
κοτόπουλο	kot**top**poolo	chicken
κοτόπουλο ψητό	kot**top**poolo pse**et**o	roast chicken
κουνέλι	koo**neh**lee	rabbit
λαγός	lah**ghoss**	hare
λαγός σιβέ	lah**ghoss** see**veh**	jugged hare
μπεκάτσα	beh**kah**tsah	woodcock
μπούτι	**boo**tee	leg
ορτύκι	or**tee**kee	quail
παπάκι	pah**pah**kee	duckling
πάπια	**pah**peeah	duck
πέρδικα	**pehr**dheekah	partridge
περιστέρι	pehree**steh**ree	pigeon
στήθος	**stee**thoss	breast
φασιανός	fahssee**ah**noss	pheasant
φτερούγα	fteh**roo**ghah	wing
χήνα	**khee**nah	goose

κοτόπουλο της κατσαρόλας (kot**top**poolo teess kahtsah**rol**lahss)	casserole of chicken with lemon sauce	
κοτόπουλο της σούβλας (kot**top**poolo teess **soov**lahss)	spit-roasted chicken	
λαγός στιφάδο (lah**ghoss** stee**fah**dho)	hare cooked with spring onions, wine or tomatoes	
πάπια γεμιστή (**pah**peeah yehmee**stee**)	stuffed duck	
μπεκάτσα (beh**kah**tsah)	woodcock casseroled in a sauce made of onions, butter, olive oil and wine	
ορτύκι (or**tee**kee)	quail baked in a wine sauce and served on a bed of rice	

Vegetables *Λαχανικά*

Vegetables occupy an important place in Greek cuisine, and are served in a multitude of different ways. A wide variety of vegetables is grown, but the season is relatively short. Keep your eyes open for artichokes, broad beans and peas in summer. Vegetables are usually eaten cold (raw or boiled, and then cooled), or tepid. Greeks like to eat them with an oil and vinegar or oil and lemon dressing. The latter is an acquired taste, but worth persevering with.

What vegetables do you recommend?	Τι λαχανικά μας συστήνετε;	tee lahkahneekah mahss seesteenehteh
αγγούρι	ahnggooree	cucumber
αγκινάρες	ahnggeenahrehss	artichokes
καλαμπόκι	kahlahmbokkee	sweetcorn
κάρδαμο	kahrdhahmo	watercress
καρόττα	kahrottah	carrots
κολοκύθα	kollokkeethah	pumpkin
κολοκύθι	kollokkeethee	marrow (zucchini)
κουνουπίδι	koonoopeedhee	cauliflower
κουκιά	kookeeah	broad beans
κρεμμύδια	krehmeedheeah	onions
λαχανάκια Βρυξελλών	lahkhahnahkeeah vreeksehlonn	Brussels sprouts
λάχανο	lahkhahno	cabbage
κόκκινο λάχανο	kokkeeno lahkhahno	red cabbage
μαϊντανός	maheendahnoss	parsley
μανιτάρια	mahneetahreeah	mushrooms
μαρούλι	mahroolee	Cos lettuce
μελιτζάνα	mehleedzahnah	aubergine (eggplant)
μπάμιες	bahmee-ehss	okra
μπιζέλια	beezehleeah	peas
ντομάτες	dommahtehss	tomatoes
παντζάρι	pahndzahree	beetroot
πατάτες	pahtahtehss	potatoes
πιπεριές	peepehreeehss	sweet peppers
πιπεριές πράσινες	peepehreeehss prahsseenehss	green peppers
πράσσα	prahssah	leeks
ραδίκι	rahdheekee	chicory (endive)
ραπανάκι	rahpahnahkee	radish
ρεβίθια	rehveetheeah	chick peas
ρύζι	reezee	rice

σέλινο	sehleeno	celery
σπαράγγια	spahrahnggeeah	asparagus
σπανάκι	spahnahkee	spinach
φακές	fahkehss	lentils
φασολάκια φρέσκα	fahssollahkeeah frehskah	green beans
φασόλια γίγοντες	fahsolleeah yeeghondehss	butter beans
χόρτα	khortah	wild, green leaf
(αντίδια)	(ahndeedheeah)	vegetable

αγγινάρες με κουκιά (ahnggeenahrehss meh kookeeah)	trimmed artichokes up-ended in a pan, cooked with broad beans, sauteed onions and herbs
κολοκύθια κεφτέδες (kollokkeetheeah kehftehdhehss)	rissoles made of minced courgettes (zucchini), potatoes, onions, cheese and herbs
κολοκύθια τηγανιτά (kollokkeetheeah teeghahneetah)	cauliflower florets deep fried in batter
μουσακάς χωρίς κρέας (moossahkahss khoreess krehahss)	vegetarian moussaka made of aubergines, tomatoes, onions and cheese, with a béchamel sauce
μπάμιες (bahmee-ehss)	ladies' fingers (okra) cooked in a tomato and onion sauce
μπριάμ (breeahm)	a selection of summer vegetables sliced and arranged in a pan, seasoned and baked
ντομάτες γεμιστές με ρίζι (dommahtehss yehmeestehss meh reezee)	tomatoes stuffed with rice, currants, pine nuts and herbs, then baked
πατάτες γεμιστές (pahtahtehss yehmeestehss)	hollowed-out boiled potatoes stuffed with cheese and bacon and covered with a béchamel sauce, and baked
σπανακόπιττα (spahnahkoppeetah)	spinach and leeks with onions and *feta* cheese baked in a *phyllo* pastry case
σπανακόριζο (spahnahkorreezo)	spinach cooked with rice and dill
φασόλια γιαχνί (fahsolleeah yeeahkhnee)	dried beans in a tomato sauce

Herbs and spices *Βότανα και μπαχαρικά*

άνηθος	ahneethoss	dill
βασσιλικός	vahsseeleekoss	basil
δάφνη	dhahfnee	bay leaves
δεντρολίβανο	dhehndhroleevahno	rose
διόσμος	dheeozmoss	mint
κάππαρη	kahpahree	capers
μαϊντανός	maheendahnoss	parsley
μουστάρδα	moostahrdhah	mustard
ρίγανη	reeghahnee	oregano
σαφράνη	sahfrahnee	saffron
σκόρδο	skordho	garlic

Sauces and dressings *Σάλτσες*

λαδόξυδο (lahdhokseedho)	vinegar and oil
μαγιονέζα (mahyeeonnehzah)	mayonnaise
σάλτσα άσπρη (sahltsah ahspree)	meat stock with milk, butter, flour
σάλτσα αυγολέμονο (sahltsah ahvghollehmonno)	meat stock with eggs, flour and lemon juice
σάλτσα κίτρινη (sahltsah keetreenee)	mayonnaise, hard-boiled egg yolks and white wine
σάλτσα λαδολέμονο (sahltsah lahdhollehmonno)	olive oil with lemon and salt to which parsley or oregano is sometimes added
σάλτσα ντομάτα (sahltsah dommahta)	tomato with olive oil, parsley, onion
σάλτσα πράσινη (sahltsah prahsseenee)	mayonnaise with minced parsley
σάλτσα ψητού (sahltsah pseetoo)	meat broth with flour and butter
τζατζίκι (dzahdzeekee)	yoghurt with cucumber, garlic, oil, mint
σκορδαλιά (skordhahleeah)	garlic with bread or potatoes, oil, parsley

Cheese   Τυρί

Greece produces many varieties of cheese, though most of them are unknown outside the country.

The Greeks are very fond of cheese and frequently eat it with the meal, depending on the type of cheese. The most popular cheese is φέτα (**feh**tah), a white cheese made from goat's milk. You can find many varieties of *feta*: soft, hard, very creamy or very salty.

What kinds of cheese do you have?	Τι είδη τυριών έχετε;	tee **ee**dhee teereee**onn** **eh**khehteh
γραβιέρα (ghrahvee**eh**rah)	Swiss-style cheese; best varieties made in Corfu and Crete	
κασέρι (kah**sse**hree)	light, yellow cheese, rich in cream with a soft texture	
κασκαβάλι (kahskah**vah**lee)	yellow cheese, very creamy and rich	
κεφαλοτύρι (kehfahlot**tee**ree)	yellow cheese, very strong and salty with tiny holes	
μανούρι (mah**noo**ree)	sort of cottage cheese, makes a tasty dessert when mixed with honey	
μυζήθρα (meez**ee**thrah)	salted white soft cheese made from ewe's milk	
τελεμές (tehleh**mehss**)	tinned (canned) white cheese	

And you will probably come across these cheese dishes:

πουρέκια από τυρί (poorehkeeah ah**po** teeree)	rolls of *phyllo* (very thin) pastry containing a mixture of Gruyère and *feta*, with eggs, parsley and nutmeg
τυράκια τηγανιτά (teerahkeeah teeghahnee**tah**)	small squares of bread topped with a cheesy mixture and deep fried
τυροπιττάκια (teeroppee**tah**keeah)	baked triangular pastries containing *feta* and another hard cheese

Fruit *Φρούτα*

Rather than finishing the meal with a sweet dessert, Greeks like to have some fruit, of which there is a great variety.

Do you have fresh fruit?	Έχετε φρέσκα φρούτα;	ehkhehteh **frehs**kah **froo**tah
What kind of fruit do you have?	Τι είδη φρούτων έχετε;	tee **ee**dhee **froo**tonn **eh**khehteh
I'd like a (fresh) fruit cocktail.	Θα ήθελα μια φρουτο- σαλάτα από (φρέσκα) φρούτα.	thah **ee**thehlah meeah frootossah**lah**tah ah**po** (**frehs**kah) **froo**tah

αμύγδαλο	ah**meegh**dhahlo	almond
ανανάς	ahnah**nahss**	pineapple
αχλάδι	ah**khlah**dhee	pear
βατόμουρο	vah**tom**mooro	raspberry
βερύκοκο	veh**ree**kokko	apricot
δαμάσκηνο	dhah**mah**skeeno	plum
γκρέιπφρουτ	**greh**eepfroot	grapefruit
καρύδα	kah**ree**dhah	coconut
καρύδι	kah**ree**dhee	walnut
καρπούζι	kahr**poo**zee	watermelon
κεράσι	keh**rah**ssee	cherry
κίτρο	**kee**tro	citron
κομπόστα φρούτων	kom**bos**tah **froo**tonn	fruit compote
κυδώνι	kee**dho**nnee	quince
λεμόνι	leh**mo**nnee	lemon
μανταρίνι	mahndah**ree**nee	tangerine
μήλο	**mee**lo	apple
μούρο	**moo**ro	blackberry
μπανάνα	bah**nah**nah	banana
πεπόνι	peh**po**nnee	melon
πορτοκάλι	porto**kkah**lee	orange
ροδάκινο	rodhah**kee**no	peach
ρόδι	**ro**dhee	pomegranate
σταφίδα	stah**fee**dhah	raisin
σταφίδα σουλτανίνα	stah**fee**dhah sooltah**nee**nah	sultana raisin
σταφύλι	stah**fee**lee	grape
άσπρο σταφύλι	**ah**spro stah**fee**lee	white grape
κόκκινο σταφύλι	**ko**kkeeno stah**fee**lee	red grape
μαύρο σταφύλι	**mah**vro stah**fee**lee	black grape
σύκο	**see**ko	fig
φουντούκι	foon**doo**kee	hazelnut
φράουλα	**frah**oolah	strawberry
χουρμάς	khoor**mahss**	date

Dessert *Επιδόρπιο*

Traditionally Greeks do not have cakes or sweets at the end of a meal, instead they eat fresh fruit or ice cream. However, they do enjoy something sweet, usually with coffee, after their siesta – and, indeed, at almost any other time of day.

I'd like a dessert, please.	Θα ήθελα ένα επιδόρπιο, παρακαλώ.	thah **ee**thehlah **eh**nah ehpee**dhor**peeo pahrahkah**lo**
Something light, please.	Κάτι ελαφρό, παρακαλώ.	**kah**tee ehlah**fro** pahrahkah**lo**
Just a small portion.	Μόνο μια μικρή μερίδα.	**mo**nno meeah mee**kree** meh**ree**dhah
Nothing more, thanks.	Τίποτε άλλο, ευχαριστώ.	**tee**potteh **ah**lo ehfkhah**rees**to
What do you have for dessert?	Τι έχετε για επιδόρπιο;	tee **eh**khehteh yeeah ehpee**dhor**peeo
γρανίτα	ghrah**nee**tah	water-ice (sherbet)
καραμέλες	kahrah**meh**lehss	sweets (candy)
καρυδόπιττα	kahree**dhop**peetah	walnut bar
κέικ	''cake''	cake
κρέμα καραμελέ	**kreh**mah kahrah**meh**leh	caramel custard
μηλόπιττα	mee**lop**peetah	apple pie
μους	mooss	mousse (custard)
μπισκότα	bees**kot**tah	biscuits (cookies)
παγωτό	pah**ghot**to	ice-cream
παγωτό βανίλια	pah**ghot**to vah**nee**leeah	vanilla ice-cream
παγωτό κασάτα	pah**ghot**to kah**ssah**tah	spumoni, cassata
παγωτό σοκολάτα	pah**ghot**to sokkol**lah**tah	chocolate ice-cream
παγωτό φράουλα	pah**ghot**to **frah**oolah	strawberry ice-cream
πάστα	**pah**stah	tart
πάστα αμυγδάλου	**pah**stah ahmeegh**dhah**loo	almond tart
πάστα με καρύδα	**pah**stah meh kah**ree**dhah	coconut tart
πάστα σοκολάτα	**pah**stah sokkol**lah**tah	chocolate tart
πες μελμπά	pehss mehl**bah**	peach melba
πουτίγκα	poo**teeng**gah	pudding
ρυζόγαλο	ree**zogha**hlo	rice pudding
φρουΐ γκλασέ	**froo**ee glah**sseh**	crystallized fruit
φρουτοσαλάτα	frootossah**lah**tah	fruit cocktail

αμυγδαλωτό (ahmeeghdhahlotto)	almond paste with sugar (marzipan)
γαλακτομπούρεκο (ghahlahktomboorehko)	flaky pastry filled with custard, steeped in syrup
κατάιφι (kahtaheefee)	shredded pastry roll filled with walnuts and steeped in syrup
κουραμπιές (koorahmbeeehss)	biscuit (cookie)
λουκουμάδες (lookoomahdhehss)	light and fluffy honey puffs powdered with cinnamon and dripping with honey
λουκούμι (lookoomee)	Turkish delight
μελομακάρονο (mehlomahkahronno)	honey and nut biscuit (cookie)
μπακλαβάς (bahklahvahss)	baklava; a flaky pastry with a nut filling
παστέλι (pahstehlee)	sesame and honey bars
ρεβανί (rehvahnee)	sponge cake
χαλβάς (khahlvahss)	pudding made of farina, chopped almonds, honey and sugar

To accompany your pastry you will be offered several different kinds of coffee, ranging from instant (known as warm Nescafe – ζεστό Nescafe, zeh**sto** Nescafe) to American and French brews. But the one drunk by Greeks is known as Greek coffee.

The beans are reduced to a fine powder which is boiled with water, and then poured, grounds and all, into a cup. You should let the grounds settle and then only drink about half the cup.

| Ελληνικό καφέ | ehleenee**ko** kah**feh** | Greek coffee |

and depending on the quantity of sugar you want, ask for:

σκέτο	**skeh**to	without sugar
μέτριο	**meh**treeo	slightly sweet
γλυκό	ghlee**ko**	sweet

Aperitifs *Απεριτίφ*

The usual Greek aperitif is ούζο (**oo**zo). It's a spirit with an aniseed flavour, containing 50° alcohol. In the provinces it's generally served neat (straight) in thimblefuls, but in town you get larger quantities and most people prefer to add water, which clouds it.

Almost always and everywhere, when you order *ouzo*, the waiter will bring you some olives, cheese, sardines, dried octopus, etc., to eat with it. These titbits are generally called μεζέδες (meh**zeh**dhess).

You'll also have the chance to taste:

ούζο μαστίχα (oozo mah**steek**hah)	sweet and scented with mastic; you can find the best *mastiha* on the isle of Chios
I'd like some *ouzo*.	**Θα ήθελα λίγο ούζο.** thah **ee**thehlah **lee**gho **oo**zo

> **ΣΤΗΝ ΥΓΕΙΑ ΣΑΣ**
> (steen eeyee**ah** sahss)
> YOUR HEALTH/CHEERS!

Beer *Μπύρα*

Most of the beer available in Greece is very good, and there's a large variety of foreign, as well as Greek, brands. If you want to try some Greek beer, ask for one of the following: Φιξ (feeks) Άλφα (**ahl**fah).

I'd like a beer, please.	**Θα ήθελα μια μπύρα, παρακαλώ.**	thah **ee**thehlah mee**ah** **beer**ah pahrahkah**lo**
Do you have ... beer?	**Έχετε ... μπύρα;**	**eh**khehteh ... **beer**ah
bottled	εμφιαλωμένη	ehmfeeahlo**mmeh**nee
draught	βαρελιού	vahrehlee**oo**
foreign	εισαγώμενη	eesah**gho**mmehnee
light/dark	ξανθή/μαύρη	ksahn**thee**/**mahv**ree

Wine   Κρασί

Many visitors are amazed by the wide range of wines available in Greece, few of which are well known abroad.

The ancient Greeks carried the love of wine to an extreme, considering it a sign of civilization. No sooner had Greek colonists set foot on foreign soil than they planted grape vines. Down through the ages, however, the custom of drinking fermented beverages became largely lost among the Greeks.

Nevertheless, ancient Greece must be considered a pioneer of viniculture, for it was the Greeks who first learned the best size for vineyards and the best terrain for the cultivation of grapes.

Today vineyards are found throughout the country, producing over 500 000 tonnes of wine annually. Following often archaic methods of wine production, the regions of Attica, Corfu, Crete, Epirus, Peloponnesus, Thrace and the islands of the Aegean Sea have extensive vineyards.

Greece produces red, white and dessert wine, and, beyond that, a typically Greek one—its resinated wine. The latter is, usually, a white wine to which a resin—from pine needles—is added during the fermentation process to preserve it in the hot Greek climate. Because of its exotic taste you may find it difficult to get used to resinated wine. Since this wine takes on a bitter taste after its first year, try a young *retsina* to start off with.

However, if you can't get used to it, ask for unresinated wine everywhere. An unfavourable latitude and hot climate often produce full-bodied wine which is too alcoholic and somewhat harsh in taste. On the other hand, Greece generally offers quite good dessert wine, best known of which is doubtless the *Muscat of Samos* which is a sweet white wine. The red *Mavrodaphni* and white *Muscat Rion* from Patras and *Vino Santo* from Santorin are among other examples.

In Athens, on the islands and in small towns you'll easily find *tavernas* that store their wine in large barrels.

I'd like a bottle of white wine/red wine.	Θα ήθελα ένα μπουκάλι άσπρο κρασί/κόκκινο κρασί.	thah eethehlah ehnah bookahlee ahspro krahssee/kokkeeno krahssee
a carafe	μια καράφα	meeah kahrahfah
a half bottle	μισό μπουκάλι	meesso bookahlee
a glass	ένα ποτήρι	ehnah potteeree
a litre	ένα λίτρο	ehnah leetro
I'd like some un-resinated wine.	Θα ήθελα λίγο αρετσίνωτο κρασί.	thah eethehlah leegho ahrehtseenotto krahssee
A glass of retsina, please.	Ένα ποτήρι ρετσίνα, παρακαλώ.	ehnah potteeree rehtseenah pahrahkahlo
Please bring me another...	Παρακαλώ φέρτε μου ακόμη...	pahrahkahlo fehrteh moo ahkommee
What's the name of this wine?	Πως λέγεται αυτό το κρασί;	poss lehyehteh ahfto to krahssee
Where does this wine come from?	Από ποια περιοχή είναι αυτό το κρασί;	ahpo peeah pehreeokhee eeneh ahfto to krahssee
How old is this wine?	Πόσο παλιό είναι αυτό το κρασί;	posso pahleeo eeneh ahfto to krahssee
How much is a bottle of...?	Πόσο κάνει ένα μπουκάλι...;	posso kahnee ehnah bookahlee
I don't want anything too sweet.	Δεν θέλω κάτι πολύ γλυκό.	dhehn thehlo kahtee pollee ghleeko

red	κόκκινο	kokkeeno
white	άσπρο	ahspro
rosé	ροζέ	rozzeh
dry	ξηρό	kseero
light	ελαφρύ	ehlahfree
full-bodied	δυνατό	dheenahto
very dry	πολύ ξηρό	pollee kseero
sweet	γλυκό	ghleeko
resinated	ρετσινομένο	rehtseenommehno
unresinated	αρετσίνωτο	ahrehtseenotto
chilled	παγωμένο	pahghomehno
at room temperature	σέ θερμοκρασία δωματίου	seh thehrmokrahsseeah dhomahteeoo

Other alcoholic drinks Άλλα οινοπνευματώδη ποτά

Most of the well-known after-dinner drinks can be found in
Greece, or as an alternative try a Greek brandy. Some taste a
little rough, but others, like Metaxa, are quite good, even though
they don't taste like French brandy.

You will probably see a range of rather lurid liqueurs – these are
based on synthetic fruit syrups and don't live up to expectations.

I'd like a...	Θα ήθελα...	thah **ee**thehlah
I'd like to try a glass of...	Θα ήθελα να δοκιμάσω ένα ποτήρι...	thah **ee**thehlah nah dhokkee**mah**sso **eh**nah pot**tee**ree
Are there any local specialities?	Υπάρχουν σπεσιαλιτέ της περιοχής;	eepahrkhoon spehsseeahlee**teh** teess pehreeo**khees**s
Bring me a glass of Metaxa, please.	Φέρτε μου ένα ποτήρι Μεταξά, παρακαλώ.	**fehr**teh moo **eh**nah pot**tee**ree mehtah**ksah** pahrahkah**lo**

κίτρο (keetro)	rather sweet, with a citrus flavour; found on the island of Naxos
Μεταξά (mehtah**ksah**)	a Greek brandy, quite enjoyable
κουμ-κουάτ (koomkoo**aht**)	yellow-coloured brandy, found on the isle of Corfu and made from tiny oranges

brandy	ένα κονιάκ	**eh**nah konnee**ahk**
gin	ένα τζιν	**eh**nah tzeen
and tonic	και τόνικ	keh **ton**neek
liqueur	ένα λικέρ	**eh**nah lee**kehr**
rum	ένα ρούμι	**eh**nah **roo**mee
sherry	ένα τσέρι	**eh**nah **tseh**ree
vermouth	ένα βερμούτ	**eh**nah vehr**moot**
vodka	μια βότκα	mee**ah votkah**
whisky	ένα ουίσκι	**eh**nah "whisky"
neat (straight)	σκέτο	**skeh**to
on the rocks	με παγάκια	meh pah**ghah**keeah
and soda	και σόδα	keh **so**dah

glass	ένα ποτήρι	**eh**nah pot**tee**ree
bottle	ένα μπουκάλι	**eh**nah boo**kah**lee
double (shot of)	ένα διπλό	**eh**nah dhee**plo**

Nonalcoholic drinks *Μη οινοπνευματώδη ποτά*

Tap water in Greece is good and not calcareous but bottled water is also available.

I'd like a/an...	Θα ήθελα...	thah **ee**thehlah
We'd like a/an...	Θα θέλαμε...	thah **theh**lahmeh
apple juice	ένα χυμό μήλου	**eh**nah kheemo **mee**loo
(hot) chocolate	μια (ζεστή) σοκολάτα	**mee**ah (zeh**stee**) sokko**llah**tah
coffee *	ένα καφέ	**eh**nah kah**feh**
instant	στιγμιαίο	steegh**meee**eho
Greek	ελληνικό	ehlee**nee**ko
black	μαύρο	**mah**vro
with cream	με κρέμα	meh **kreh**mah
with milk	με γάλα	meh **ghah**lah
decaffeinated	χωρίς καφεΐνη	khor**eess** kahfeh**ee**nee
fruit juice	ένα χυμό φρούτων	**eh**nah kheemo **froo**tonn
grapefruit juice	ένα χυμό κρέιπφρουτ	**eh**nah kheemo "grapefruit"
herb tea	ένα τσάι από βότανα	**eh**nah tsahee ahpo **vot**tahnah
lemon juice	ένα χυμό λεμονιού	**eh**nah kheemo lehmon**nee**oo
lemonade	μια λεμονάδα	**mee**ah lehmon**nah**dhah
milk	ένα ποτήρι γάλα	**eh**nah pot**tee**ree **ghah**lah
milkshake	ένα μιλκσέικ	**eh**nah "milkshake"
mineral water	ένα μεταλλικό νερό	**eh**nah mehtahl**lee**ko nehro
fizzy (carbonated)	αεριούχο	ahehree**oo**kho
still	κανονικό	kahnon**nee**ko
orange juice	ένα χυμό πορτοκαλιού	**eh**nah kheemo portokkah**lee**oo
orangeade	μια πορτοκαλάδα	**mee**ah portokkah**lah**dhah
tea	ένα τσάι	**eh**nah tsahee
cup of tea	ένα φλιτζάνι τσάι	**eh**nah fleed**zah**nee tsahee
with milk	με γάλα	meh **ghah**lah
with lemon	με λεμόνι	meh lehmonnee
iced tea	ένα παγωμένο τσάι	**eh**nah pahghom**meh**no tsahee
tomato juice	ένα χυμό ντομάτας	**eh**nah kheemo dommah**tahss**
tonic water	ένα τόνικ	**eh**nah tonneek

---

* read about coffee on page 55

Complaints   Παράπονα

There is a plate/ glass missing.	Λείπει ένα πιάτο/ ποτήρι.	leepee ehnah peeahto/ potteeree
I don't have a knife/ fork/spoon.	Δεν έχω μαχαίρι/ πηρούνι/κουτάλι.	dhehn ehkho mahkhehree/ peeroonee/kootahlee
That's not what I ordered.	Δεν είναι αυτό που παράγγειλα.	dhehn eeneh ahfto poo pahrahnggeelah
I asked for...	Ζήτησα...	zeeteessah
There must be some mistake.	Πρέπει να έγινε κάποιο λάθος.	prehpee nah ehyeeneh kahpeeo lahthoss
May I change this?	Μπορώ να αλλάξω αυτό;	borro nah ahlahkso ahfto
I asked for a small portion (for the child).	Ζήτησα μια μικρή μερίδα (για το παιδί).	zeeteessah meeah meekree mehreedhah (yeeah to pehdhee)
The meat is...	Το κρέας είναι...	to krehahss eeneh
overdone underdone too tough	πολύ ψημένο άψητο πολύ σκληρό	pollee pseemehno ahpseeto pollee skleero
This is too...	Αυτό είναι πολύ...	ahfto eeneh pollee
bitter/salty/sweet	πικρό/αλμυρό/γλυκό	peekro/ahlmeero/ ghleeko
I don't like this.	Δεν μου αρέσει αυτό.	dhehn moo ahrehssee ahfto
The food is cold.	Το φαγητό είναι κρύο.	to fahyeeto eeneh kreeo
This isn't fresh.	Δεν είναι φρέσκο.	dhehn eeneh frehsko
What's taking so long?	Γιατί αργεί τόσο;	yeeahtee ahrghee tosso
Have you forgotten our drinks?	Έχετε ξεχάσει τα ποτά μας;	ehkhehteh ksehkhahssee tah pottah mahss
The wine tastes of cork.	Το κρασί μυρίζει φελλό.	to krahssee meereezee fehlo
This isn't clean.	Αυτό δεν είναι καθαρό.	ahfto dhehn eeneh kahthahro
Would you ask the head waiter to come over?	Μπορείτε να ζητήσετε στον αρχισερβιτόρο να έλθη εδώ;	borreeteh nah zeeteessehteh stonn ahrkheessehrveetorro nah ehlthee ehdho

The bill (check) *Ο λογαριασμός*

By law all service charges must be included in the bill, but there is nothing to stop you offering a tip if the service has been particularly attentive.

I'd like to pay.	Θα ήθελα να πληρώσω.	thah **ee**thehlah nah pleer**o**sso
We'd like to pay separately.	Θα θέλαμε να πληρώσουμε χωριστά.	thah **theh**lahmeh nah pleer**o**ssoomeh khorree**stah**
I think there is a mistake in this bill.	Νομίζω υπάρχει λάθος σε αυτό τον λογαριασμό.	nomm**ee**zo eepahrkhee **lah**thoss seh ahfto tonn loghahree**ah**zmo
What's this amount for?	Γιατί είναι αυτή η τιμή;	yeeaht**ee ee**neh ahft**ee** ee teem**ee**
Is service included?	Συμπεριλαμβάνεται το σερβίρισμα;	seembehreelahmv**ah**nehteh to sehr**vee**reezmah
Is the cover charge included?	Συμπεριλαμβάνεται το κουβέρ;	seembehreelahmv**ah**nehteh to koo**vehr**
Is everything included?	Συμπεριλαμβάνονται τα πάντα;	seembehreelahmv**ah**nondeh tah **pahn**dah
Do you accept traveller's cheques?	Δέχεστε τράβελερς τσεκ;	**dheh**khehsteh **trah**vehlehrss tsehk
Can I pay with this credit card?	Μπορώ να πληρώσω με αυτή την πιστωτική κάρτα;	borr**o** nah pleer**o**sso meh ahft**ee** teen peestotee**kee kahr**tah
Thank you, this is for you.	Ευχαριστώ, αυτό είναι για σας.	ehfkhahree**sto** ahft**o ee**neh yeeah sahss
Keep the change.	Κρατήστε τα ρέστα.	krah**tee**steh tah **reh**stah
That was a delicious meal.	Το γεύμα ήταν πολύ νόστιμο.	to **yehv**mah **ee**tahn poll**ee no**steemo
We enjoyed it, thank you.	Το απολαύσαμε, ευχαριστούμε.	to ahpoll**ahf**sahmeh ehfkhahree**stoo**meh

> **ΤΟ ΦΙΛΟΔΩΡΗΜΑ ΣΥΜΠΕΡΙΛΑΜΒΑΝΕΤΑΙ**
> SERVICE INCLUDED

TIPPING, see inside back-cover

Εστιατόριο – Φαγητά

Snacks – Picnic Σνακς – πικ-νικ

There is a wide variety of snacks available in Greece, and many of them are made with layers of wafer-thin *phyllo* pastry. They are usually baked or deep-fried, and fillings range from spinach and cheese to chicken and other kinds of meat.

Another typically Greek snack is σουβλάκι (soovlahkee) which consists of slices of meat grilled on a spit and served with tomatoes, onions and parsley, all wrapped in a type of bread called πίττα (**pee**tah). It's very cheap and tasty and can be found almost anywhere in the country.

I'll have one of these, please.	Θα πάρω ένα από αυτά, παρακαλώ.	thah **pah**ro **eh**nah ahpo ahf**tah** pahrahkah**lo**
Give me two of these and one of those, please.	Δώστε μου δύο από αυτά και ένα από αυτό, παρακαλώ.	**dhos**teh moo **dhee**o ahpo ahf**tah** keh **eh**nah ahpo ahf**to** pahrahkah**lo**
to the left/right/ above/below	στα αριστερά/δεξιά/ από πάνω/από κάτω	stah ahreesteh**rah**/ dhehk**see**ah/ ahpo **pah**no/ahpo **kah**to
It's to take-away.	Είναι για να το πάρω μαζί μου.	**ee**neh **yee**ah nah to **pah**ro mah**zee** moo
Do you have any cold drinks?	Έχετε παγομένα ποτά;	**eh**khehteh pahgho**mmeh**nah pot**tah**
May I have a straw?	Μπορώ να έχω ένα καλαμάκι;	bor**ro** nah **eh**kho **eh**nah kahlah**mah**kee
How much is that?	Πόσο κάνει αυτό;	**pos**so **kah**nee ahf**to**
I'd like a...	Θα ήθελα...	thah **ee**thehlah
cheese pie	μια τυρόπιττα	meeah tee**rop**peetah
chicken pie	μια κοτόπιττα	meeah kot**top**peetah
meat pie	μια κρεατόπιττα	meeah krehahto**ppee**tah
spinach pie	μια σπανακόπιττα	meeah spahnahk**kop**peetah
hamburger	ένα χάμπουργκερ	**eh**nah **khahm**boohrgehr
hot dog	ένα χοτ-ντογκ	**eh**nah ''hot-dog''
pastry	μια πάστα	meeah **pah**stah
pie	μια πίττα	meeah **pee**tah
roll	ένα ψωμάκι	**eh**nah pso**mah**kee
salad	μια σαλάτα	meeah sah**lah**tah
sandwich	ένα σάντουϊτς	**eh**nah **sahn**dooeetss
cheese	από τυρί	ahpo tee**ree**
ham	από ζαμπόν	ahpo zahm**bonn**

Here's a basic list of food and drink that might come in useful when shopping for a picnic.

May I help myself?	Μπορώ να εξυπηρετηθώ μόνος/-η μου;	borro nah ehksee peereh-teetho monnass/-ee moo
Please give me a/ an/some...	Παρακαλώ, μου δίνετε...	pahrahkahlo moo dheenehteh
apples	μήλα	meelah
bananas	μπανάνες	bahnahnehss
biscuits	μπισκότα	beeskottah
beer	μια μπύρα	meeah beerah
bread	ψωμί	psommee
butter	βούτυρο	vooteero
cake	ένα κέικ	ehnah "cake"
cheese	τυρί	teeree
chips (Am.)	τσιπς (πατατάκια)	"chips" (pahtahtahkeeah)
chocolate bar	μια σοκολάτα	meeah sokkollahtah
coffee	καφέ	kahfeh
cold cuts	αλαντικά κομμένα σε φέτες	ahlahndeekah kommehnah seh fehtehss
cookies	μπισκότα	beeskottah
crackers	κράκερς	krahkehrss
crisps	τσιπς (πατατάκια)	"chips" (pahtahtahkeeah)
eggs	αυγά	ahvghah
gherkins (pickles)	αγγούρια ξυδάτα	ahnggooreeah kseedhahtah
grapes	σταφύλια	stahfeeleeah
ham	ζαμπόν	zahmbonn
ice-cream	παγωτό	pahghotto
lemon	ένα λεμόνι	ehnah lehmonnee
lemonade	μια λεμονάδα	meeah lehmonnahdhah
milk	γάλα	ghahlah
mineral water	μεταλλικό νερό	mehtahleeko nehro
mustard	μουστάρδα	moostahrdhah
oranges	πορτοκάλια	portokkahleeah
pastries	πάστες	pahstehss
pepper	πιπέρι	peepehree
roll	ένα ψωμάκι	ehnah psommahkee
salt	αλάτι	ahlahtee
sausages	λουκάνικα	lookahneekah
soft drink	ένα αναψυκτικό	ehnah ahnahpseekteeko
sugar	ζαχάρη	zahkhahree
tea	τσάι	tsahee
wine	κρασί	krahssee
yoghurt	γιαούρτι	yeeahoortee

Travelling around

Plane *Αεροπλάνο*

Is there a flight to Athens?	Υπάρχει πτήση για την Αθήνα;	eepahrkhee pteessee yeeah teen ahtheenah
Is it a direct flight?	Είναι κατευθείας η πτήση;	eeneh kahtehftheeahss ee pteessee
When's the next plane to Rhodes?	Πότε είναι το επόμενο αεροπλάνο για τη Ρόδο;	potteh eeneh to ehpomehno ahehroplahno yeeah tee rodho
Do I have to change planes?	Πρέπει να αλλάξω αεροπλάνα;	prehpee nah ahlahkso ahehroplahnah
Can I make a connection to Cos?	Μπορώ να έχω αντα- πόκριση για τη Κω;	borro nah ehkho ahndahpokreessee yeeah tee ko
What time do we take off?	Τι ώρα απογειώνεται το αεροπλάνο;	tee orrah ahpoyeeonnehteh to ahehroplahno
What time do I have to check in?	Τι ώρα πρέπει να είμαι στο αεροδρόμιο;	tee orrah prehpee nah eemeh sto ahehrodhrommeeo
Is there a bus to the airport?	Υπάρχει λεωφορείο για το αεροδρόμιο;	eepahrkhee lehofforreeo yeeah to ahehrodhrommeeo
What's the flight number?	Ποιος είναι ο αριθμός της πτήσης;	peeoss eeneh o ahreethmoss teess pteesseess
What time do we arrive?	Τι ώρα φθάνουμε;	tee orrah fthahnoomeh
I'd like to ... my reservation on flight no 123.	Θα ήθελα να... την κράτηση μου για την πτήση υπ'αριθμό 123.	thah eethehlah nah... teen krahteessee moo yeeah teen pteessee eepahreethmo 123
cancel	ακυρώσω	ahkeerosso
change	αλλάξω	ahlahkso
confirm	επιβεβαιώσω	ehpeevehvehosso

ΑΦΙΞΗ	ΑΝΑΧΩΡΗΣΗ
ARRIVAL	DEPARTURE

TICKETS, see page 68

Train *Τραίνο*

The Greek rail network is not particularly extensive. However, there are lines between Athens and northern Greece, and Athens and the Peloponnese. Always book in advance as trains get very crowded.

To the railway station *Για τον σιδηροδρομικό σταθμό*

Where's the railway station?	Που είναι ο σιδηροδρομικός σταθμός;	poo **ee**neh o seedheerodhrommee**koss** stahth**moss**
Taxi!	Ταξί!	tah**ksee**
Take me to the railway station.	Να με πάτε στο σιδηροδρομικό σταθμό.	nah meh **pah**teh sto seedheerodhrommee**ko** stahth**mo**
What's the fare?	Πόσο κάνει;	**posso kah**nee

ΕΙΣΟΔΟΣ	ENTRANCE
ΕΞΟΔΟΣ	EXIT
ΠΡΟΣ ΤΙΣ ΑΠΟΒΑΘΡΕΣ	TO THE PLATFORMS
ΠΛΗΡΟΦΟΡΙΕΣ	INFORMATION

Where's the...? *Που είναι...;*

Where is/are the...?	Που είναι...;	poo **ee**neh
bar	το μπαρ	to ''bar''
booking office	το γραφείο κρατήσεως	to grah**fee**o krah**tee**ssehoss
left luggage office (baggage check)	το γραφείο αποσκευών	to grah**fee**o ahposkeh**vonn**
lost property (lost and found) office	το γραφείο απωλεσθέντων αντικειμένων	to grah**fee**o ahpollehs**thehn**donn ahndeekee**meh**nonn
luggage lockers	το τμήμα αποσκευών	to **tmee**mah ahposkeh**vonn**
newsstand	το περίπτερο	to pehr**eep**tehro
platform 7	η αποβάθρα 7	ee ahpo**vvahth**rah 7
reservations office	το γραφείο κρατήσεως	to grah**fee**o krah**tee**ssehoss
restaurant	το εστιατόριο	to ehsteeah**tor**reeo
snack bar	το σνακ-μπαρ	to ''snack bar''

TAXI, see page 21

ticket office	το γραφείο εισιτηρίων	to ghrahfeeo eesseeteereeonn
waiting room	η αίθουσα αναμονής	ee ehthoossah ahnahmonneess
Where are the toilets?	Που είναι οι τουαλέττες;	poo eeneh ee tooahlehtehss

Inquiries Πληροφορίες

When is the ... train to Patras?	Πότε είναι το... τραίνο για τη Πάτρα;	potteh eeneh to... trehno yeeah tee pahtrah
first/last/next	πρώτο/τελευταίο/ επόμενο	protto/tehlehfteho/ ehpommehno
What time does the train to Athens leave?	Τι ώρα φεύγει το τραίνο για Αθήνα;	tee orrah fehvyee to trehno yeeah ahtheenah
What's the fare to Volos?	Πόσο κάνει το εισιτήριο για Βόλο;	posso kahnee to eesseeteereeo yeeah vollo
Is it an express train?	Είναι εζπρές το τραίνο;	eeneh ehksprehss to trehno
Is there a connection to...?	Υπάρχει ανταπόκριση για...;	eepahrkhee ahndahpokreessee yeeah
Do I have to change trains?	Πρέπει να αλλάξω τραίνο;	prehpee nah ahlahkso trehno
Is there enough time to change?	Είναι αρκετός ο χρόνος για την αλλαγή τραίνου;	eeneh ahrkehtoss o khronnoss yeeah teen ahlahyee trehnoo
Is the train running on time?	Φεύγουν τα τραίνα στην ώρα τους;	fehvghoon tah trehnah steen orrah tooss
What time does the train arrive in Patras?	Τι ώρα φθάνει το τραίνο στην Πάτρα;	tee orrah fthahnee to trehno steen pahtrah
Does the train stop in Argos?	Αυτό το τραίνο σταματά στο Άργος;	ahfto to trehno stahmahtah sto ahrghoss
What platform does the train to Patras leave from?	Από ποια αποβάθρα φεύγει το τραίνο για την Πάτρα;	ahpo peeah ahpovvahthrah fehvyee to trehno yeeah teen pahtrah
What platform does the train from Paris arrive at?	Σε ποια αποβάθρα φθάνει το τραίνο από το Παρίσι;	seh peeah ahpovvahthrah fthahnee to trehno ahpo to pahreessee
I'd like to buy a timetable.	Θα ήθελα να αγοράσω ένα ωράριο.	thah eethehlah nah ahghorrahsso ehnah orrahreeo

Το τραίνο είναι κατευθείαν.	It's a direct train.
Πρέπει να αλλάξετε στο...	You have to change at...
Να αλλάξετε στο... και να πάρετε ένα τοπικό τραίνο.	Change at ... and get a local train.
Η αποβάθρα 7 είναι...	Platform 7 is...
προς τα εκεί/πάνω αριστερά/δεξιά	over there/upstairs on the left/on the right
Υπάρχει τραίνο για... στις...	There's a train to... at...
Το τραίνο σας φεύγει από την αποβάθρα 8.	Your train will leave from platform 8.
Υπάρχει καθυστέρηση ... λεπτών.	There will be a delay of ... minutes.
Η πρώτη θέση μπροστά/στο κέντρο/στο πίσω μέρος.	First class at the front/in the middle/at the end.

Tickets   *Εισιτήρια*

I'd like a ticket to ...	Θα ήθελα ένα εισιτήριο για ...	thah **ee**thehlah **eh**nah eesseet**ee**reeo yeeah
single (one-way)	απλό	ahplo
return (roundtrip)	μετ' επιστροφής	meht ehpeestrof**fee**ss
first/second class	πρώτη/δεύτερη θέση	**prot**tee/**dheh**ftehree **theh**ssee
half price	μισή τιμή	mee**ssee** tee**mee**

Reservation   *Κράτηση*

I'd like to reserve a...	Θα ήθελα να κρατήσω...	thah **ee**thehlah nah krah**tee**sso
seat (by the window)	μια θέση (στο παράθυρο)	**mee**ah **theh**ssee (sto pahr**ah**theero)
berth	ένα κρεββάτι	**eh**nah kreh**vah**tee
upper	στο πάνω μέρος	sto **pah**no **meh**ross
middle	στη μέση	stee **meh**ssee
lower	στο κάτω μέρος	sto **kah**to **meh**ross
berth in the sleeping car	ένα κρεββάτι στο βαγκόν-λι	**eh**nah kreh**vah**tee sto vah**gonn** lee

All aboard *Επιβίβαση*

Is this the right platform for the train to Paris?	Είναι αυτή η σωστή αποβάθρα για το τραίνο για το Παρίσι;	eeneh ahftee ee sostee ahpovvahthrah yeeah to trehno yeeah to pahreessee
Is this the train to Tripolis?	Είναι αυτό το τραίνο για την Τρίπολη;	eeneh ahfto to trehno yeeah teen treepollee
Excuse me. May I get by?	Με συγχωρείτε. Μπορώ να περάσω;	meh seengkhorreeteh. borro nah pehrrahsso
Is this seat taken?	Είναι κατειλημμένη αυτή η θέση;	eeneh kahteeleemehnee ahftee ee thehssee

ΚΑΠΝΙΣΤΕΣ	ΜΗ ΚΑΠΝΙΣΤΕΣ
SMOKER	NONSMOKER

I think that's my seat.	Νομίζω ότι αυτή είναι η θέση μου.	nommeezo ottee ahftee eeneh ee thehssee moo
Would you let me know before we get to Mycenae?	Μπορείτε να με ειδοποιήσετε πριν φθάσουμε στις Μυκήνες;	borreeteh nah meh eedhoppeeeessehteh preen fthahssoomeh steess meekeenehss
What station is this?	Ποιος σταθμός είναι αυτός;	peeoss stahthmoss eeneh ahftoss
How long does the train stop here?	Για πόση ώρα σταματά το τραίνο εδώ;	yeeah possee orrah stahmahtah to trehno ehdho
When do we arrive in Athens?	Πότε φθάνουμε στην Αθήνα;	potteh fthahnoomeh steen ahtheenah

Sleeping *Στο βαγκόν-λι*

Are there free compartments in the sleeping car?	Υπάρχουν ελεύθερα διαμερίσματα στο βαγκόν-λι;	eepahrkhoon ehlehfthehrah dheeahmehreezmahtah sto vahgonn lee
Where's the sleeping car?	Που είναι το βαγκόν-λι;	poo eeneh to vahgonn lee
Where's my berth?	Που είναι το κρεββάτι μου;	poo eeneh to krehvahtee moo

I'd like a lower berth.	Θα ήθελα ένα κρεββάτι στο κάτω μέρος.	thah eetehlah ehnah krehvahtee sto kahto mehross
Would you make up our berths?	Θα μπορούσατε να μας φτιάξετε τα κρεββάτια;	thah borroossahteh nah mahss fteeahksehteh tah krehvahteeah
Would you wake me at 7 o'clock?	Μπορείτε να με ξυπνήσετε στις 7;	borreeteh nah meh kseepneessehteh steess 7

Eating Γεύμα

| Is there a dining-car/buffet on the train? | Υπάρχει βαγόνι-εστιατόριο/μπουφέ στο τραίνο; | eepahrkhee vahgonnee-ehsteeahtorreeo/''buffet'' sto trehno |

Baggage and porters Αποσκευές και αχθοφόροι

Porter!	Αχθοφόρε!	ahkhthofforreh
Can you help me with my luggage?	Μπορείτε να με βοηθήσετε με τις αποσκευές μου;	borreeteh nah meh voeetheessehteh meh teess ahposkehvehss moo
Where are the luggage trolleys (carts)?	Που είναι τα καροτσάκια αποσκευών;	poo eeneh tah kahrotsahkeeah ahposkehvonn
Where are the luggage lockers?	Που είναι το τμήμα αποσκευών;	poo eeneh to tmeemah ahposkehvonn
Where's the left-luggage office (baggage check)?	Που είναι το γραφείο διαφυλάξεως αποσκευών;	poo eeneh to ghrahfeeo dheeahfeelahksehoss ahposkehvonn
I'd like to leave my luggage, please.	Θα ήθελα να αφήσω τις αποσκευές μου, παρακαλώ.	thah eetehlah nah ahfeesso teess ahposkehvehss moo pahrahkahlo
I'd like to register (check) my luggage.	Θα ήθελα να παραδώσω συστημένες τις αποσκευές μου.	thah eetehlah nah pahrahdhosso seesteemehnehss teess ahposkehvehss moo

---

ΚΑΤΑΓΡΑΦΗ ΑΠΟΣΚΕΥΩΝ
REGISTERING (CHECKING) BAGGAGE

PORTERS, see also page 18

Ταξιδεύοντας

Coach (long-distance bus)   *Υπεραστικό λεωφορείο*

Coach is the ideal way of getting around Greece, as there is only a very limited rail network. Even the smallest towns can be reached, although the service is not so frequent. Coaches are cheap, fast, comfortable, and often crowded.

To find out about schedules, go to one of the larger bus stations.

For more phrases look under the train section, they should also apply to coach travel.

Inquiries   *Πληροφορίες*

When is the... coach to Patras?	Πότε φεύγει το... λεωφορείο για Πάτρα;	potteh fehvyee to... lehofforreeo yeeah pahtrah
first/last/next	πρώτο/τελευταίο/ επόμενο	protto/tehlefteho/ ehpommehno
What time does the coach to Volos leave?	Τι ώρα φεύγει το λεωφορείο για Βόλο;	tee orrah fehvyee to lehofforreeo yeeah vollo
What's the fare to Argos?	Πόσο κάνει το εισιτήριο για Άργος;	posso kahnee to eessee-teereeo yeeah ahrghoss
Do I have to change coaches?	Πρέπει να αλλάξω λεωφορείο;	prehpee nah ahlahkso lehofforreeo
What time does the coach arrive in ...?	Τι ώρα φθάνει το λεωφορείο στην ...;	tee orrah fthahnee to lehofforreeo steen
Does the coach stop in Volos?	Σταματά το λεωφορείο στον Βόλο;	stahmahtah to lehofforreeo stonn vollo
How long does the journey (trip) take?	Πόση ώρα διαρκεί το ταξίδι;	possee orrah dheeahr-kee to tahkseedhee
I'd like to buy a time table.	Θα ήθελα να αγοράσω ένα ωράριο.	thah eethehlah nah ahghorrahsso ehnah orrahreeo

Kilometres into miles												
1 kilometre (km.) = 0.62 miles												
km.	10	20	30	40	50	60	70	80	90	100	110	120	130
miles	6	12	19	25	31	37	44	50	56	62	68	75	81

Bus *Λεωφορείο*

Local buses are cheap and cheerful. If you want a seat then you should get to the bus stop early. In big cities enter the bus at the front and deposit the correct fare in the box provided. When you want to get off, press a button that makes a "stop" sign light up. Travel in Athens is free before 8 a.m.

Which bus goes to the centre of town?	Ποιο λεωφορείο πηγαίνει στο κέντρο της πόλης;	peeo lehofforreeo peeyehnee sto **kehn**dro teess **poll**eess
Where can I get a bus to the opera?	Που μπορώ να πάρω το λεωφορείο για την Όπερα;	poo borro nah **pah**ro to lehofforreeo yeeah teen oppehrah
Which bus do I take to Syntagma?	Ποιο λεωφορείο πρέπει να πάρω για το Σύνταγμα;	peeo lehofforreeo **preh**pee nah **pah**ro yeeah to **seen**dahghmah
How often do the buses to ... run?	Πόσο συχνά υπαρχει λεωφορείο για ...;	**poss**o seekhnah eepahr-khee lehofforreeo yeeah
Where's the bus stop?	Που σταματά το λεωφορείο;	poo stahmahtah to lehofforreeo
When is the ... bus to Halandri?	Πότε είναι το λεωφορείο για το Χαλάνδρι;	**pott**eh **een**eh to... lehofforreeo yeeah to khahlahndhree
first/last/next	πρώτο/τελευταίο/ επόμενο	**prott**o/tehleh**fteh**o/ ehpommehno
How much is the fare to...?	Πόσο κάνει το εισι-τήριο για...;	**poss**o **kahn**ee to eessee-**teer**eeo yeeah
Do I have to change buses?	Πρέπει να αλλάξω λεωφορείο;	**preh**pee nah ahlahkso lehofforreeo
How many bus stops are there to...?	Πόσες στάσεις είναι μέχρι...;	possehss stahsseess **een**eh **mehkh**ree
Will you tell me when to get off?	Θα μου πείτε που να κατέβω;	thah moo **peet**eh poo nah kahtehvo
I want to get off at the National Garden.	Θέλω να κατέβω στον Εθνικό κήπο.	**theh**lo nah kahtehvo stonn ehthneeko **keep**o

```
ΣΤΑΣΗ ΛΕΩΦΟΡΕΙΟΥ
BUS STOP
```

Ταξιδεύοντας

Underground (subway) *Ηλεκτρικός*

There is a long underground line in Athens called Ηλεκτρικός (eelehktreekoss). It is fast and economical, but should be avoided during lunch hours. Cancel your ticket just before going on the platform, and keep it until the end of your journey as you will be asked for it at the exit.

Where's the nearest underground station?	Που είναι ο κοντινότερος σταθμός του Ηλεκτρικού;	poo **ee**neh o kondee-**not**tehross staht**hmoss** too eelehktree**koo**
Does this train go to...?	Πηγαίνει αυτό το τραίνο στο...;	peey**eh**nee ahft**o** to **treh**no sto
Is the next station ...?	Ο επόμενος σταθμός είναι...;	o ehp**om**mehnoss staht**hmoss ee**neh

Boat service *Υπηρεσία πλοίου*

Most people like to do a bit of island-hopping while on holiday, and it's certainly not expensive to do so. There are up to four fare classes – the cheapest is usually fine for a daytrip. If you are travelling overnight then it makes sense to book a first or second class cabin. If you want to get around more quickly then catch a hydrofoil from Zéa harbour in Athens – but it's more expensive.

For those on a budget, buy soft drinks and sandwiches before boarding.

When does the next boat to ... leave?	Πότε φεύγει το επόμενο πλοίο για...;	**pott**eh **fehv**yee to ehp**om**mehno pl**ee**o yeeah
Where's the embarkation point?	Που είναι το σημείο επιβιβάσεως;	poo **ee**neh to seem**ee**o ehpeeveev**ahs**sehoss
How long does the crossing take?	Πόση ώρα διαρκεί η διαδρομή;	**poss**ee orrah dheeahr-**kee** ee dheeahdhrom**mee**
At which ports do we stop?	Σε ποια λιμάνια σταματάμε;	seh peeah leem**ahn**eeah stahmaht**ahm**eh
Does the boat stop at...?	Σταματά το πλοίο στο...;	stahmaht**ah** to pl**ee**o sto

I'd like a... ticket.	Θα ήθελα ένα εισητήριο...	thah **ee**thehlah **eh**nah eesseet**ee**reeo
first/second/third/ fourth class	πρώτης/δεύτερης/ τρίτης/τέταρτης θέσης	prott**ee**ss/dheh**ft**ehreess/tr**ee**teess/ t**eh**tahrteess thehss**ee**ss
I'd like to take a tour of the harbour/ cruise.	Θα ήθελα να κάνω ένα ταξίδι στα λιμάνια/ μια κρουαζιέρα.	thah **ee**thehlah nah **kah**no **eh**nah tahks**ee**-dhee stah leem**ah**neeah/ m**ee**ah krooahz**ee**ehrah
boat	η βάρκα	ee **vah**rkah
cabin	η καμπίνα	ee kahmb**ee**nah
single/double	μονή/διπλή	mon**ee**/dheepl**ee**
deck	το κατάστρωμα	to kaht**ah**strommah
ferry	το φέρρυ-μποτ	to "ferry boat"
hydrofoil	το ιπτάμενο δελφίνι	to eept**ah**mehno dhehl-f**ee**nee
life belt/boat	το σωσίβιο/η ναυαγο-σωστική λέμβος	to soss**ee**veeo/ee nahvah-ghoss**oste**ek**ee** **leh**mvoss
ship	το πλοίο	to pl**ee**o

Bicycle hire *Ενοικίαση ποδηλάτου*

Bicycles have become popular over the last few years, particularly on the islands, but it's not always possible to hire one in high season. In low season you may be able to get a reduction.

| I'd like to hire a bicycle. | Θα ήθελα να νοικιάσω ένα ποδήλατο. | thah **ee**thehlah nah neekee**ah**sso **eh**nah podh**ee**lahto |

Other means of transport *Άλλα μέσα μεταφοράς*

cable car	εναέριο βαγκόνι	ehnah**eh**reeo vahg**o**nnee
helicopter	ελικόπτερο	ehleek**o**ptehro
moped	μοτοποδήλατο	mottoppodh**ee**lahto
motorbike	μοτοσυκλέτα	mottosseek**leh**tah
scooter	βέσπα	**veh**spah

Or perhaps you prefer:

| to hitchhike | κάνω ωτοστόπ | **kah**no otto**stop** |
| to walk | περπατώ | pehrpah**to** |

Car *Αυτοκίνητο*

The condition of roads varies in Greece. Motorways (express-ways) tend to be good, and tolls are charged according to distance. Secondary roads on the main tourist routes are also reasonably well-maintained, but many country roads may be little more than dirt tracks. Carry a red warning-triangle, first-aid kit and fire extinguisher, and wear your seat belt.

Where's the nearest filling station?	Που είναι το κοντινό-τερο πρατήριο βενζί-νης;	poo **ee**neh to kondee-**no**ttehro praht**ee**reeo vehnz**ee**neess
Full tank, please.	Γέμισμα, παρακαλώ.	**yeh**meezmah pahrah-**kah**lo
I'd like ... litres of petrol (gasoline).	Θα ήθελα ... λίτρα βενζίνη.	thah **ee**thehlah ... **lee**trah vehnz**ee**nee
super (premium/ regular/unleaded/ diesel	σούπερ/απλή/χωρίς μόλυβδο/πετρέλαιο	s**oo**pehr/ah**plee**/ khor**reess** m**o**lleevdho/ peht**reh**leho
Please check the...	Παρακαλώ ελέγξτε...	pahrahk**ah**lo ehl**eh**ngksteh
battery	την μπαταρία	teen bahtah**ree**ah
brake fluid	το λάδι των φρένων	to **lah**dhee tonn **freh**nonn
oil	το λάδι	to **lah**dhee
water	το νερό	to neh**ro**
Would you check the tyre pressure?	Μπορείτε να ελέγχετε την πίεση των τροχών;	borr**ee**teh nah ehl**eh**ng-ksehteh teen **pee**-ehssee tonn tro**khonn**
1.6 front, 1.8 rear.	1.6 μπροστά, 1.8 πίσω.	1 k**o**mmah 6 bro**stah** 1 k**o**mmah 8 pe**esso**
Please check the spare tyre, too.	Παρακαλώ ελέγξτε και την ρεζέρβα.	parahk**ah**lo ehl**eh**ngksteh keh teen reh**zehr**vah
Can you mend this puncture (fix this flat)?	Το λάστιχο έχει τρυ-πήσει. Μπορείτε να το διορθώσετε;	to **lah**steekho **eh**khee treep**ee**ssee. borr**ee**teh nah to dheeortho-**sseh**teh
Would you change the ..., please?	Μπορείτε να αλλάξετε ..., παρακαλώ;	borr**ee**teh nah ahl**ah**-ksehteh ... pahrahk**ah**lo
bulb	τα φώτα	tah **fo**ttah
fan belt	τον ιμάντα του ανεμιστήρα	tonn eem**ah**ndah too ahnehm**ee**steerah

CAR HIRE, see page 20

spark(ing) plugs	τα μπουζί	tah boozee
tyre	το λάστιχο	to lahsteekho
wipers	τους καθαριστήρες	tooss kahthahreesteerehss
Would you clean the windscreen (windshield)?	Μπορείτε να καθαρίσετε το παρ-μπριζ;	borreeteh nah kahthahreessehteh to pahrbreez

Asking the way – Directions   Ερωτόντας για την κατεύθυνση

Can you tell me the way to...?	Μπορείτε να μου δείξετε το δρόμο για...;	borreeteh nah moo dheeksehteh to dhrommo yeeah
How do I get to...?	Πως μπορώ να πάω στο...;	poss borro nah paho sto
Are we on the right road for...?	Είμαστε στο σωστό δρόμο για...;	eemahsteh sto sosto dhrommo yeeah
How far is the next village?	Πόσο μακρυά είναι το επόμενο χωριό;	posso mahkreeah eeneh to ehpommehno khorreeo
Is there a road with little traffic?	Υπάρχει δρόμος με λιγότερη κίνηση;	eepahrkhee dhrommoss meh leeghottehree keeneessee
How far is it to... from here?	Πόσο μακρυά είναι... από εδώ;	posso mahkreeah eeneh ... ahpo ehdho
Is there a motorway (expressway)?	Υπάρχει αυτοκινητό-δρομος;	eepahrkhee ahfto-kkeeneetodhrommoss
How long does it take by car/on foot?	Πόσο μακρυά είναι με το αυτοκίνητο/ με τα πόδια;	posso mahkreeah eeneh meh to ahftokkeeneeto/ meh tah podheeah
Can I drive to the centre of town?	Μπορώ να οδηγήσω μέχρι το κέντρο της πόλης;	borro nah odheeyeesso mehkhree to kehndro teess polleess
Can you tell me where ... is?	Μπορείτε να μου πείτε που είναι...;	borreeteh nah moo peeteh poo eeneh
How can I find this place/address?	Πως μπορώ να βρω αυτό το μέρος/αυτήν την διεύθυνση;	poss borro nah vro ahfto to mehross/ahfteen teen dheeehftheensee
Where's this?	Που είναι αυτό;	poo eeneh ahfto
Can you show me on this map where I am?	Μπορείτε να μου δείξετε που είμαι σ'αυτό το χάρτη;	borreeteh nah moo dheeksehteh poo eemeh sahfto to khahrtee

Έχετε πάρει λάθος δρόμο.	You're on the wrong road.
Να πάτε ίσια.	Go straight ahead.
βορράς/νότος/ανατολή/δύσις	north/south/east/west
Είναι εκεί κάτω αριστερά/δεξιά.	It's down there on the left/right.
αντίθετα/πίσω... δίπλα από/μετά...	opposite/behind... next to/after...
Να πάτε στο πρώτο/δεύτερο σταυροδρόμι.	Go to the first/second crossroads (intersection).
Στρίψτε αριστερά στα φανάρια.	Turn left at the traffic lights.
Στρίψτε δεξιά στην επόμενη γωνία.	Turn right at the next corner.
Πάρτε την οδό...	Take the ... road.
Πρέπει να γυρίσετε πίσω στο...	You have to go back to...
Ακολουθήστε τα σήματα για Αθήνα.	Follow signs for Athens.

Parking   *Στάθμευση*

Parking in the capital can be a bit of a problem, although some hotels have car parks. Traffic police can give on-the-spot fines for parking offences.

Where can I park?	Που μπορούμε να σταθμεύσουμε;	poo borroomeh nah stahthmehfsoomeh
Is there a car park nearby?	Υπάρχει εδώ κοντά πάρκινγκ;	eepahrkhee ehdho kondah ''parking''
May I park here?	Μπορώ να σταθμεύσω εδώ;	borro nah stahthmehfso ehdho
How long can I park here?	Πόση ώρα μπορώ να σταθμεύσω εδώ;	possee orrah borro nah stahthmehfso ehdho
What's the charge per hour?	Πόσο κάνει την ώρα;	posso kahnee teen orrah
Do you have some change for the parking meter?	Μήπως έχετε ψιλά για το παρκόμετρο;	meeposs ehkhehteh pseelah yeeah to pahrkommehtro

Breakdown – Road assistance *Βλάβη – Οδική βοήθεια*

Where's the nearest garage?	Που είναι το κοντινό-τερο γκαράζ;	poo **ee**neh to kondeeno-ttehro gah**rahz**
Excuse me. My car has broken down.	Με συγχωρείτε. Το αυτοκίνητο μου έχει μια βλάβη.	meh seengkhor**ree**teh. to ahf**tok**keeneeto moo **eh**khee **mee**ah vlah**vee**.
I've had a break-down at...	Έπαθα μια βλάβη στο...	**eh**pahthah **mee**ah vlah**vee** sto
Can you send a mechanic?	Μπορείτε να στείλετε ένα μηχανικό;	bor**ree**teh nah **stee**lehteh **eh**nah meekhah**nee**ko
My car won't start.	Το αυτοκίνητο μου δεν ξεκινά.	to ahf**tok**keeneeto moo dhen kseh**kee**nah
The battery is dead.	Μου τελείωσε η μπαταρία.	moo teh**lee**osseh ee bahtah**ree**ah
I've run out of petrol (gasoline).	Μου τελείωσε η βενζίνη.	moo teh**lee**osseh ee vehn**zee**nee
I have a flat tyre.	Έμεινα από λάστιχο.	**eh**meenah ahpo **lah**steekho
The engine is over-heating.	Η μηχανή είναι πολύ ζεστή.	ee meekhah**nee ee**neh pol**lee** zeh**stee**
There is something wrong with the...	Κάτι συμβαίνει με...	**kah**tee seem**veh**nee meh
brakes	τα φρένα	tah **freh**nah
carburettor	το καρμπυρατέρ	to kahrbeerah**tehr**
exhaust pipe	την εξάτμιση	teen ehk**saht**meessee
radiator	το ψυγείο	to psee**yee**o
wheel	τον τροχό	tonn tro**kho**
Can you send a break-down van (tow truck)?	Μπορείτε να στείλετε ένα ρυμουλκό;	bor**ree**teh nah **stee**lehteh **eh**nah reemool**ko**
How long will you be?	Πόση ώρα θα κάνετε;	**possee orrah** thah **kah**nehteh

Accident – Police *Δυστύχημα – Αστυνομία*

| Please call the police. | Παρακαλώ, καλέστε την αστυνομία. | pahrahkah**lo** kah**leh**steh teen ahsteenom**meeah** |
| There's been an accident. | Έγινε ένα δυστύχημα. | **eh**yeeneh **eh**nah dhee-**steek**heemah |

It's about 2 kilometres from...	Περίπου 2 χιλιόμετρα από...	pehreepoo 2 kheeleeommeehtrah ahpo
Where is there a telephone?	Υπάρχει εδώ κοντά τηλέφωνο;	eepahrkhee ehdho kondah teelehfonno
Call a doctor/an ambulance, quickly.	Καλέστε ένα γιατρό/ ένα ασθενοφόρο, γρήγορα.	kahlehsteh ehnah yeeahtro/ehnah ahsthehnofforro ghreeghorrah
There are people injured.	Υπάρχουν τραυματίες.	eepahrkhoon trahvmahteeehss
What's your name and address?	Ποιο είναι το όνομα και η διεύθυνση σας;	peeo eeneh to onnommah keh ee dheeehftheensee sahss
What's your insurance company?	Ποια είναι η ασφαλιστική εταιρία σας;	peeah eeneh ee ahsfahleesteekee ehtehreeah sahss

Road signs Σήματα τροχαίας

ΑΛΑΓΗ ΠΟΡΕΙΑΣ	Diversion (detour)
ΑΝΑΨΤΕ ΤΑ ΦΩΤΑ	Switch on headlights
ΑΠΑΓΟΡΕΥΕΤΑΙ Η ΣΤΑΘΜΕΥΣΗ	No parking
ΑΠΑΓΟΡΕΥΕΤΑΙ ΤΟ ΠΡΟΣΠΕΡΑΣΜΑ	No overtaking (no passing)
ΑΠΟΤΟΜΗ ΑΝΩΦΕΡΕΙΑ/ ΚΑΤΩΦΕΡΕΙΑ	Steep hill
ΑΡΓΑ/ΚΟΞΤΕ ΤΑΧΥΤΗΤΑ	Slow down
ΒΑΡΕΙΑ ΟΧΗΜΑΤΑ	Heavy vehicles
ΔΙΑΣΤΑΥΡΩΣΗ ΜΕ ΣΙΔΗΡΟΔΡΟΜΙΚΗ	Level (railroad) crossing
ΔΙΟΔΙΑ	Toll
ΔΥΣΚΟΛΗ ΔΙΑΒΑΣΗ/ΑΡΓΑ	Slow traffic
ΔΩΣΤΕ ΠΡΩΤΟΠΟΡΕΙΑ	Give way (yield)
ΕΠΙΤΡΕΠΕΤΑΙ Η ΣΤΑΘΜΕΥΣΗ	Parking allowed
ΕΡΓΑ ΕΠΙ ΤΗΣ ΟΔΟΥ	Road works ahead (men working)
ΕΞΟΔΟΣ ΒΑΡΕΩΝ ΟΧΗΜΑΤΩΝ	Lorry (truck) exit
ΚΑΤΟΛΙΣΘΗΣΗ ΛΙΘΩΝ	Falling rocks
ΚΙΝΔΥΝΟΣ	Danger
ΚΡΑΤΑΤΕ ΔΕΞΙΑ	Keep right
ΛΑΚΟΥΒΕΣ	Potholes
ΜΟΝΟ ΓΙΑ ΠΕΖΟΥΣ	Pedestrians only
ΟΔΙΚΗ ΓΡΑΜΜΗ ΓΙΑ ΔΗΜΟΣΙΕΣ ΜΕΤΑΦΟΡΕΣ	Lane reserved for public transport
ΠΡΟΣΟΧΗ ΣΧΟΛΕΙΟ	Caution, school
ΣΤΡΟΦΕΣ	Bends (curves)
ΤΕΛΟΣ ΑΠΑΓΟΡΕΥΜΕΝΗΣ ΖΩΝΗΣ	End of restricted area
ΧΑΛΑΣΜΕΝΟΣ ΔΡΟΜΟΣ	Poor road surface

Sightseeing

Where's the tourist office?	Που είναι το γραφείο τουρισμού;	poo **ee**neh to ghrah**fee**o **too**reesmoss
What are the main points of interest?	Ποια είναι τα πιο ενδιαφέροντα μέρη;	peeah **ee**neh tah peeo ehndheeah**feh**ronndah **meh**ree
We're only here for...	Είμαστε εδώ μόνο για...	**ee**mahsteh eh**dho** monno yeeah
a few hours	λίγες ώρες	**lee**yehss orrehss
a day	μια μέρα	**mee**ah **meh**rah
a week	μια βδομάδα	**mee**ah vdhom**mah**dhah
Can you recommend a sightseeing tour/ an excursion?	Μπορείτε να προτείνετε μια περιοδεία στα αξιοθέατα/μια εκδρομή;	bor**ree**teh nah prot**tee**neh-teh **mee**ah pehree**o**dheeah stah ahkseeo**theh**ahtah/ **mee**ah ehk**dhro**mmee
Where do we leave from?	Από που θα φύγουμε;	ah**po** poo thah **fee**-ghoomeh
Will the bus pick us up at the hotel?	Μπορεί να μας πάρει το λεωφορείο από το ξενοδοχείο;	bor**ree** nah mahss **pah**ree to lehofo**rree**o ah**po** to ksehnodho**khee**o
How much does the tour cost?	Πόσο κοστίζει η εκδρομή;	**po**sso kos**tee**zee ee ehk**dhro**mmee
What time does the tour start?	Τι ώρα αρχίζει η εκδρομή;	tee **orr**ah ahr**khee**zee ee ehk**dhro**mmee
Is lunch included?	Συμπεριλαμβάνεται το γεύμα;	seembehreelahmvah-nehteh to **yehv**mah
What time do we get back?	Τι ώρα θα επιστρέψουμε;	tee **orr**ah thah ehpee-**streh**psoomeh
Do we have free time in...?	Έχουμε ελεύθερη ώρα στο...;	**ehk**hoomeh eh**lehf**-thehree **orr**ah sto
Is there an English-speaking guide?	Υπάρχει ξεναγός που να μιλάει Αγγλικά;	ee**pahr**khee ksehnah-**ghoss** poo nah mee**lah**ee ahngg**lee**kah
I'd like to hire a private guide for...	Θα ήθελα να νοικιάσω έναν ιδιωτικό ξεναγό για...	thah **ee**thehlah nah nee-**kee**ahsso **eh**nahn eedheeot**tee**ko ksehnah**gho** yeeah
half a day	μισή μέρα	mees**see** **meh**rah
a full day	μια μέρα	**mee**ah **meh**rah

Where's/Where are the...?	Που είναι...;	poo eeneh
abbey	το μοναστήρι	to monnahsteeree
art gallery	η γκαλερί τέχνης	ee gahlehree tehkhneess
artists' quarter	η συνοικία των καλλι-τεχνών	ee seeneekeeah tonn kahleetehkhnonn
botanical gardens	ο βοτανικός κήπος	o vottahneekoss keeposs
building	το κτίριο	to kteereeo
business quarter	το εμπορικό κέντρο	to ehmborreeko kehndro
castle	ο πύργος	o peerghoss
cathedral	η μητρόπολη	ee meetroppollee
cave	το σπήλαιο	to speeleho
cemetery	το νεκροταφείο	to nehkrottahfeeo
chapel	το παρεκκλήσι	to pahrehkleessee
church	η εκκλησία	ee ehkleesseeah
city centre	το κέντρο της πόλης	to kehndro teess polleess
concert hall	η αίθουσα συναυλιών	ee ehthoossah seenahvleeonn
convent	το μοναστήρι	to monnahsteeree
court house	το δικαστήριο	to dheekahsteereeo
downtown area	το κέντρο της πόλης	to kehndro teess polleess
embankment	το φράγμα	to frahghmah
exhibition	η έκθεση	ee ehkthehssee
factory	το εργοστάσιο	to ehrghostahsseeo
fair	το πανηγύρι	to pahneeyeeree
flea market	η λαϊκή αγορά	ee laheekee ahghorrah
fortress	το φρούριο	to frooreeo
fountain	η πηγή	ee peeyee
gardens	το πάρκο	to pahrko
harbour	το λιμάνι	to leemahnee
library	η βιβλιοθήκη	ee veevleeotheekee
market	η αγορά	ee ahghorrah
monastery	το μοναστήρι	to monnahsteeree
monument	το μνημείο	to mneemeeo
museum	το μουσείο	to moosseeo
old town	η παλιά πόλη	ee pahleeah pollee
opera house	η όπερα	ee oppehrah
palace	το παλάτι	to pahlahtee
park	το πάρκο	to pahrko
parliament building	η βουλή	ee voolee
planetarium	το αστεροσκοπείο	to ahstehrosskoppeeo
royal palace	το βασιλικό παλάτι	to vahsseeleeko pahlahtee
ruins	τα ερείπια	tah ehreepeeah
shopping area	η περιοχή για ψώνια	ee pehreeokhee yeeah psonneeah

square	η πλατεία	ee plahteeah
stadium	το στάδιο	to stahdheeo
statue	το άγαλμα	to ahghahlmah
stock exchange	το χρηματιστήριο	to khreemahteesteereeo
theatre	το θέατρο	to thehahtro
tomb	ο τάφος	o tahfoss
tower	ο πύργος	o peerghoss
town hall	το δημαρχείο	to dheemahrkheeo
university	το πανεπιστήμιο	to pahnehpeesteemeeo
zoo	ο ζωολογικός κήπος	o zo-olloyeekoss keeposs

Admission   Η είσοδος

Is ... open on Sundays?	Είναι ανοικτό... τις Κυριακές;	eeneh ahneekto... teess keereeahkehss
What are the opening hours?	Ποιες ώρες είναι ανοικτά τα καταστήματα;	peeehss orrehss eeneh ahneektah tah kahtahsteemahtah
When does it close?	Πότε κλείνει;	potteh kleenee
How much is the entrance fee?	Πόσο κοστίζει η είσοδος;	posso kosteezee ee eessodhoss
Is there any reduction for...?	Υπάρχει έκπτωση γιά...;	eepahrkhee ehkptossee yeeah
children	τα παιδιά	tah pehdheeah
the disabled	τους ανάπηρους	tooss ahnahpeerooss
groups	τις ομάδες	teess ommahdhehss
pensioners	τους συνταξιούχους	tooss seendahkseeoo-khooss
students	τους φοιτητές	tooss feeteetehss
Do you have a guidebook in English?	Έχετε οδηγό στα Αγγλικά;	ehkhehteh odheegho stah ahnggleekah
Can I buy a catalogue?	Μπορώ να αγοράσω ένα κατάλογο;	borro nah ahghorrahsso ehnah kahtahlogho
Is it all right to take pictures?	Επιτρέπεται να πάρω φωτογραφίες;	ehpeetrehpehteh nah pahro fottoghrahfeeehss

| ΕΙΣΟΔΟΣ ΕΛΕΥΘΕΡΑ | ADMISSION FREE |
| ΑΠΑΓΟΡΕΥΕΤΑΙ Η ΦΩΤΟΓΡΑΦΗΣΗ | TAKING PHOTOGRAPHS IS PROHIBITED |

Who – What – When?   Ποιος – Τι – Πότε;

What's that building?	Ποιο είναι αυτό το κτίριο;	peeo **ee**neh ahfto to **ktee**reeo
Who was the...?	Ποιος ήταν ο...;	pee**oss ee**tahn o
architect	αρχιτέκτονας	ahrkhee**tehk**tonnahss
artist	καλλιτέχνης	kahlee**tehk**hneess
painter	ζωγράφος	zogh**rahf**oss
sculptor	γλύπτης	gh**leep**teess
Who built it?	Ποιος το έκτισε;	pee**oss** to **ehk**teesseh
Who painted that picture?	Ποιος ζωγράφισε αυτό τον πίνακα;	pee**oss** zogh**rahf**eesseh ahfto tonn **pee**nahkah
When did he live?	Πότε έζησε;	**pot**teh **ehz**eesseh
When was it built?	Πότε κτίστηκε;	**pot**teh **ktee**steekeh
Where's the house where ... lived?	Που είναι το σπίτι που έζησε ο/η...;	poo **ee**neh to **spee**tee poo **ehz**eesseh o/ee*
We're interested in...	Ενδιαφερόμαστε για...	ehndheeahfeh**rom**mahsteh yee**ah**
antiques	αντίκες	ahn**dee**kehss
archaeology	αρχαιολογία	ahrkheholl**oy**eeah
art	τέχνη	**tehk**hnee
botany	βοτανική	vottahnee**kee**
ceramics	κεραμική	kehrahmee**kee**
coins	νομίσματα	nom**meez**mahtah
fine arts	καλές τέχνες	kah**lehss tehk**hnehss
furniture	έπιπλα	**ehp**eeplah
geology	γεωλογία	yeholl**oy**eeah
handicrafts	χειροτεχνία	kheerottehk**hnee**ah
history	ιστορία	eestorr**ee**ah
medicine	ιατρική	eeahtree**kee**
music	μουσική	moossee**kee**
natural history	φυσική ιστορία	feessee**kee** eestorr**ee**ah
ornithology	ορνιθολογία	orneetholl**oy**eeah
painting	ζωγραφική	zoghrahfee**kee**
pottery	αγγειοπλαστική	ahnggeeoplahstee**kee**
religion	θρησκεία	threes**kee**ah
sculpture	γλυπτική	ghleeptee**kee**
zoology	ζωολογία	zo-olloy**ee**ah
Where's the... department?	Που είναι το τμήμα...;	poo **ee**neh to **tmee**mah

---

* When referring to a man use **o** (o), to a woman say **η** (ee)

It's...	Είναι...	eeneh
amazing	καταπληκτικό	kahtahpleekteeko
awful	τρομερό	trommehro
beautiful	ωραίο	orreho
gloomy	σκοτεινό	skotteeno
impressive	επιβλητικό	ehpeevleeteeko
interesting	ενδιαφέρον	ehndheeahfehronn
magnificent	μεγαλοπρεπές	mehghahloprehpehss
pretty	όμορφο	ommorfo
strange	παράξενο	pahrahksehno
superb	θαυμάσιο	thahvmahsseeo
terrifying	τρομακτικό	trommahkteeko
tremendous	εξαιρετικό	ehksehrehteeko
ugly	άσχημο	ahskheemo

Religious services   *Θρησκευτική λειτουργία*

The national religion is Greek Orthodox. In Athens and other large towns you will also find Catholic and Protestant churches, and some synagogues. During the high season, part of the service may be in English, but normally they are held in Greek.

Is there a... near here?	Υπάρχει μια... εδώ κοντά;	eepahrkhee meeah... ehdho kondah
Catholic church	καθολική εκκλησία	kahtholleekee ehklee-sseeah
Orthodox church	ορθόδοξη εκκλησία	orthodhoksee ehklee-sseeah
synagogue	συναγωγή	seenahghoyee
mosque	τζαμί	dzahmee
Protestant church	εκκλησία διαμαρ-τυρομένων	ehkleesseeah dheeah-mahrteerommehnonn
At what time is...?	Τι ώρα είναι...;	tee orrah eeneh
mass/the service	η λειτουργία	ee leetooryeeah
Where can I find a... who speaks English?	Που μπορώ να βρω ένα... που να μιλάει Αγγλικά;	poo borro nah vro ehnah... poo nah meelahee ahnggleekah
priest/minister/rabbi	παπά/προτεστάντη κληρικό/ραββίνο	pahpah/prottehstahndee kleereeko/rahveeno
I'd like to visit the church.	Θα ήθελα να επισκεπτώ την εκκλησία.	thah eethehlah nah ehpeeskehpto teen ehkleesseeah

In the countryside   Στήν ύπεθρο

Is there a scenic route to...?	Υπάρχει γραφική διαδρομή για...;	eepahrkhee ghrahfeekee dheeahdhrommee yeeah
How far is it to...?	Πόσο μακρυά είναι μέχρι το/τη...;	posso mahkreeah eeneh mehkhree to/tee
Can we walk?	Μπορούμε να περπατήσουμε;	borroomeh nah pehrpahteessoomeh
How high is that mountain?	Πόσο ύψος έχει αυτό το βουνό;	posso eepsoss ehkhee ahfto to voono
What's the name of that...?	Πως λέγεται αυτό ...;	poss lehyehteh ahfto
animal/bird	το ζώο/το πουλί	to zo-o/to poolee
flower/tree	το λουλούδι/το δέντρο	to looloodhee/to dhehndro

Landmarks   Ορόσημα

bridge	γέφυρα	yehfeerah
canal	κανάλι	kahnahlee
cliff	γκρεμός	grehmoss
farm	αγρόκτημα	ahghrokteemah
field	χωράφι	khorrahfee
footpath	μονοπάτι	monnoppahtee
forest	δάσος	dhahssoss
garden	κήπος	keeposs
hill	λόφος	loffoss
house	σπίτι	speetee
lake	λίμνη	leemnee
meadow	λιβάδι	leevahdhee
mountain	βουνό	voono
(mountain) pass	(ορεινή) διάβαση	(orreenee) dheeahvahssee
path	μονοπάτι	monnoppahtee
peak	κορυφή	korreefee
pond	μικρή λίμνη	meekree leemnee
river	ποταμός	pottahmoss
road	δρόμος	dhrommoss
sea	θάλασσα	thahlahssah
spring	πηγή	peeyee
valley	κοιλάδα	keelahdhah
village	χωριό	khorreeo
vineyard	αμπέλι	ahmbehlee
wall	τοίχος	teekhoss
waterfall	καταρράκτης	kahtahrahkteess
wood	δάσος	dhahssoss

ASKING THE WAY, see page 76

Αξιοθέατα

Relaxing

Cinema (movies) – Theatre Κινηματογράφος – Θέατρο

You may still find some beautiful open-air cinemas in the countryside and suburbs. Foreign films are usually shown in the original version with Greek subtitles. It's not normally possible to reserve seats. Like cinemas, theatres are also often open-air in summer, but here you should book in advance.

What's on at the cinema tonight?	Τι παίζουν στον κινηματογράφο απόψε;	tee **peh**zoon stonn keeneemahto**grah**fo ah**pop**seh
What's playing at the ... Theatre?	Τι παίζουν στο... Θέατρο;	tee **peh**zoon sto... the**hah**tro
What sort of play is it?	Τι είδους έργο είναι;	tee **eed**hooss **eh**rgho **ee**neh
Who's it by?	Ποιος είναι ο συγγραφέας;	pee**oss ee**neh o seenggrah**feh**ahss
Can you recommend a ...?	Μπορείτε να μου προτείνετε ...;	borr**ee**teh nah moo protte**en**ehteh
good film	ένα καλό φιλμ	**eh**nah kah**lo** feelm
comedy	μια κωμωδία	mee**ah** kommod**hee**ah
musical	ένα μουσικοχορευτικό	**eh**nah moosseekokhorrehf**tee**ko
Where's that new film directed by... being shown?	Που παίζετε αυτό το νέο έργο του...;	poo **peh**zehteh ah**fto** to **neh**o **eh**rgho too
Who's in it?	Ποιος παίζει;	pee**oss peh**zee
Who's playing the lead?	Ποιος είναι ο πρωταγωνιστής;	pee**oss ee**neh o prottahghonnee**steess**
Who's the director?	Ποιος είναι ο σκηνοθέτης;	pee**oss ee**neh o skeeno**theh**teess
At which theatre is that new play by... being performed?	Σε ποιο θέατρο παίζετε αυτό το νέο έργο του...;	seh pee**o** the**hah**tro **peh**zehteh ah**fto** to **neh**o **eh**rgho too
Is there a sound-and-light show on somewhere?	Υπάρχει πουθενά παράσταση ήχος και φως;	ee**pahr**khee poothe**nah** pah**rah**stahssee **ee**khoss keh foss

What time does it begin?	Τι ώρα αρχίζει;	tee **orr**ah ahr**kee**zee
Are there any seats for tonight?	Υπάρχουν θέσεις για απόψε;	eepahr**khoon thehss**eess **yeeah** ah**pop**seh
How much are the seats?	Πόσο κοστίζει η είσοδος;	**posso** kos**tee**zee ee **ees**sodhoss
I want to reserve 2 seats for the show on Friday evening.	Θέλω να κρατήσω 2 θέσεις για τη βραδυνή παράσταση της Παρασκευής.	**theh**lo nah krah**tee**sso 2 **thehss**eess yeeah tee vrah**dhee**nee pahrah-**stah**ssee teess pahrah-skeh**veess**
Can I have a ticket for the matinee on Tuesday?	Μπορώ να έχω ένα εισιτήριο για την απογευματινή της Τρίτης;	bor**ro** nah **eh**kho **eh**nah eesseeteereeo yeeah teen ahpoyehvmahtee**nee** teess **tree**teess
I want a seat in the stalls (the orchestra).	Θέλω μια θέση στη πλατεία.	**theh**lo **mee**ah **theh**ssee stee plah**tee**ah
Not too far back.	Όχι πολύ πίσω.	**okh**ee pol**lee pee**sso
Somewhere in the middle.	Κάπου στο κέντρο.	**kah**poo sto **kehn**dro
How much are the seats in the circle (mezzanine)?	Πόσο κάνουν οι θέσεις στον εξώστη;	**posso kah**noon ee **thehss**eess stonn eh**ksos**tee
May I have a pro- gramme, please?	Μπορώ να έχω ένα πρό- γραμμα, παρακαλώ;	bor**ro** nah **eh**kho **eh**nah **progh**rahmah pahrah-**kah**lo
Where's the cloak- room?	Που είναι η γκαρντε- ρόμπα;	poo **ee**neh ee gahrndeh-**ro**bah

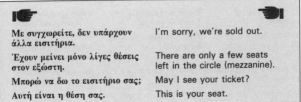

Με συγχωρείτε, δεν υπάρχουν άλλα εισιτήρια.	I'm sorry, we're sold out.
Έχουν μείνει μόνο λίγες θέσεις στον εξώστη.	There are only a few seats left in the circle (mezzanine).
Μπορώ να δω το εισιτήριο σας;	May I see your ticket?
Αυτή είναι η θέση σας.	This is your seat.

Ξεκούραση

DAYS OF THE WEEK, see page 150

Opera – Ballet – Concert   Όπερα – Μπαλέτο – Συναυλία

Can you recommend a/an...?	Μπορείτε να μου προτείνετε...;	borreeteh nah moo protteenehteh
ballet	ένα μπαλέτο	ehnah bahlehto
concert	μια συναυλία	meeah seenahvleeah
opera	μια όπερα	meeah oppehrah
operetta	μια οπερέττα	meeah oppehrehtah
Where's the opera house/the concert hall?	Που είναι η όπερα/ η αίθουσα συναυλίας;	poo eeneh ee oppehrah/ ee ehthoossah seenahvleeahss
What's on at the opera tonight?	Τι παίζεται στην Όπερα απόψε;	tee pehzehteh steen oppehrah ahpopseh
Who's singing/ dancing?	Ποιος τραγουδά/ χορεύει;	peeoss trahghoodhah/ khorrehvee
Which orchestra is playing?	Ποια ορχήστρα παίζει;	peeah orkheestrah pehzee
Who's the conductor/ soloist?	Ποιος είναι ο διευθηντής της ορχήστρας/ ο σολίστας;	peeoss eeneh o dheeehftheendeess teess orkheestrahss/ o solleestahss

Nightclubs – Discos   Νυκτερινά κέντρα – Δισκοθήκη

Can you recommend a good nightclub?	Μπορείτε να μου συστήσετε ένα καλό νυκτερινό κέντρο (νάιτ-κλαμπ);	borreeteh nah moo seesteessehteh ehnah kahlo neektehreeno kehndro ("night club")
Is there a floor show?	Έχει επιθεώρηση πίστας;	ehkhee ehpeethehorreessee peestahss
What time does the show start?	Τι ώρα αρχίζει το πρόγραμμα;	tee orrah ahrkheezee to proghrahmah
Is evening dress required?	Είναι απαραίτητο το βραδυνό ρούχο;	eeneh ahpahrehteeto to vrahdheeno rookho
Where can we go dancing?	Που μπορούμε να πάμε να χορέψουμε;	poo borroomeh nah pahmeh nah khorrehpsoomeh
Is there a discotheque in town?	Υπάρχει δισκοθήκη στην πόλη;	eepahrkhee dheeskotheekee steen pollee
Would you like to dance?	Θα θέλατε να χορέψετε;	thah thehlahteh nah khorrehpsehteh

Sports *Αθλητισμός*

Very popular in Greece are watersports. From swimming to water-skiing, almost every watersport imaginable is available, including water polo. If you want to use underwater equipment, check with the local tourist office as strict rules govern its use.

Yachting: there are plenty of pleasure ports with many facilities where you can dock your own yacht, ship or sailing boat or hire one.

Is there a soccer match anywhere this Sunday?	Υπάρχει πουθενά ποδοσφαιρικός αγώνας αυτή τη Κυριακή;	eepahrkhee poothehnah podhosfehreekoss ahghonnahss ahftee tee keereeahkee
Which teams are playing?	Ποιες ομάδες παίζουν;	peeehss ommahdhehss pehzoon
Can you get me a ticket?	Μπορείτε να μου πάρετε ένα εισητήριο;	borreeteh nah moo pahrehteh ehnah eesseeteereeo

basketball	καλαθόσφαιρα/ μπάσκετ	kahlahthossfehrah/ "basket"
boxing	πυγμαχία/μποξ	peeghmahkheeah/"box"
cycling	ποδηλασία	podheelahsseeah
football (soccer)	ποδόσφαιρο	podhosfehro
horse racing	ιπποδρομία	eepodhrommeeah
(horseback) riding	ιππασία	eepahsseeah
mountaineering	ορειβασία	orreevahsseeah
sailing	ιστιοπλοΐα	eesteeoploeeah
skiing	χιονοδρομία	kheeonnodhrommeeah
swimming	κολύμβηση	kolleemveessee
tennis	τέννις	"tennis"
volleyball	βόλεϋ	volleh-ee
water polo	υδατόσφαιρα/πόλο	eedhahtosfehrah/"polo"

...d like to see a ...oxing match.	Θα ήθελα να δω ένα αγώνα πυγμαχίας.	thah eethehlah nah dho ehnah ahghonnah peeghmahkheeahss
...hat's the admis- ...on charge?	Πόσο κοστίζει η είσοδος;	posso kosteezee ee eessodhoss

Where's the nearest golf course?	Που είναι το κοντινό- τερο γήπεδο γκολφ;	poo **ee**neh to kondeeno- ttehro **yee**pehdho ''golf''
Where are the tennis courts?	Που είναι τα γήπεδα του τέννις;	poo **ee**nah tah **yee**- pehdhah too ''tennis''
What's the charge per...?	Πόσο κοστίζει...;	**posso** kost**ee**zee
day/round/hour	την μέρα/τον γύρος/ την ώρα	teen **meh**rah/tonn **yee**ross/teen **or**rah
Can I hire (rent) rackets?	Μπορώ να νοικιάσω ρακέτες;	**borro** nah neekee**ah**sso rah**keh**tehss
Where's the race course (track)?	Που είναι ο ιππό- δρομος;	poo **ee**neh o eepo- dhr**om**moss
Is there any good fishing/hunting around here?	Υπάρχει καλό ψάρεμα/ κυνήγι εδώ κοντά;	eep**ah**rkhee kahlo ps**ah**rehmah/k**ee**n**ee**yee ehdho kond**ah**
Do I need a permit?	Χρειάζομαι άδεια;	khree**ah**zommeh **ah**dheeah
Where can I get one?	Που μπορώ να βγάλω μια;	poo **borro** nah v**gah**hlo m**ee**ah
Is there a swimming pool here?	Υπάρχει πισίνα εδώ;	eep**ah**rkhee pees**ee**nah ehdho
Is it open-air or indoor?	Είναι ανοικτή ή σκεπαστή;	**ee**neh ahn**ee**kt**ee** ee skehpah**stee**
Is it heated?	Είναι θερμενόμενη;	**ee**neh thehrmehno- **mm**ehnee
What's the tempera- ture of the water?	Ποια είναι η θερμο- κρασία του νερού;	pe**eah ee**neh ee thehrmo- kkrah**ssee**ah too nehroo
What's the beach like – sandy, shingle, rocky?	Πως είναι η πλαζ – έχει άμμο, χαλίκια, βράχια;	poss **ee**neh ee plahz – **ehk**hee **ah**mo, khahl**ee**keeah, **vrah**kheeah

On the beach Στη παραλία

Is it safe for swim- ming?	Μπορούμε να κολυμπή- σουμε χωρίς κίνδυνο;	bor**roo**meh nah kolleem- **bee**ssoomeh khorr**ess** **keen**dheeno
Is there a lifeguard?	Υπάρχει ακτοφύ- λακας;	eep**ah**rkhee ahktoffee- l**ah**kahss
Is it safe for children?	Είναι ακίνδυνα για τα παιδιά;	**ee**neh ah**keen**dheenah yee**ah** tah pehdh**ee**ah

The sea is very calm.	Η θάλασσα είναι πολύ ήσυχη.	ee thahlahssah eeneh pollee eesseekhee
There are some big waves.	Υπάρχουν μεγάλα κύματα.	eepahrkhoon mehghah-lah keemahtah
Are there any dangerous currents?	Υπάρχουν επικίνδυνα ρεύματα;	eepahrkhoon ehpeekeen-dheenah rehvmahtah
What time is high tide/low tide?	Τι ώρα έχει παλίρροια/ άμπωτη;	tee orrah ehkee pahleereeah/ahmbottee
I want to hire a/an/ some...	Θα ήθελα να νοικιάσω...	thah eethehlah nah neekeeahsso
bathing hut (cabana)	μια καμπίνα	meeah kahmbeenah
deck chair	μια πολυθρόνα	meeah polleethronnah
motorboat	μια βάρκα με μηχανή	meeah vahrkah meh meekhahnnee
rowing boat	μια βάρκα με κουπιά	meeah vahrkah meh koopeeah
sailing boat	μια βάρκα με πανί	meeah vahrkah meh pahnee
skin-diving equipment	μια εξάρτηση για υποβρύχιο ψάρεμα	meeah ehksahrteessee yeeah eepovreekheeo psahrehmah
sunshade (umbrella)	μια τέντα για τον ήλιο	meeah tehndah yeeah tonn eeleeo
surfboard	ένα κάνω για σερφ	ehnah kahno yeeah sehrf
water-skis	θαλάσσια σκι	thahlahsseah "ski"
windsurfer	ένα γουϊντσέρφερ	ehnah "windsurfer"

| ΙΔΙΩΤΙΚΗ ΠΛΑΖ | PRIVATE BEACH |
| ΑΠΑΓΟΡΕΥΕΤΑΙ Η ΚΟΛΥΜΠΗΣΗ | NO SWIMMING |

Winter sports Χειμερινά σπορ

s there a skating ink near here?	Υπάρχει εδώ κοντά πίστα πάγου;	eepahrkhee ehdho kondah peestah pahghoo
Are there ski lifts?	Υπάρχουν σκι αναβατήρες;	eepahrkhoon "ski" ahnahvahteerehss
Can I take skiing essons?	Μπορώ να παρακο-λουθήσω μαθήματα σκι;	borro nah pahrahko-llootheesso mathee-mahtah "ski"

Making friends

Introductions Συστάσεις

May I introduce...?	Μπορώ να σας γνωρίσω...;	borro nah sahss ghnorreesso
John, this is...	Τζων, από εδώ...	"John" ahpo ehdho
My name's...	Ονομάζομαι...	onnommahzommeh
Pleased to meet you.	Χαίρομαι που σας γνωρίζω.	khehrommeh poo sahss ghnorreezo
What's your name?	Πως σας λένε;	poss sahss lehneh
How are you?	Πως είστε;	poss eesteh
Fine, thanks. And you?	Καλά, ευχαριστώ. Και σεις;	kahlah, ehfkhahreesto keh seess

Follow up Καλύτερη γνωριμία

Where do you come from?	Από που είστε;	ahpo poo eesteh
I'm from...	Είμαι από το/την...	eemeh ahpo to/teen
What nationality are you?	Ποια είναι η εθνικότητα σας;	peeah eeneh ee ehthneekotteetah sahss
I'm...	Είμαι...	eemeh
American	Αμερικάνος/-ίδα*	ahmehreekahnoss/ -eedhah
British	Βρεττανός/-ίδα	vrehtahnoss/-eedhah
Canadian	Καναδός/-έζα	kahnahdhoss/-ehzah
English	Άγγλος/-ίδα	ahnggloss/-eedhah
Irish	Ιρλανδός/-έζα	eerlahndhoss/-ehzah
Scottish	Σκωτζέζος/-α	skotzehzoss/-ah
How long have you been here?	Πόσο καιρό είστε εδώ;	posso kehro eesteh ehdho
Is this your first visit?	Έρχεστε για πρώτη φορά;	ehrkhehsteh yeeah prottee forrah

---

* Where there is a different ending for the feminine gender, we have indicated the by printing first the masculine, and then the feminine ending. For example ahmehreekahnoss/ahmehreekahneedah. See the grammar section for a more detaile explanation.

COUNTRIES, see page 145

Are you enjoying your stay?	Είστε ευχαριστημένος/-η από την διαμονή σας;	eesteh ehfkhahreestee-mehnoss/-ee ahpo teen dheeahmonnee sahss
I like the landscape a lot.	Μου αρέσει πολύ η φύση.	moo ahrehssee pollee ee feessee
What do you think of the country/people?	Τι γνώμη έχετε για την χώρα/τους ανθρώπους;	tee ghnommee ehkheh-teh yeeah teen khorrah/tooss ahnthroppooss
Where are you staying?	Που μένετε;	poo mehnehteh
Are you on your own?	Είστε μόνος/-η σας;	eesteh monnoss/-ee sahss
I'm with my...	Είμαι με... μου.	eemeh meh... moo
wife	την γυναίκα	teen yeenehkah
husband	τον άνδρα	tonn ahndrah
family	την οικογένεια	teen eekoyehneeah
parents	τους γονείς	tooss ghonneess
boyfriend/girlfriend	τον φίλο/την φίλη	tonn feelo/teen feelee

father/mother	ο πατέρας/η μητέρα	o pahtehrahss/ee meetehrah
son/daughter	ο γιός/η κόρη	o yeeoss/ee korree
brother/sister	ο αδελφός/η αδελφή	o ahdhehlfoss/ee ahdhehlfee
uncle/aunt	ο θείος/η θεία	o theeoss/ee theeah
nephew/niece	ο ανεψιός/η ανεψιά	o ahnehpseeoss/ee ahneh-pseeah
cousin	ο ξάδελφος/η ξαδέλφη	o ksahdhehlfoss/ee ksah-dhehlfee

Are you married?	Είστε παντρεμένος/-η;	eesteh pahndrehmeh-noss/-ee
Are you single?	Είστε ελεύθερος/-η;	eesteh ehlehftheh-ross/-ee
Do you have children?	Έχετε παιδιά;	ehkhehteh pehdheeah
I'm a student.	Είμαι φοιτητής/φοι-τήτρια.	eemeh feeteeteess/feeteetreeah
What are you studying?	Τι σπουδάζετε;	tee spoodhahzehteh
Do you travel a lot?	Ταξιδεύετε πολύ;	tahkseedhehvehteh pollee
Do you play cards/chess?	Παίζετε χαρτιά/σκάκι;	pehzehteh khahrteeah/skahkee

The weather *Ο καιρός*

What a lovely day!	Τι υπέροχη μέρα!	tee eepehrokhee mehrah
What awful weather!	Τι απαίσιος καιρός!	tee ahpehsseeoss kehross
Isn't it cold/hot today?	Κάνει κρύο/ζέστη σήμερα.	kahnee kreeo/zehstee seemehrah
Is it usually as warm as this?	Συνήθως ο καιρός είναι τόσο ζεστός όπως τώρα;	seeneethoss o kehross eeneh tosso zehstoss oposs torrah
Do you think it's going to ...?	Τι λέτε θα...;	tee lehteh thah
be a nice day	είναι ωραία μέρα	eeneh orrehah mehrah
rain	βρέξει	vrehksee
What is the weather forecast?	Ποια είναι η πρόβλεψη κερού;	peeah eeneh ee provlehpsee kehroo

cloud	το σύνεφο	to seenehfo
fog	η ομίχλη	ee ommeekhlee
frost	ο παγετός	o pahyehtoss
ice	ο πάγος	o pahghoss
lightning	η αστραπή	ee ahstrahpee
moon	το φεγγάρι/η σελήνη	to fehnggahree/ee sehleenee
sky	ο ουρανός	o oorahnoss
snow	το χιόνι	to kheeonnee
star	το αστέρι/το άστρο	to ahstehree/to ahstro
sun	ο ήλιος	o eeleeoss
thunder	η βροντή	ee vrondee
thunderstorm	η θύελλα	ee theeehlah
wind	ο άνεμος	o ahnehmoss

Invitations *Προσκλήσεις*

Would you like to have dinner with us on...?	Θα θέλατε να δειπνήσετε μαζί μας την...;	thah thehlahteh nah dheepneessehteh mahzee mahss teen
May I invite you for lunch?	Μπορώ να σας προσκαλέσω για γεύμα;	borro nah sahss proskahlehsso yeeah yehvmah
Can you come over for a drink this evening?	Μπορείτε να έλθετε για ένα ποτό απόψε;	borreeteh nah ehlthehteh yeeah ehnah potto ahpopseh

DAYS OF THE WEEK, see page 150

There's a party. Are you coming?	Γίνεται ένα πάρτυ. Έρχεστε;	yeenehteh ehnah pahrtee. ehrkhehsteh
That's very kind of you.	Πολύ ευγενικό από μέρους σας.	pollee ehvyehneeko ahpo mehrooss sahss
Great. I'd love to come.	Περίφημα. Θα ήθελα πολύ να έλθω.	pehreefeemah. thah eethehlah pollee nah ehltho
What time shall we come?	Τι ώρα να έλθουμε;	tee orrah nah ehl-thoomeh
May I bring a friend/ a girlfriend?	Μπορώ να φέρω ένα φίλο/μια φίλη;	borro nah fehro ehnah feelo/meeah feelee
I'm afraid we have to leave now.	Νομίζω ότι πρέπει να φύγουμε τώρα.	nommeezo ottee prehpee nah feeghoomeh torrah
Next time you must come to visit us.	Την επόμενη φορά πρέπει εσείς να μας επισκεφτείτε.	teen ehpommehnee fo-rrah prehpee ehseess nah mahss ehpeeskehfteeteh
Thanks for the evening. It was great.	Ευχαριστώ για την βραδυά. Ήταν υπέροχη.	ehfkhahreesto yeeah teen vrahdheeah. eetahn eepehrokhee

Dating   *Ραντε-βού*

Do you mind if I smoke?	Σας ενοχλεί εάν καπνίζω;	sahss ehnokhlee ehahn kahpneezo
Would you like a cigarette?	Θα θέλατε ένα τσιγάρο;	thah thehlahteh ehnah tseeghahro
Do you have a light, please?	Έχετε φωτιά, παρακαλώ;	ehkhehteh fotteeah pahrahkahlo
Why are you laughing?	Γιατί γελάτε;	yeeahtee yehlahteh
Is my Greek that bad?	Είναι τα Ελληνικά μου τόσο άσχημα;	eeneh tah ehleeneekah moo tosso ahskheemah
Do you mind if I sit here?	Σας ενοχλεί εάν καθήσω εδώ;	sahss ehnokhlee ehahn kahtheeso ehdho
Can I get you a drink?	Μπορώ να σας φέρω ένα ποτό;	borro nah sahss fehro ehnah potto
Are you waiting for someone?	Περιμένετε κάποιον;	pehreemehnehteh kah-peeonn
Are you free this evening?	Είστε ελεύθερος/-η απόψε;	eesteh ehlehfthehross/-ee ahpopseh

Would you like to go out with me tonight?	Θα θέλατε να βγούμε έξω μαζί απόψε;	thah **theh**lahteh nah **vghoo**meh **ehk**so mah**zee** ah**pop**seh
Would you like to go dancing?	Θα θέλατε να πάμε να χορέψουμε;	thah **theh**lahteh nah **pah**meh nah khorreh- **psoo**meh
Shall we go to the cinema (movies)?	Πάμε στον κινηματο- γράφο;	**pah**meh stonn keenee- mahto**ghrah**fo
Would you like to go for a drive?	Θα θέλατε να πάμε βόλτα με το αυτοκίνητο;	thah **theh**lahteh nah **pah**meh **vol**tah meh to ahfto**kkee**neeto
Where shall we meet?	Που θα συναντηθούμε;	poo thah seenahndee- **thoo**meh
I'll pick you up at your hotel.	Θα σας πάρω από το ξενοδοχείο σας.	thah sahss **pah**ro ahpo to ksehnodho**kheeo** sahss
I'll call for you at 8.	Θα περάσω να σας πάρω στις 8.	thah peh**rah**sso nah sahss **pah**ro steess 8
May I take you home?	Μπορώ να σας πάω στο σπίτι σας;	bor**ro** nah sahss **pa**ho sto **spee**tee sahss
Can I see you again tomorrow?	Μπορώ να σας ξαναδώ αύριο;	bor**ro** nah sahss ksah- **nah**dho ah**vree**o
I hope we'll meet again.	Ελπίζω να ξανά- συναντηθούμε;	ehl**pee**zo nah ksahnah- seenahndee**thoo**meh

... and you might answer:

I'd love to, thank you.	Θα μου άρεσε πολύ, ευχαριστώ.	thah moo **ah**rehsseh pol**lee** ehfkhah**ree**sto
Thank you, but I'm busy.	Ευχαριστώ, αλλά είμαι πολύ απασχολημένος/-η.	ehfkhah**ree**sto ahlah **ee**meh pol**lee** ahpah- skholleeme**hnoss**/-ee
No, I'm not inter- ested, thank you.	Όχι, δεν με ενδιαφέρει, ευχαριστώ.	**o**khee dhehn meh ehndheeah**feh**ree ehfkhah**ree**sto
Thank you, it's been a wonderful evening.	Ευχαριστώ, ήταν μια υπέροχη βραδιά.	ehfkhah**ree**sto **ee**tahn **mee**ah ee**peh**rokhee vrah**dhee**ah
I've enjoyed myself.	Διασκέδασα πολύ.	dheeahs**kehd**hahssah pol**lee**

Shopping Guide

This shopping guide is designed to help you find what you want with ease, accuracy and speed. It features:

1. A list of all major shops, stores and services (p. 98).
2. Some general expressions required when shopping to allow you to be specific and selective (p. 100).
3. Full details of the shops and services most likely to concern you. Here you'll find advice, alphabetical lists of items and conversion charts listed under the headings below.

LAUNDRY, see page 29/HAIRDRESSER'S, see page 30

Οδηγός για ψώνια

Shops, stores and services   Μαγαζιά και εξυπηρέτηση

Opening times vary from place to place, and are particularly erratic on the islands. Many shops open from 7.30 or 8 a.m. until 2.30 p.m. on Mondays and Wednesdays, and 1.30 p.m. on Saturdays. On the other days they close for a long siesta until 5 p.m., opening afterwards until 8 or 8.30 p.m.

Where's the nearest...?	Που είναι ο κοντινό-τερος/η κοντινότερη/ το κοντινότερο...;	poo **ee**neh o kondeeno-ttehross/ee kondee-**no**ttehree/to kondee-**no**ttehro
antique shop	το κατάστημα για αντίκες*	to kaht**ah**steemah yee**ah** ahnd**ee**ekehss
art gallery	η γκαλερί τέχνης	ee gahleh**ree** tehkhneess
baker's	το αρτοποιείο (ο φούρνος)	to ahrtoppee**eeo** (o **foor**noss)
bank	η τράπεζα	ee tr**ah**pehzah
barber's	το κουρείο	to koor**eeo**
beauty salon	το ινστιτούτο καλλονής	to eensteet**oo**to kahlo-**nn**eess
bookshop	το βιβλιοπωλείο	to veevleeoppoll**eeo**
butcher's	το κρεοπωλείο	to krehoppoll**eeo**
cake shop	το ζαχαροπλαστείο	to zahkhahroplahst**eeo**
camera shop	το φωτογραφείο	to fottoghrahf**eeo**
chemist's	το φαρμακείο	to fahrmahk**eeo**
dairy shop	το γαλακτοπωλείο	to ghahlahktoppoll**eeo**
delicatessen	το μπακάλικο	to bahkahl**eeo**
dentist	ο οδοντίατρος	o odhond**eeah**tross
department store	το μεγάλο εμπορικό κατάστημα	to meh**ghah**lo ehmborr**ee**ko kaht**ah**steemah
drugstore	το φαρμακείο	to fahrmahk**eeo**
dry cleaner's	το καθαριστήριο	to kahthahreest**eer**eeo
electrician	ο ηλεκτρολόγος	o eelehktroll**o**ghoss
fishmonger's	το ιχθυοπωλείο	to eekhtheeoppoll**eeo**
florist's	το ανθοπωλείο	to ahnthoppoll**eeo**
furrier's	το γουναράδικο	to ghoonahrahd**ee**eeko
greengrocer's	το μανάβικο	to mahnahv**ee**eeko
grocery	το παντοπωλείο	to pahndoppoll**eeo**

---

* The article before each noun should only be used as a guide to the correct gender and not be pronounced; e.g. Where is the nearest bank? Που είναι η κοντινότερη τράπεζα; — poo **ee**neh ee kondee**no**ttehree tr**ah**pehzah

hairdresser's (ladies/men)	το κομμωτήριο	to kommotteereeo
health food shop	το κατάστημα δίαιτας	to kahtahsteemah dheeehtahss
hospital	το νοσοκομείο	to nossokkommeeo
jeweller's	το κοσμηματοπωλείο	to kozmeemahtoppolleeo
launderette	το αυτόματο πλυντήριο	to ahftommahto pleendeereeo
laundry	το πλυντήριο	to pleendeereeo
library	η βιβλιοθήκη	ee veevleeotheekee
market	η αγορά	ee aghorrah
newsagent's	το πρακτορείο	to prahktorreeo
newsstand	το περίπτερο	to pehreeptehro
optician	ο οπτικός	o opteekoss
pastry shop	το ζαχαροπλαστείο	to zahkhahroplahsteeo
photographer's	ο φωτογράφος	o fottoghrahfoss
police station	το αστυνομικό τμήμα	to ahsteenommeeko tmeemah
post office	το ταχυδρομείο	to tahkheedhrommeeo
shoemaker's (repairs)	ο τσαγκάρης	o tsahnggahreess
shoe shop	το υποδηματοποιείο	to eepodheemahtoppeeeeo
shopping centre	τα κεντρικά καταστήματα	tah kehndreekah kahtahsteemahtah
souvenir shop	το κατάστημα σουβενίρ	to kahtahsteemah soovehneer
sporting goods shop	το κατάστημα αθλητικών ειδών	to kahtahsteemah ahthleeteekonn eedhonn
stationer's	το χαρτοπωλείο	to khahrtoppolleeo
supermarket	το σούπερ μάρκετ	to "supermarket"
tailor's	το ραφείο	to rahfeeo
telegraph office	το τηλεγραφείο	to teelehghrahfeeo
tobacconist's	το καπνοπωλείο	to kahpnoppolleeo
toy shop	το κατάστημα παιχνιδιών	to kahtahsteemah pehkhneedheeonn
travel agency	το πρακτορείο ταξιδίων	to prahktorreeo tahkseedheeonn
vegetable store	το μανάβικο	to mahnahveeko
veterinarian	ο κτηνίατρος	o kteeneeahtross
watchmaker's	το ωρολογοποιείο	to orrolloghoppeeeeo
wine merchant	το οινοπωλείο	to eenoppolleeo

ΕΙΣΟΔΟΣ	ENTRANCE
ΕΞΟΔΟΣ	EXIT
ΕΞΟΔΟΣ ΚΙΝΔΥΝΟΥ	EMERGENCY EXIT

General expressions   *Γενικές εκφράσεις*

Where?   *Που;*

Where's there a good ...?	Που υπάρχει ένα καλό...;	poo eepahrkhee ehnah kahlo
Where can I find a ...?	Που μπορώ να βρω ένα...;	poo borro nah vro ehnah
Where's the shopping area?	Που είναι η περιοχή για ψώνια;	poo eeneh ee pehreeokhee yeeah psonneeah
Is it far from here?	Είναι μακρυά από εδώ;	eeneh mahkreeah ahpo ehdho
How do I get there?	Πως μπορώ να πάω εκεί;	poss borro nah paho ehkee

Service   *Εξυπηρέτηση*

Can you help me?	Μπορείτε να με βοηθήσετε;	borreeteh nah meh vo-ee-theessehteh
I'm just looking.	Απλώς κοιτάζω.	ahploss keetahzo
Do you sell...?	Πωλείτε...;	polleeteh
I want...	Θέλω...	thehlo
Can you show me some...?	Μπορείτε να μου δείξετε μερικά...;	borreeteh nah moo dheeksehteh mehreekah
Do you have any...?	Έχετε μερικά...;	ehkhehteh mehreekah
Where's the ... department?	Που είναι το τμήμα...;	poo eeneh to tmeemah
Where is the lift (elevator)/escalator?	Που είναι το ασανσέρ (ο αναβατήρας)/ η κινητή σκάλα;	poo eeneh to ahssahn-ssehr (o ahnah-vahteerahss)/ee keeneetee skahlah

That one   *Εκείνο*

Can you show me...?	Μπορείτε να μου δείξετε...;	borreeteh nah moo dheeksehteh
this/that	αυτό/εκείνο	ahfto/ehkeeno
the one in the window/in the display case	αυτό εκεί στη βιτρίνα/στο ράφι	ahfto ehkee stee veetreenah/sto rahfee

Defining the article   *Περιγραφή του είδους*

I'd like a ... one.	θα ήθελα ένα/μια...	thah **ee**thehlah **eh**nah/**mee**ah
big	μεγάλο/-λη	mehg**hah**lo/-lee
cheap	φθηνό/-νή	fthee**no**/-**nee**
dark	σκούρο/-ρα	**skoo**ro/-rah
good	καλό/-λή	kah**lo**/-**lee**
heavy	βαρύ/-ριά	vah**ree**/-**reeah**
large	φαρδύ/-διά	fahr**dhee**/-**dheeah**
light (weight)	ελαφρό/-ριά	ehlah**fro**/-**reeah**
light (colour)	ανοιχτό/-ή	ahneekh**to**/-**ee**
oval	οβάλ	o**vahl**
rectangular	μακρόστενο/-νη	mahk**ro**stehno/-nee
round	στρογγυλό/-λή	stronggee**lo**/-**lee**
small	μικρό/-κρή	meek**ro**/-**kree**
square	τετράγωνο/-νη	tehtrah**ghon**no/-nee
sturdy	ανθεκτικό/-κή	ahnthehk**tee**ko/-**kee**
I don't want anything too expensive.	Δεν θέλω κάτι πολύ ακριβό.	dhehn **theh**lo **kah**tee pollee ahkree**vo**

Preference   *Προτίμηση*

Can you show me some more?	Μπορείτε να μου δείξετε κι' άλλα;	bor**ree**teh nah moo **dheek**sehteh kee' **ah**lah
Haven't you anything...?	Δεν έχετε κάτι...;	dhehn **eh**khehteh **kah**tee
cheaper/better	φτηνότερο/καλύτερο	ftee**not**tehro/kah**lee**tehro
larger/smaller	μεγαλύτερο/μικρότερο	mehghah**lee**tehro/meek**ro**ttehro

How much?   *Πόσο κάνει;*

How much is this?	Πόσο κάνει αυτό;	**pos**so **kah**nee ahf**to**
How much are they?	Πόσο κάνουν αυτά;	**pos**so **kah**noon ahf**tah**
I don't understand.	Δεν καταλαβαίνω.	dhehn kahtahlah**veh**no
Please write it down.	Παρακαλώ, γράψτε το.	pahrah**kah**lo **ghrahps**teh to
I don't want to spend more than... drachmas.	Δεν θέλω να ξοδέψω περισσότερο από... δραχμές.	dhehn **theh**lo nah kso**dheh**pso pehree**ssot**tehro ahpo... drahk**mehss**

ΕΚΠΤΩΣΕΙΣ   SALE

COLOURS, see page 113

Decision Απόφαση

It's not quite what I want.	Δεν είναι ακριβώς αυτό που θέλω.	dhehn eeneh ahkreevoss ahfto poo thehlo
No, I don't like it.	Όχι, δεν μου αρέσει.	okhee dhehn moo ahrehssee

Ordering Παραγγελεία

Can you order it for me?	Μπορείτε να μου το παραγγείλετε;	borreeteh nah moo to pahrahnggeelehteh
How long will it take?	Πόσο καιρό χρειάζεται;	posso kehro khreeahzehteh

Delivery Παράδοση

I'll take it with me.	Θα το πάρω μαζί μου.	thah to pahro mahzee moo
Deliver it to the ...Hotel.	Στείλτε το στο ξενοδοχείο...	steelteh to sto ksehnodhohkheeo
Please send it to this address.	Παρακαλώ, στείλτε το σ'αυτή τη διεύθυνση.	pahrahkahlo steelteh to sahftee tee dheeehftheensee
Will I have any difficulty with the customs?	Θα έχω καμμιά δυσκολία στο τελωνείο;	thah ehkho kahmeeah dheeskolleeah sto tehlonneeo

Paying Πληρωμή

How much is it?	Πόσο κάνει;	posso kahnee
Can I pay by traveller's cheque?	Μπορώ να πληρώσω με τράβελερς τσεκ;	borro nah pleerosso meh trahvehlehrs tsehk
Do you accept...?	Δέχεστε...;	dhehkhehsteh
dollars	δολλάρια	dhollahreeah
pounds	Αγγλικές λίρες	ahnggleekehss leerehss
credit cards	πιστωτικές κάρτες	peestotteekehss kahrtehss
Do I have to pay the VAT (sales tax)?	Πρέπει να πληρώσω φόρο;	prehpee nah pleerosso forro
I think there's a mistake in the bill.	Νομίζω κάνατε λάθος στον λογαριασμό;	nommeezo kahnahteh lahthoss stonn loghahreeahzmo

Anything else?   Τίποτα άλλο;

No, thanks, that's all.	Όχι, ευχαριστώ, τίποτε άλλο.	okhee ehfkhahreesto teepotteh ahlo
Yes, I want ...	Ναι, θέλω ...	neh thehlo
Show me ...	Δείξτε μου ...	dheeksteh moo
May I have a bag, please?	Μπορώ να έχω μια τσάντα παρακαλώ;	borro nah ehkho meeah tsahndah pahrahkahlo
Could you wrap it up for me, please?	Μου το τυλίγετε, παρακαλώ;	moo to teeleeyehteh pahrahkahlo

Dissatisfied?   Δυσαρεστημένος;

Can you exchange this, please?	Μπορείτε να το αλλάξετε παρακαλώ;	borreeteh nah to ahlahksehteh pahrahkahlo
I want to return this.	Θέλω να επιστρέψω αυτό.	thehlo nah ehpeestrehpso ahfto
I'd like a refund. Here's the receipt.	Θα ήθελα να μου επιστρέψετε τα χρήματα. Να η απόδειξη.	thah eethehlah nah moo ehpeestrehpsehteh tah khreemahtah. nah ee ahpodheeksee

---

Μπορώ να σας βοηθήσω;	Can I help you?
Τι θα θέλατε;	What would you like?
Τι ... θα θέλατε;	What ... would you like?
χρώμα/σχήμα ποιότητα/ποσότητα	colour/shape quality/quantity
Λυπούμαι, δεν έχομε άλλο.	I'm sorry, we don't have any.
Μας έχει εξαντληθή.	We're out of stock.
Να σας το παραγγείλουμε;	Shall we order it for you?
Θα το πάρετε ή να σας το στείλουμε;	Will you take it with you or shall we send it?
Τίποτα άλλο;	Anything else?
... δραχμές, παρακαλώ.	That's ... drachmas, please.
Το ταμείο είναι προς τα εκεί.	The cash desk is over there.

104

Bookshop – Stationer's   Βιβλιοπωλείο – Χαρτοπωλείο

In Greece, bookshops and stationer's are the same shop.
Newspapers and magazines are sold at kiosks and newsstands.

Where's the nearest...?	Που είναι το κοντινό- τερο...;	poo **ee**neh to kondee- **no**ttehro
bookshop	βιβλιοπωλείο	veevleeoppolleeo
stationer's	χαρτοπωλείο	khahrtoppolleeo
newsstand	χερίπτερο	pehr**ee**ptehro
Where can I buy an English-language newspaper?	Που μπορώ να αγοράσω μια εφημερίδα στα Αγγλικά;	poo borro nah aghghorrah- sso meeah ehfeemehree- dhah stah ahnggleekah
Where's the guide- book section?	Που είναι το τμήμα των τουριστικών οδηγών;	poo **ee**neh to **tmee**mah tonn tooreesteek**onn** odheeghonn
Where do you keep the English books?	Που έχετε τα Αγγλικά βιβλία;	poo eh**kheh**teh tah ahng- gleekah veevleeah
Do you have any of ...'s books in English?	Έχετε βιβλία του... στα Αγγλικά;	eh**kheh**teh veevleeah too ... stah ahnggleekah
Do you have second- hand books?	Έχετε μεταχειρισμένα βιβλία;	eh**kheh**teh mehtahkhee- reezmehnah veevleeah
I want to buy a/an/ some...	Θέλω να αγοράσω...	**theh**lo nah aghghorrahsso
ball-point pen	ένα στυλό διαρκείας	**eh**nah steelo dheeahr- **kee**ahss
book	ένα βιβλίο	**eh**nah veevleeo
calendar	ένα ημερολόγιο	**eh**nah eemehrolloyeeo
cellophane tape	σελοτέιπ	"Sellotape"
crayons	χρωματιστά μολύβια	khrommahteestah mollee- veeah
dictionary	ένα λεξικό	**eh**nah lehkseeko
Greek-English	Ελληνοαγγλικό	ehleeno–ahnggleeko
pocket	τσέπης	tsehpeess
drawing paper	χαρτί σχεδίου	khahr**tee** skhehdheeoo
envelopes	μερικούς φακέλλους	mehreekooss fahkehlooss
eraser	μια γομολάστιχα	**mee**ah ghommollah- steekhah
exercise book	ένα τετράδιο ασκήσεων	**eh**nah tehtrahdheeo ahs**kee**ssehonn
felt-tip pen	ένα μαρκαδόρο	**eh**nah mahrkahdhorro
fountain pen	ένα πενοφόρο	**eh**nah pehnofforro

glue	κόλλα	kollah
grammar book	ένα βιβλίο γραμματικής	ehnah veevleeo ghrahmahteekeess
guide book	ένα τουριστικό οδηγό	ehnah tooreesteeko odheegho
ink	μελάνι	mehlahnee
black/red/blue	μαύρο/κόκκινο/μπλε	mahvro/kokkeeno/bleh
(adhesive) labels	(αυτοκόλλητες) ετικέττες	(ahftokkolleeteess) ehteekehtehss
magazine	ένα περιοδικό	ehnah pehreeodheeko
map	ένα χάρτη	ehnah khahrtee
map of the town	ένα χάρτη της πόλης	ehnah khahrtee teess polleess
road map of ...	ένα οδηκό χάρτη της...	ehnah odheeko khahrtee teess
newspaper	μια εφημερίδα	meeah ehfeemehreedhah
American/English	Αμερικανική/Αγγλική	ahmehreekahneekee/ ahnggleekee
notebook	ένα τετράδιο	ehnah tehtrahdheeo
note paper	ένα μπλοκ	ehnah blok
paintbox	ένα κουτί μπογιές	ehnah kootee boyeeehss
paper	μερικές κόλλες χαρτί	mehreekehss kollehss khahrtee
paperback	ένα φτηνό βιβλίο	ehnah fteeno veevleeo
paperclips	συνδετήρες	seendhehteerehss
paper napkins	χαρτοπετσέτες	khahrtoppehtsehtehss
paste	μια κόλλα	meeah kollah
pen	ένα στυλό	ehnah steelo
pencil	ένα μολύβι	ehnah molleevee
playing cards	μια τράπουλα	meeah trahpoolah
pocket calculator	μια υπολογιστική μηχανή τσέπης	meeah eepolloyeesteekee meekhahnee tsehpeess
postcard	μια καρτ-ποστάλ	meeah kahrt postahl
refill (for a pen)	ένα ανταλλακτικό για στυλό	ehnah ahndahlahkteeko yeeah steelo
rubber	μια γομολάστιχα	meeah ghommollah- steekhah
ruler	ένα χάρακα	ehnah khahrahkah
string	σπάγγο	spahnggo
travel guide	ένα ταξιδιωτικό οδηγό	ehnah tahkseedheeotteeko odheegho
typing paper	χαρτί γραφομηχανής	khahrtee ghrahfommee- khahneess
writing pad	ένα μπλοκ αλληλογραφίας	ehnah blok ahleeloghrahfeeahss

Camping equipment   Εφοδιασμός για κατασκήνωση

I'd like a/an/some...	Θα ήθελα...	thah eethehlah
bottle opener	ένα ανοιχτήρι για μπούκαλια	ehnah ahneekhteeree yeeah bookahleeah
butane gas	μια φιάλη υγραερίου	meeah feeahlee eeghrah-ehreeoo
campbed	ένα κρεββάτι εκστρατείας	ehnah krehvahtee ehkstrahteeahss
can opener	ένα ανοιχτήρι κονσέρβας	ehnah ahneekhteeree konsehrvahss
candles	μερικά κεριά	mehreekah kehreeah
(folding) chair	μια (πτυσόμενη) καρέκλα	meeah (pteessommehnee) kahrehklah
charcoal	μερικά κάρβουνα	mehreekah kahrvoonah
clothes pegs	μερικά μανδαλάκια	mehreekah mahndhahlahkeeah
compass	μια πυξίδα	meeah peekseedhah
cool box	ένα ψυγείο	ehnah pseeyeeo
corkscrew	ένα τιρ-μπουσόν	ehnah teerboossonn
deck chair	μια πολυθρόνα	meeah polleethronnah
dishwashing detergent	ένα απολυμαντικό πιάτων	ehnah ahpolleemahndeeko peeahtonn
first-aid kit	ένα φαρμακείο για πρώτες βοήθειες	ehnah fahrmahkeeo yeeah protehss voeethee-ehss
fishing tackle	ένα εξοπλισμό για ψάρεμα	ehnah ehksopleezmo yeeah psahrehmah
flashlight	ένα φακό	ehnah fahko
food box	ένα δοχείο για τρόφιμα	ehnah dhokheeoo yeeah troffeemah
frying pan	ένα τηγάνι	ehnah teeghahnee
groundsheet	ένα χαλί τέντας	ehnah khahlee tehndahss
hammock	μια κούνια	meeah kooneeah
haversack	ένα οδοιπορικό σάκο	ehnah odheeporeeko sahko
ice pack	μια παγοτιέρα	meeah pahghotteeehrah
kerosene	φωτιστικό πετρέλαιο	fotteesteeko pehtrehleho
knapsack	ένα οδοιπορικό σάκο	ehnah odheeporeeko sahko
lamp	μια λάμπα	meeah lahmbah
lantern	ένα φανάρι	ehnah fahnahree
matches	μερικά σπίρτα	mehreekah speertah
mattress	ένα στρώμα	ehnah strommah
methylated spirits	πράσινο οινόπνευμα	prahsseeno eenopnehvmah
mosquito net	μια κουνουπιέρα	meeah koonoopeeehrah

CAMPING, see page 32

paraffin	φωτιστικό πετρέλαιο	fotteesteeko pehtrehleho
penknife	ένα σουγιά	ehnah sooyeeah
picnic basket	ένα καλάθι για πικ-νικ	ehnah kahlahthee yeeah ''picnic''
plastic bag	μια πλαστική τσάντα	meeah plahsteekee tsahndah
rope	ένα σχοινί	ehnah skheenee
rucksack	ένα ταξιδιωτικό σάκκο	ehnah tahkseedheeotteeko sahko
saucepan	μια κατσαρόλα	meeah kahtsahrollah
scissors	ένα ψαλίδι	ehnah psahleedhee
screwdriver	ένα κατσαβίδι	ehnah kahtsahveedhee
sleeping bag	ένα σάκο ύπνου	ehnah sahko eepnoo
(folding) table	ένα (πτυσσόμενο) τραπέζι	ehnah (pteessommehno) trahpehzee
tent	μια σκηνή	meeah skeenee
tent peg	ένα πάσσαλο	ehnah pahssahlo
tent pole	ένα κοντάρι	ehnah kondahree
tinfoil	αλλουμινόχαρτο	ahloomeenokhahrto
tin opener	ένα ανοιχτήρι κονσέρβας	ehnah ahneekhteeree konsehrvahss
tongs	μια τσιμπίδα	meeah tseembeedhah
torch	ένα φακό	ehnah fahko
vacuum flask	ένα θερμός	ehnah thehrmoss
washing powder	σκόνη πλυσίματος	skonnee pleesseemahtoss
water flask	ένα παγούρι	ehnah pahghooree
wood alcohol	οινόπευμα	eenopnehvmah

Crockery   Πιατικά

cups	φλυτζάνια	fleedzahneeah
mugs	κύπελλα	keepehlah
plates	πιάτα	peeahtah
saucers	πιατάκια	peeahtahkeeah
tumblers	ποτήρια	potteereeah

Cutlery   Μαχαιροπήρουνα

forks	πηρούνια	peerooneeah
knives	μαχαίρια	mahkhehreeah
spoons	κουτάλια	kootahleeah
teaspoons	κουταλάκια	kootahlahkeeah
(made of) plastic	από πλαστικό	ahpo plahsteeko
(made of) stainless steel	από ανοξείδωτο ατσάλι	ahpo ahnokseedhotto ahtsahlee

Chemist's (drugstore)   Φαρμακείο

You will recognize a chemist's by the sign outside—a red or green cross, which is lit at night. In the window you'll see a notice telling you where the nearest all-night chemist's is.

Go to a κατάστημα καλλυντικών (kah**tah**steemah kahleendee-**konn**) for perfume and cosmetics.

This section is divided into two parts:

1. Pharmaceutical—medicine, first-aid, etc.
2. Toiletry—toilet articles, cosmetics

General   Γενικά

Where's the nearest (all-night) chemist's?	Που είναι το κοντινότερο (διανυκτερεύον) φαρμακείο;	poo **ee**neh to kondeenottehro (dheeahneekteh-**reh**vonn) fahrmah**kee**o
What time does the chemist's open/close?	Τι ώρα ανοίγει/κλείνει το φαρμακείο;	tee orrah ahn**ee**yee/**klee**nee to fahrmah**kee**o

Part 1 – Pharmaceutical   Φαρμακευτικά

I want something for...	Θέλω κάτι για...	**theh**lo **kah**tee yeeah
a cold	το κρυολόγημα	to kreeo**lloy**eemah
a cough	το βήχα	to **vee**khah
hay fever	το αλλεργικό συνάχι	to ahlehr**yee**ko seenah**khee**
insect bites	τα κεντρίσματα	tah kehnd**ree**zmahtah
a headache	τον πονοκέφαλο	tonn ponno**keh**fahlo
sunburn	το ηλιακό έγκαυμα	to eeleeah**ko eh**ngahvmah
travel sickness	τη ναυτία	tee nahf**tee**ah
an upset stomach	την στομαχική ανωμαλία	teen stommahkhee**kee** ahnommah**lee**ah
Can you make up this prescription for me?	Μπορείτε να μου ετοιμάσετε αυτή τη συνταγή;	borr**ee**teh nah moo ehtee-**mah**ssehteh ahf**tee** tee seendah**yee**
Can I get it without a prescription?	Μπορώ να το πάρω χωρίς συνταγή;	bor**ro** nah to **pah**ro khorr**eess** seendah**yee**
Shall I wait?	Πρέπει να περιμένω;	**preh**pee nah pehree**meh**nn—

DOCTOR, see page 136

Can I have a/an/some...?	Μπορώ να έχω...;	borro nah ehkho
analgesic	μερικά παυσίπονα	mehreekah pahf-seeponnah
antiseptic cream	αντισηπτική κρέμα	ahndeesseepteekee krehmah
aspirin	ασπιρίνη	ahspeereenee
(elastic) bandage	ένα (ελαστικό) επίδεσμο	ehnah (ehlahsteeko) ehpeedhehzmo
Band-Aids	λευκοπλάστη	lehfkoplahstee
contraceptives	αντισυλληπτικά	ahndeesseeleepteekah
corn plasters	έμπλαστρα για κάλλους	ehmblahstrah yeeah kahlooss
cotton wool (absorbent cotton)	μπαμπάκι	bahmbahkee
cough drops	παστίλλιες για το βήχα	pahsteelee-ehss yeeah to veekhah
disinfectant	απολυμαντικό	ahpolleemahndeeko
Elastoplast	ένα λευκοπλάστη	ehnah lehfkoplahstee
eye drops	κολλύριο	kolleereeo
gauze	γάζα αντισηπτική	ghahzah ahndeesseepteekee
insect repellent/spray	εντομοκτόνο/ένα εντομοκτόνο σπρέι	ehndommoktonno/ehnah ehndommoktonno "spray"
iodine	ιώδιο	eeodheeo
laxative	καθαρκτικό	kahthahrkteeko
mouthwash	υγρό για την πλύση του στόματος	eeghro yeeah teen pleessee too stommahtoss
nose drops	σταγόνες για τη μύτη	stahghonnehss yeeah tee meetee
sanitary towels (napkins)	σερβιέττες υγείας	sehrveeehtehss eeyeeahss
suppositories	ένα υπόθετο	ehnah eepothehto
... tablets	...χάπια	...khahpeeah
tampons	μερικά ταμπόν	mehreekah tahmbonn
thermometer	ένα θερμόμετρο	ehnah thehrmommehtro
throat lozenges	παστίλλιες για το λαιμό	pahsteeleeehss yeeah to lehmo
vitamin pills	βιταμίνες	veetahmeenehss

ΔΗΛΗΤΗΡΙΟ	POISON
ΓΙΑ ΕΞΩΤΕΡΙΚΗ ΧΡΗΣΗ ΜΟΝΟ	FOR EXTERNAL USE ONLY

Part 2—Toiletry Καλλυντικά

I'd like a/an/some...	Θα ήθελα...	thah eethehlah
after-shave lotion	μια λοσιόν για μετά το ξύρισμα	meeah losseeonn yeeah mehtah to kseereezmah
astringent	μια στυπτική λοσιόν	meeah steepteekee losseeonn
blusher	ρουζ	rooz
bubble bath	ένα αφρόλουτρο	ehnah ahfrolootro
cream	μια κρέμα	meeah krehmah
cleansing cream	ένα γαλάκτωμα	ehnah ghahlahktommah
foundation cream	μια βάση	meeah vahssee
moisturizing cream	μια κρέμα υδατική	meeah krehmah eedhahteekee
night cream	μια κρέμα νύκτας	meeah krehmah neektahss
deodorant	ένα αποσμητικό	ehnah ahpozmeeteeko
emery board	ένα γυαλόχαρτο για τα νύχια	ehnah yeeahlokhahrto yeeah tah neekheeah
eye liner	μια γραμμή για τα μάτια	meeah ghrahmee yeeah tah mahteeah
eyebrow pencil	ένα μολύβι για τα μάτια	ehnah moleevee yeeah tah mahteeah
eye shadow	μια σκιά για τα μάτια	meeah skeeah yeeah tah mahteeah
face powder	μια πούδρα για το πρόσωπο	meeah poodhrah yeeah to prossoppo
foot/hand cream	κρέμα γιά τα πόδια/χέρια	krehmah yeeah tah podheeah/khehreeah
lipsalve	μια κρέμα για τα χείλια	meeah krehmah yeeah tah kheeleeah
lipstick	ένα κραγιόν για τα χείλια	ehnah krahyeeonn yeeah tah kheeleeah
nail brush	μια βούρτσα για τα νύχια	meeah voortsah yeeah tah neekheeah
nail clippers/scissors	ένα νυχοκόπτη	ehnah neekhokkoptee
nail file	μια λίμα για τα νύχια	meeah leemah yeeah tah neekheeah
nail polish	ένα βερνίκι για τα νύχια	ehnah vehrneekee yeeah tah neekheeah
nail polish remover	ένα ασετόν για τα νύχια	ehnah ahssehtonn yeeah tah neekheeah
perfume	ένα άρωμα	ehnah ahrommah
powder	μια πούδρα	meeah poodhrah
razor	μια ξυριστική μηχανή	meeah kseereesteekee meekhahnee

razor blades	ξυραφάκια για το ξύρισμα	kseerahfahkeeah yeeah to kseereezmah
safety pins	παραμάνες	pahrahmahnehss
shaving cream	μια κρέμα ξυρίσματος	meeah krehmah kseereezmahtoss
soap	ένα σαπούνι	ehnah sahpoonee
sponge	ένα σφουγγάρι	ehnah sfoonggahree
sun-tan cream	μια κρέμα για τον ήλιο	meeah krehmah yeeah tonn eeleeo
sun-tan oil	ένα λάδι για τον ήλιο	ehnah lahdhee yeeah tonn eeleeo
talcum powder	ταλκ	tahlk
tissues	μερικά χαρτομάντηλα	mehreekah khahrtommahndeelah
toilet paper	χαρτί υγείας	khahrtee eeyeeahss
toilet water	ω ντε τουαλέτ	o deh tooahleht
toothbrush	μια οδοντόβουρτσα	meeah odhondovoortsah
toothpaste	μια οδοντόπαστα	meeah odhondoppahstah
towel	μια πετσέτα	meeah pehtsehtah
tweezers	ένα τσιμπίδι για τα φρύδια	ehnah tseembeedhee yeeah tah freedheeah

For your hair   Για τα μαλλιά σας

bobby pins	τσιμπιδάκια	tseembeedhahkeeah
comb	μια χτένα	meeah khtehnah
dry shampoo	ένα στεγνό σαμπουάν	ehnah stehghno sahmbooahn
hairbrush	μια βούρτσα	meeah voortsah
hairgrips	τσιμπιδάκια	tseembeedhahkeeah
hair lotion	μια λοσιόν για τα μαλλιά	meeah losseeonn yeeah tah mahleeah
hair slide	κοκκαλάκια για τα μαλλιά	kokkahlahkeeah yeeah tah mahleeah
shampoo	σαμπουάν	sahmbooahn
for dry/greasy (oily) hair	για ξηρά/ λιπαρά μαλλιά	yeeah kseerah/ leepahrah mahleeah
tint	μια ελαφριά βαφή	meeah ehlahfreeah vahfee
wig	μια περούκα	meeah pehrookah

For the baby   Για το παιδί

baby food	παιδική τροφή	pehdheekee troffee
dummy (pacifier)	μια κούκλα	meeah kooklah
feeding bottle	ένα πιπερό	ehnah peepehro
nappies (diapers)	πάννες	pahnehss

Clothing *Ενδύματα*

If you want to buy something specific, prepare yourself in advance. Look at the list of clothing on page 116. Get some idea of the colour, material and size you want. They're all listed on the next few pages.

General *Γενικά*

I'd like ...	Θα ήθελα...	thah **ee**thehlah
I want ... for a 10-year-old boy/girl.	Θέλω ... για ένα αγόρι/κορίτσι 10 ετών.	**theh**lo ... yeeah **eh**nah ah**ghor**ree/korree**tsee** 10 eh**tonn**
I want something like this.	Θέλω κάτι σαν κι'αυτό.	**theh**lo **kah**tee sahn keeah**fto**
I like the one in the window.	Μου αρέσει αυτό στη βιτρίνα.	moo ah**reh**ssee ah**fto** stee veet**ree**nah
How much is that per metre?	Πόσο κάνει το μέτρο;	**poss**o **kah**nee to **meh**tro

1 centimetre (cm.) =	0.39 in.	1 inch = 2.54 cm.
1 metre (m.)	= 39.37 in.	1 foot = 30.5 cm.
10 metres	= 32.81 ft.	1 yard = 0.91 m.

Colour *Χρώμα*

I want something in ...	Θέλω κάτι σε...	**theh**lo **kah**tee seh
I want a darker/lighter shade.	Θέλω μια ποιο σκοτεινή/πιο ανοικτή απόχρωση	**theh**lo **mee**ah **peo** skot**tee**nee/**peo** ahn**neek**tee ahpokh**ross**ee
I want something to match this.	Θέλω κάτι να ταιριάζη με αυτό.	**theh**lo **kah**tee nah tehree**ah**zee meh ah**fto**
I don't like the colour.	Δεν μου αρέσει το χρώμα.	dhehn moo ah**reh**ssee to **khromm**ah

μονόχρωμο
(monno**khromm**o)

ριγέ
(ree**yeh**)

πουά
(poo**ah**)

καρρώ
(**kah**ro)

εμπριμέ
(ehmbree**meh**)

beige	μπεζ	behz
black	μαύρο	**mah**vro
blue	μπλε	bleh
brown	καφέ	kah**feh**
fawn	μπεζ σκούρο	behz **skoo**ro
golden	χρυσαφένιο	khreessah**feh**neeo
green	πράσινο	**prah**sseeno
grey	γκρίζο	**gree**zo
mauve	μωβ	movv
orange	πορτοκαλί	portokkah**lee**
pink	ροζ	rozz
purple	πορφυρό	por**fee**ro
red	κόκκινο	**kokk**eeno
scarlet	κόκκινο της φωτιάς	**kokk**eeno teess fotte**eahss**
silver	ασημένιο	ahssee**meh**neeo
turquoise	τουρκουάζ	teerkoo**ahz**
white	άσπρο	**ahs**pro
yellow	κίτρινο	**kee**treeno
light...	ανοιχτός...	ahnee**kh**toss...
dark...	σκούρος...	**skoo**ross...

Fabric Ύφασμα

Do you have anything in ...?	Έχετε κάτι σε...;	**eh**khehteh **kah**tee seh
Is that ...?	Είναι ...;	**ee**neh
handmade	χειροποίητο	kheero**ppee**-eeto
imported	εισαγώμενο	eessah**ghom**mehno
made in Greece	ελληνικής κατασκευής	ehleenee**keess** kahtahskeh**veess**
pure cotton/wool	βαμβακερό/μάλλινο	vahmvahkeh**ro**/**mah**leeno
synthetic	συνθετικό	seenseh**teeko**
colourfast	ύφασμα που δεν ξεβάφει	**ee**fahzmah poo dhehn kseh**vah**fee
wrinkle resistant	ύφασμα που δεν ζαρώνει	**ee**fahzmah poo dhehn zah**ronn**ee
I want something thinner.	Θέλω κάτι λεπτότερο.	**theh**lo **kah**tee lehp**tott**ehro
Do you have anything of better quality?	Έχετε κάτι καλύτερης ποιότητας;	**eh**khehteh **kah**tee kah**lee**tehreess peeoteetahss

Is it hand washable/ machine washable?	Πλένεται στα χέρια/ στη μηχανή;	**pleh**nehteh stah **kheh**reeah/stee meekhah**nee**
Will it shrink?	Μαζεύει;	mah**zeh**vee
What's it made of?	Τι ύφασμα είναι;	tee **ee**fahzmah **ee**neh

cambric	βατίστα	vah**tee**stah
camel-hair	καμηλό	kahmee**lo**
chiffon	μουσελίνα μεταξωτή	moossehle**ee**nah mehtah-k**sot**tee
corduroy	βελούδο κοτλέ	veh**loo**dho kotleh
cotton	βαμβακερό	vahmvahkehro
crepe	ύφασμα κρεπ	**ee**fahzmah "crepe"
denim	χονδρό βαμβακερό ύφασμα	khon**dhro** vahmvahkehro **ee**fahzmah
felt	τσόχα	**tso**khah
flannel	φανέλλα	fah**neh**lah
gabardine	καμπαρντίνα	kahbahr**dee**nah
lace	δαντέλλα	dhahn**teh**lah
leather	δέρμα	**dher**hmah
linen	λινό	**lee**no
poplin	ποπλίνα	po**plee**nah
satin	σατέν	sah**tehn**
silk	μεταξωτό	mehtahk**sot**to
suede	σουέτ	soo**eht**
towelling	πετσετέ	pehtseh**teh**
velvet	βελούδο	veh**loo**dho
velveteen	βελούδο βαμβακερό	veh**loo**dho vahmvahkehro
wool	μαλλί	mah**lee**
worsted	μάλλινο υφαντό	**mah**leeno eefah**ndo**

Size Μέγεθος

Sizes can vary from one manufacturer to another, so be sure to try on shoes and clothing before you buy.

Could you measure me?	Θέλετε να μου πάρετε μέτρα;	**theh**lehteh nah moo **pah**rehteh **meh**trah
I don't know the Greek sizes.	Δεν ξέρω τα Ελληνικά μεγέθη.	dhehn **kseh**ro tah ehleen-**eekah** mehy**eh**thee

A good fit? *Ταιριάζει;*

Can I try it on?	Μπορώ να το δοκιμάσω;	borro nah to dhokkee**mahs**so
Where's the fitting room?	Που είναι το δοκιμαστήριο;	poo **ee**neh to dhokkee-mah**stee**reeo
Is there a mirror?	Υπάρχει καθρέφτης;	ee**pahr**khee kah**threhf**teess
It fits very well.	Μου ταιριάζει πολύ καλά.	moo tehree**ah**zee pol**lee** kah**lah**
It doesn't fit.	Δεν μου ταιριάζει.	dhehn moo tehree**ah**zee
It's too ...	Είναι πολύ ...	**ee**neh pol**lee**
short/long	κοντό/μακρύ	kon**do**/mah**kree**
tight/loose	στενό/φαρδύ	steh**no**/fahr**dhee**
How long will it take to alter?	Σε πόσες μέρες μπορείτε να μου το διορθώσετε;	seh **pos**sehss **meh**rehss bor**ree**teh nah moo to dheeor**thos**sehteh

Women *Γυναίκες*

	Dresses/suits					
American	8	10	12	14	16	18
British	10	12	14	16	18	20
Greek	42	44	46	48	50	52

	Stockings						Shoes			
American British	8	8½	9	9½	10	10½	5½ 4	6½ 5	7½ 6	8½ 7
Greek	0		1		2	3	37	38	39	40

Men *Άνδρες*

	Suits/overcoats						Shirts			
American British	36	38	40	42	44	46	15	16	17	18
Greek	46	48	50	52	54	56	38	40	42	44

	Shoes									
American British	5	6	7	8	8½	9	9½	10	11
Greek	38	39	40	41	41½	42	42½	43	44

NUMBERS, see page 146

Clothes and accessories   Ρούχα και αξεσουάρ

I'd like a/an/ some ...	Θα ήθελα...	thah eethehlah
anorak	ένα αδιάβροχο τζάκετ	ehnah ahdheeahvrokho dzahkeht
bathing cap	μια σκούφια για το μπάνιο	meeah skoofeeah yeeah to bahneeo
bathrobe	ένα μπουρνούζι	ehnah boornoozee
blouse	μια μπλούζα	meeah bloozah
bow tie	ένα παπιγιόν	ehnah pahpeeyeeonn
bra	ένα σουτιέν	ehnah sooteeehn
braces	τιράντες	teerahndehss
briefs	κυλότες	keelottehss
cap	μια κασκέτα	meeah kahskehtah
cardigan	μια πλεκτή ζακέττα	meeah plehktee zahkehtah
coat	ένα παλτό	ehnah pahlto
dress	ένα φόρεμα	ehnah forrehmah
evening dress (woman's)	ένα βραδυνό φόρεμα	ehnah vrahdheeno forrehmah
girdle	ένα λαστέξ	ehnah lahstehkss
gloves	γάντια	ghahndeeah
handbag	μια τσάντα	meeah tsahndah
handkerchief	ένα μαντήλι	ehnah mahndeelee
hat	ένα καπέλλο	ehnah kahpehlo
jacket	μια ζακέτα	meeah zahkehtah
jeans	μπλου-τζήν	bloodzeen
kneesocks	κάλτσες μέχρι τα γόνατα	kahltsehss mehkhree tah ghonnahtah
nightdress	ένα νυκτικό	ehnah neekteeko
pair of ...	ένα ζευγάρι...	ehnah zehvghahree
panties	κυλότες	keelottehss
pants (Am.)	ένα παντελόνι	ehnah pahndehlonnee
panty-girdle	ένα λαστέξ	ehnah lahstehks
panty hose	ένα καλτσόν	ehnah kahltsonn
pullover	ένα πουλόβερ	ehnah poolovehr
roll-neck (turtle-neck)	με ζιβάνγκο	meh zeevahnggo
round neck	με λαιμόκοψη	meh lehmokkopsee
V-neck	με ανοιχτό λαιμό	meh ahneekhto lehmo
with long/short	με μακρυά/κοντά	meh mahkreeah/kondah
sleeves	μανίκια	mahneekeeah
sleeveless	χωρίς μανίκια	khorreess mahneekeeah

pyjamas	μια πυτζάμα	meeah peedzahmah
raincoat	ένα αδιάβροχο	ehnah ahdheeahvrokho
scarf	ένα κασκόλ	ehnah kahskoll
shirt	ένα πουκάμισο	ehnah pookahmeesso
shorts	ένα σορτς	ehnah sorts
skirt	μια φούστα	meeah foostah
slip	ένα κομπιναιζόν	ehnah kombeenehzonn
socks	κάλτσες	kahltsehss
sports jacket	ένα σακκάκι σπόρ	ehnah sahkahkee spor
stockings	κάλτσες γυναικείες	kahltsehss yeenehkeeehss
suit (man's)	ένα κοστούμι	ehnah kostoomee
suit (woman's)	ένα ταγιέρ	ehnah tahyeeehr
suspenders (Am.)	τιράντες	teerahndehss
sweater	ένα πουλόβερ	ehnah poolovvehr
sweatshirt	ένα φανελάκι σπορ	ehnah fahnehlahkee spor
swimming trunks	ένα μαγιό	ehnah mahyeeo
swimsuit	ένα μαγιό	ehnah mahyeeo
T-shirt	ένα τι-σερτ	ehnah teessehrt
tie	μια γραβάτα	meeah ghrahvahtah
tights	ένα καλσόν	ehnah kahlsonn
tracksuit	μια φόρμα	meeah formah
trousers	ένα παντελόνι	ehnah pahndehlonnee
umbrella	μια ομπρέλα	meeah ombrehlah
underpants (men)	ένα σώβρακο	ehnah sovrahko
undershirt	μια φανέλλα εσώρουχο	meeah fahnehlah ehssorrookho
vest (Am.)	ένα γιλέκο	ehnah yeelehko
vest (Br.)	μια φανέλλα εσώρουχο	meeah fahnehlah ehssorrookho
waistcoat	ένα γιλέκο	ehnah yeelehko

belt	μια ζώνη	meeah zonnee
buckle	μια εγγράφα ζώνης	meeah ehnggrahfah zonneess
button	ένα κουμπί	ehnah koombee
collar	ένα γιακά	ehnah yeeahkah
pocket	μια τσέπη	meeah tsehpee
press stud (snap fastener)	μια σούστα	meeah soostah
zip (zipper)	ένα φερμουάρ	ehnah fehrmooahr

Shoes Παπούτσια

I'd-like a pair of ...	Θα ήθελα ένα ζευγάρι...	thah **ee**thehlah **e**hnah zehv**gha**hree
boots	μπότες	**bo**ttehss
moccasins	μοκασίν	mokka**see**n
plimsolls (sneakers)	αθλητικά παπούτσια	ahthleetee**kah** pah**poo**tseeah
sandals	σάνδαλα	**sah**ndahlah
shoes	παπούτσια	pah**poo**tseeah
flat/with a heel	ίσια/με τακούνι	**ee**sseeah/meh ta**koo**nee
slippers	παντόφλες	pahn**do**flehss
These are too ...	Είναι πολύ ...	**ee**neh po**lee**
narrow/wide	στενά/φαρδιά	ste**hnah**/fahr**dhee**ah
large/small	μεγάλα/μικρά	meh**ghah**lah/mee**krah**
Do you have a larger/ smaller size?	Έχετε ένα μέγεθος μεγαλήτερο/μικρότερο;	**eh**khehteh **e**hnah **meh**yehthoss mehghah**lee**tehro/mee**kro**tehro
Do you have the same in black?	Έχετε το ίδιο σε μαύρο;	**eh**khehteh to **ee**dheeo seh **mah**vro
cloth	ύφασμα	**ee**fahzmah
leather	δέρμα	**dheh**rmah
rubber	λάστικο	**lah**steeko
suede	σουέτ	soo**eh**t
Is it genuine leather?	Είναι από γνήσιο δέρμα;	**ee**neh ah**po** ghnee**ss**eeo **dheh**rmah
I need some shoe polish/shoelaces.	Χρειάζομαι μια μπογιά/ κορδόνια υποδημάτων.	khree**ah**zommeh meeah bo**yeah**/kord**ho**neeah eepodhee**mah**tonn

Shoes worn out? Here's the key to getting them fixed again:

Can you repair these shoes?	Μπορείτε να επιδιορθώ-σετε αυτά τα παπούτσια;	bor**ree**teh nah ehpeedhee-or**tho**ssehteh ahf**tah** tah pah**poo**tseeah
Can you stitch this?	Μπορείτε να το ράψετε;	bor**ree**teh nah to **rah**psehteh
I want new soles and heels.	Θέλω νέες σόλες και τακούνια.	**the**hlo **ne**hehss **so**llehss keh ta**koo**neeah
When will they be ready?	Πότε θα είναι έτοιμα;	**po**tteh thah **ee**neh **e**hteemah

Electrical appliances   *Ηλεκτρικές συσκευές*

The general rule in Greece is 220-volt, 50-cycle AC current.

What's the voltage?	Πόσα βολτ είναι το ρεύμα;	possah volt **ee**neh to **reh**vmah
Do you have a battery for this?	Έχετε μια μπαταρία γι'αυτό;	**eh**kheteh **mee**ah bahtah**ree**ah yeeah**f**to
This is broken. Can you repair it?	Έχει σπάσει. Μπορείτε να το διορθώσετε;	**eh**khee **spah**ssee. bo**ree**teh nah to dheeor**thoss**ehteh
Can you show me how it works?	Μπορείτε να μου δείξετε πως λειτουργεί;	bo**ree**teh nah moo dhee-**ksehteh poss leetooryee**
I'd like a/an/some...	Θα ήθελα...	thah **ee**thehlah
adaptor	ένα μετασχηματιστή πρίζας	**eh**nah mehtahskhee-mah**tees**tee **pree**zahss
amplifier	ένα ενισχυτή	**eh**nah ehnees**khee**tee
clock-radio	ένα ραδιοξυπνητήρι	**eh**nah rahdheeokseep-nee**tee**ree
electric toothbrush	μια ηλεκτρική οδοντόβουρτσα	mee**ah** eelehktree**kee** odhon**do**voortsah
extension lead (cord)	μια μπαλαντέζα	**mee**ah bahlahn**deh**zah
hair dryer	ένα στεγνωτήρα μαλλιών	**eh**nah stehgno**tee**rah mahlee**onn**
headphones	ακουστικά	ahkoostee**kah**
(travelling) iron	ένα σίδερο (για ταξίδι)	**eh**nah **see**dhehro (yeeah tah**ksee**dhee)
lamp	μια λάμπα	**mee**ah **lahm**bah
plug	μια πρίζα	**mee**ah **pree**zah
portable ...	ένα φορητό ...	**eh**nah forre**to**
radio	ράδιο	**rah**dheeo
record player	ένα πικ-απ	**eh**nah peek-ahp
shaver	μια ξυριστική μηχανή	**mee**ah kseereestee**kee** meekhah**nee**
speakers	μεγάφωνα	meh**ghah**fonnah
(cassette) tape recorder	ένα κασεττόφωνο	**eh**nah kahsseh**toff**onno
(colour) television	μια (έγχρωμη) τηλεόραση	**mee**ah (**ehng**khrommee) teeleho**rah**ssee
transformer	ένα μετασχηματιστή	**eh**nah mehtahskhee-mah**tees**tee
video cassette	μια βίντεο-κασέττα	**mee**ah **vee**deho-kah**sseh**tah
video recorder	ένα βίντεο	**eh**nah **vee**deho

Grocery Παντοπωλείον

I'd like some bread, please.	Θα ήθελα λίγο ψωμί, παρακαλώ.	thah eethehlah leegho psommee pahrahkahlo
What sort of cheese do you have?	Τι είδους τυριά έχετε;	tee eedhooss teereeah ehkhehteh
A piece of ...	Ένα κομμάτι από...	ehnah kommahtee ahpo
that one	αυτό	ahfto
the one on the shelf	αυτό στο ράφι	ahfto sto rahfee
I'll have one of those, please.	Θα πάρω ένα από αυτά, παρακαλώ.	thah pahro ehnah ahpo ahftah pahrahkahlo
May I help myself?	Μπορώ να εξυπηρετηθώ μόνος/-η μου;	borro nah ehkseepeerehteetho monnoss/-ee moo
I'd like ...	Θα ήθελα...	thah eethehlah
a kilo of apples	ένα κιλό μήλα	ehnah keelo meelah
half a kilo of tomatoes	μισό κιλό ντομάτες	meesso keelo dommahtehss
100 grams of butter	100 γραμμάρια βούτυρο	100 ghrahmahreeah vooteero
a litre of milk	ένα λίτρο γάλα	ehnah leetro ghahlah
4 slices of ham	4 φέτες ζαμπόν	4 fehtehss zahmbonn
a packet of tea	ένα κουτί τσάι	ehnah kootee tsahee
a jar of jam	ένα κουτί μαρμελάδα	ehnah kootee mahrmehlahdhah
a tin (can) of peaches	μια κονσέρβα ροδάκινα	meeah konsehrvah rodhahkeenah
a box of chocolates	ένα κουτί σοκολάτες	ehnah kootee sokkollahtehss
a tube of mustard	μια μουστάρδα σε σωληνάριο	meeah moostahrdhah seh solleenahreeo

---

1 kilogram or kilo (kg.) = 1000 grams (g.)

100 g. = 3.5 oz.	¹/₂ kg. = 1.1 lb.
200 g. = 7.0 oz.	1 kg. = 2.2 lb.

1 oz. = 28.35 g.
1 lb. = 453.60 g.

---

1 litre (l.) = 0.88 imp. quarts = 1.06 U.S. quarts

1 imp. quart = 1.14 l.	1 U.S. quart = 0.95 l.
1 imp. gallon = 4.55 l.	1 U.S. gallon = 3.8 l.

FOOD, see also page 63

Jeweller's – Watchmaker's   *Κοσμηματοπωλείο – Ωρολογοποιείον*

Could I see that, please?	Μπορώ να δω εκείνο παρακαλώ;	borro nah dho ehkeeno pahrahkahlo
Do you have anything in gold?	Έχετε κάτι σε χρυσό;	ehkhehteh kahtee seh khreesso
How many carats is this?	Πόσων καρατίων είναι αυτό;	possonn kahrahteeonn eeneh ahfto
Is this real silver?	Αυτό είναι αληθινό ασήμι;	ahfto eeneh ahleetheeno ahsseemee
Can you repair this watch?	Μπορείτε να επιδιορθώσετε αυτό το ρολόι;	borreeteh nah ehpeedheeorthossehteh ahfto to rolloee
I'd like a/an/some...	Θα ήθελα...	thah eethehlah
alarm clock	ένα ξυπνητήρι	ehnah kseepneeteeree
bangle	ένα βραχιόλι	ehnah vrahkheeollee
battery	μια μπαταρία	meeah bahtahreeah
bracelet	ένα βραχιόλι	ehnah vrahkheeollee
chain bracelet	μια αλυσίδα του χεριού	meeah ahleesseedhah too khehreeoo
charm bracelet	ένα μπρελόκ βραχιόλι	ehnah brehlok vrahkheeollee
brooch	μια καρφίτσα	meeah kahrfeetsah
chain	μια αλυσίδα	meeah ahleesseedhah
charm	ένα μπρελόκ	ehnah brehlok
cigarette case	μια τσιγαροθήκη	meeah tseeghahrotheekee
cigarette lighter	έναν αναπτήρα	ehnahn ahnahpteerah
clip	ένα κλιπς	ehnah kleeps
clock	ένα ρολόι	ehnah rolloee
cross	ένα σταυρό	ehnah stahvro
cuff-links	ένα ζευγάρι μανικετόκουμπα	ehnah zehvghahree mahneekehtokoombah
cutlery	μαχαιροπήρουνα	mahkhehroppeeroonah
earrings	ένα ζευγάρι σκουλαρίκια	ehnah zehvghahree skoolahreekeeah
gem	ένα πολύτιμο λίθο	ehnah polleeteemo leetho
jewel box	μια μπιζουτιέρα	meeah beezooteeehrah
necklace	ένα κολλιέ	ehnah kolleeeh
pendant	ένα παντατίφ	ehnah pahndahteef
pin	μια καρφίτσα	meeah kahrfeetsah
pocket watch	ένα ρολόι τσέπης	ehnah rolloee tsehpeess
powder compact	μια πουδριέρα	meeah poodhreeehrah

ring	ένα δακτυλίδι	**eh**nah dhahkteel**ee**dhee
engagement ring	ένα δακτυλίδι	**eh**nah dhahkteel**ee**dhee
	αρραβώνα	ahrahvonnah
signet ring	ένα δακτυλίδι με	**eh**nah dhahkteel**ee**dhee
	οικόσημο	meh eek**oss**eemo
wedding ring	μια βέρα	mee**ah** **veh**rah
rosary	ένα κομπολόι για	**eh**nah komb**oll**oee yee**ah**
	προσευχές	prosseh**fkheh**ss
silverware	μερικά ασημικά	mehree**kah**
		ahsseemee**kah**
watch	ένα ρολόϊ	**eh**nah r**oll**oee
automatic	αυτόματο	ahf**tomm**ahto
digital	ψηφιακό	pseefeea**hko**
quartz	χαλαζία	khahlah**zee**ah
with a second hand	με δείκτη για	meh **dheek**tee yee**ah**
	δευτερόλεπτα	dhehftehr**oll**ehptah
waterproof	αδιάβροχο	ahdhee**ah**vrokho
watchstrap	ένα μπρασελέ για ρολόι	**eh**nah brahsehl**eh** yee**ah**
		r**oll**oee
wristwatch	ένα ρολόι χεριού	**eh**nah r**oll**oee khehree**oo**

amber	κεχριμπάρι	kehkhreemb**ah**ree
amethyst	αμέθυστος	ahm**eh**theestoss
chromium	χρώμιο	**khromm**eeo
copper	χαλκός	khahl**koss**
coral	κοράλι	korr**ah**lee
crystal	κρύσταλλο	**krees**tahlo
cut glass	κρύσταλλο ταγιέ	**krees**tahlo tahyee**eh**
diamond	διαμάντι	dheeah**mahn**dee
emerald	σμαράγδι	zmahr**ah**ghdhee
enamel	σμάλτο	**zmahl**to
gold	χρυσός	khree**ssoss**
gold plated	επίχρυσο	ehpee**khreess**o
ivory	ελεφαντόδοντο	ehlehfahnd**o**dhondo
jade	ζαντ	zahnd
onyx	όνυχας	onn**ee**khahss
pearl	μαργαριτάρι	mahrghahreet**ah**ree
pewter	κασσίτερος	kahss**ee**tehross
platinum	πλατίνα	plaht**ee**nah
ruby	ρουμπίνι	roomb**ee**nee
sapphire	σαφείρι	zahf**ee**ree
silver	ασήμι	ahss**ee**mee
silver plated	επάργυρο	ehp**ah**ryeero
topaz	τοπάζι	toh**pah**zee
turquoise	τουρκουάζ	teerkoo**ah**z

Optician   Οπτικός

I've broken my glasses.	Έσπασα τα γυαλιά μου.	ehspahssah tah yeeahleeah moo
Can you repair them for me?	Μπορείτε να μου τα επιδιορθώσετε;	borreeteh nah moo tah ehpeedheeorthossehteh
Can you change the lenses?	Μπορείτε να αλλάξετε τους φακούς;	borreeteh nah ahlahksehteh tooss fahkooss
I want tinted lenses.	Θέλω φακούς φιμέ.	thehlo fahkooss feemeh
The frame is broken.	Έσπασε ο σκελετός.	ehspahsseh o skehlehtoss
I'd like a spectacle case.	Θα ήθελα μια θήκη για τα γυαλιά.	thah eethehlah meeah theekee yeeah tah yeeahleeah
I'd like to have my eyesight checked.	Θα ήθελα να κάνω ένα τεστ για τα μάτια μου.	thah eethehlah nah kahno ehnah tehsst yeeah tah mahteeah moo
I'm short-sighted/ long-sighted.	Είμαι μύωπας/ πρεσβύωπας.	eemeh meeoppahss/ prehzveeoppahss
I want some contact lenses.	Θέλω φακού επαφής.	thehlo fahkooss ehpahfeess
I've lost one of my contact lenses.	Έχασα ένα από τους φακούς επαφής μου.	ehkhahssah ehnah ahpo tooss fahkooss ehpahfeess moo
Could you give me another one?	Μπορείτε να μου δώσετε έναν άλλο;	borreeteh nah moo dhossehteh ehnahn ahlo
I have hard/soft lenses.	Έχω σκληρούς/ μαλακούς φακούς.	ehkho skleerooss/ mahlahkooss fahkooss
Do you have any contact-lens fluid?	Έχετε υγρό για τους φακούς επαφής;	ehkhehteh eeghro yeeah tooss fahkooss ehpahfeess
I'd like to buy a pair of sunglasses.	Θα ήθελα να αγοράσω ένα ζευγάρι γυαλιά ήλιου.	thah eethehlah nah aghorrahsso ehnah zehvghahree yeeahleeah eeleeoo
May I look in a mirror?	Μπορώ να κοιτάξω στον καθρέφτη;	borro nah keetahkso stonn kahthrehftee
I'd like to buy a pair of binoculars.	Θα ήθελα να αγοράσω ένα ζευγάρι κυάλια.	thah eethehlah nah aghorrahsso ehnah zehvghahree keeahleeah

Photography   Φωτογραφείο

I want a(n) ... camera.	Θέλω μια ... φωτο-γραφική μηχανή.	thehlo meeah ... fotto-ghrahfeekee meekhahnee
automatic	αυτόματη	ahftommahtee
inexpensive	φθηνή	ftheenee
simple	απλή	ahplee
Show me some cine (movie) cameras, please.	Δείξτε μου μερικές κινηματογραφικές μηχανές, παρακαλώ.	dheeksteh moo mehreekehss keenee-mahtoghrahfeekehss meekhahnehss pahrahkahlo
I'd like to have some passport photos taken.	Θα ήθελα να βγάλω μερικές φωτογραφίες για το διαβατήριο.	thah eethehlah nah vghahlo mehreekehss fottoghrahfeeehss yeeah to dheeahvahteereeo

Film   Φιλμ

I'd like a film for this camera.	Θα ήθελα ένα φιλμ γι'αυτή τη μηχανή.	thah eethehlah ehnah feelm yeeahftee tee meekhahnee
black and white	ασπρόμαυρο	ahsprommahvro
colour	έγχρωμο	ehngkhrommo
colour negative	έγχρωμο αρνητικό	ehngkhrommo ahrneeteeko
colour slide	έγχρωμο σλάιντς	ehngkhrommo "slides"
cartridge	ένα φιλμ κασέττα	ehnah feelm kahssehtah
disc film	μια ντισκέττα	meeah deeskehtah
roll film	ένα φιλμ ρολό	ehnah feelm rollo
video cassette	ένα βίντεο-κασέττα	ehnah veedeho-kahssehtah
24/36 exposures	ένα εικοσιτεσσάρι τριανταεξάρι φιλμ	ehnah eekosseetehssahree treeahndahehksahree feelm
this size	αυτό το μέγεθος	ahfto to mehyehthoss
this ASA/DIN number	αυτό τον αριθμό ASA/DIN	ahfto tonn ahreethmo "ASA/DIN"
artificial light type	για τεχνητό φως	yeeah tehkhneeto foss
daylight type	για φως της μέρας	yeeah foss teess mehrahss
fast (high-speed)	υψηλής ταχύτητας	eepseeleess tahkheeteetahss
fine grain	λεπτού κόκου	lehptoo kokkoo

Processing   *Εμφάνιση*

How much do you charge for developing?	Πόσο κοστίζει η εμφάνιση;	**posso** kost**ee**zee ee ehm**fah**neessee
I want ... prints of each negative.	Θέλω ... φωτογραφίες από κάθε αρνητικό.	**thehlo** ... fottoghrah**fee**ehss ah**po kah**theh ahrneeteeko
with a mat finish	ματ	maht
with a glossy finish	γυαλιστερές	yeeahleestehrehss
Will you enlarge this, please?	Μπορείτε να μου μεγεθύνετε αυτό παρακαλώ;	borreeteh nah moo mehyehntheenehteh ahfto pahrahkahlo
When will the photos be ready?	Πότε θα είναι έτοιμες οι φωτογραφίες;	potteh thah eeneh ehteemehss ee fottoghrahfeeehss

Accessories and repairs   *Αξεσουάρ και επισκευές*

I want a/an/some...	Θέλω ...	**thehlo**
battery	μια μπαταρία	meeah bahtahreeah
(electronic) flash	ένα (ηλεκτρονικό) φλας	ehnah (eelehktronneeko) flahss
filter	ένα φίλτρο	ehnah feeltro
for black and white	για ασπρόμαυρο	yeeah ahsprommahvro
for colour	για έχρωμο	yeeah ehkhrommo
lens	ένα φακό	ehnah fahko
telephoto lens	ένα τηλεφακό	ehnah teelehfahko
wide-angle lens	ένα ευρυγώνιο φακό	ehnah ehvreeghonneeo fahko
Can you repair this camera?	Μπορείτε να διορθώσετε αυτή την φωτογραφική μηχανή;	borreeteh nah dheeorthossehteh ahftee teen fottoghrahfeekee meekhahnee
The film is jammed.	Το φιλμ έχει μπλεχτεί.	to feelm ehkhee blehkhtee
There's something wrong with the ...	Κάτι δεν λειτουργεί καλά στο ...	kahtee dhehn leetooryee kahlah sto
exposure counter	μετρητή των φωτογραφιών	mehtreetee tonn fottoghrahfeeonn
film winder	γύρισμα του φιλμ	yeereezmah too feelm
flash attachment	μια υποδοχή για φλας φακό	meeah eepodhokhee yeeah flahss fahko
light meter	φωτόμετρο	fottomehtro
rangefinder	αποστασιόμετρο	ahpostahsseeommehtro
shutter	διάφραγμα	dheeahfrahghmah

NUMBERS, see page 146

Tobacconist's Καπνοπωλείον

Greek tobacco products, of good quality and generally mild, are far cheaper than the few foreign brands (manufactured under licence) available.

A packet of cigarettes, please.	Ένα κουτί τσιγάρα, παρακαλώ.	ehnah kootee tseeghahrah pahrahkahlo
Do you have any American/English cigarettes?	Έχετε Αμερικάνικα/ Αγγλικά τσιγάρα;	ehkhehteh ahmehreekah-neekah/ahnggleekah tseeghahrah
I'd like a carton.	Θα ήθελα μια κούτα.	thah eethehlah meeah kootah
Give me a/some ... please.	Δώστε μου ... παρακαλώ.	dhosteh moo ... pahrahkahlo
candy	καραμέλες	kahrahmehlehss
chewing gum	μια τσίχλα	meeah tseekhlah
chocolate	μια σοκολάτα	meeah sokkollahtah
cigarette case	μια τσιγαροθήκη	meeah tseeghahrotheekee
cigarette holder	μια πίπα για στιγάρα	meeah peepah yeeah tseeghahrah
cigarettes	τσιγάρα	tseeghahrah
filter-tipped	με φίλτρο	meh feeltro
without filter	χωρίς φίλτρο	khorreess feeltro
light/dark tobacco	ξανθό/μαύρο καπνό	ksahntho/mahvro kahpno
mild/strong	ελαφρυά/βαρυά	ehlahfreeah/vahreeah
menthol	μεντόλ	mehndoll
king-size	κιγκ-σάιζ	"king-size"
cigars	πούρα	poorah
lighter	ένα αναπτήρα	ehnah ahnahpteerah
lighter fluid/gas	υγραέριο/αέριο για αναπτήρα	eeghrahehreeo/ ahehreeo yeeah ahnahpteerah
matches	σπίρτα	speertah
pipe	μια πίπα	meeah peepah
pipe cleaners	καθαριστήρες πίπας	kahthahreesteerehss peepahss
pipe tobacco	καπνό πίπας	kahpno peepahss
pipe tool	πανί πίπας	pahnee peepahss
postcard	μια καρτ-ποστάλ	meeah kahrt-postahl
stamps	γραμματόσημα	ghrahmahtoseemah
sweets	καραμέλες	kahrahmehlehss
wick	ένα φιτίλι	ehnah feeteelee

Miscellaneous   Διάφορα

Souvenirs   Σουβενίρς (Ενθύμια)

Greece offers a wide range of handicrafts, particularly hand-woven textiles, costumed dolls and embroidered blouses and tablecloths. Ceramics and costume jewellery are most often designed in classic Greek styles. The flea markets offer countless antiques, including all sorts of copper, brass, bronze and other metallic objects. However, the exportation of ancient artifacts is strictly controlled, and it's virtually impossible to take any out of the country.

For those who like fine furs, Greece is noted for its marten—and especially stone marten—pelts.

alabaster objects	αλάβαστρο	ahlahvahstro
backgammon	τάβλι	tahvlee
bed rug	κάλυμμα κρεβατιού	kahleemah krehvahteeoo
brass	μπρούντζινα είδη	broondzeenah eedhee
ceramics	κεραμικά	kehrahmeekah
copper bells	χάλκινα κουδούνια	khahlkeenah koodhooneeah
dolls in national costumes (evzon)	κούκλες με εθνικές στολές (εύζωνος)	kooklehss meh ehthneekehss stollehss (ehvzonnoss)
embroidery	κέντημα	kehndeemah
floor rug	χαλί	khahlee
fur	γούνα	ghoonah
hand-knotted carpet	κιλίμι (χειροποίητο χαλί)	keeleemee (kheeropeeeeto khahlee)
honey	μέλι	mehlee
icon	εικόνα	eekonnah
long-fleeced woollen rug	φλοκάτη	flokkahtee
olive oil	ελαιόλαδο	ehlehollahdho
pottery	είδη αγγειοπλαστικής	eedhee ahnggeeoplahsteekeess
shepherd's coat	κάπα	kahpah
silverware	ασημικά	ahsseemeekah
tote bag	ταγάρι	tahghahree
wine	κρασί	krahssee
worry-beads	κομπολόι	kombolloee

Records – Cassettes   Δίσκοι – Κασέττες

Do you have any records by ...?	Έχετε δίσκους του...;	ehkhehteh dheeskooss too
I'd like a	Θα ήθελα ...	thah eethehlah
cassette	μια κασέττα	meeah kahssehtah
compact disc	ένα δίσκο για πικ-απ λέιζερ	ehnah dheesko yeeah "pick-up laser"
Do you have any songs by ...?	Έχετε τραγούδια του...;	ehkhehteh trahghoodheeah too
Can I listen to this record?	Μπορώ να ακούσω αυτό το δίσκο;	borro nah ahkoosso ahfto to dheesko
chamber music	μουσική δωματίου	moosseekee dhommah-teeoo
classical music	κλασσική μουσική	klahsseekee moosseekee
folk music	λαϊκή μουσική	laheekee moosseekee
instrumental music	ενορχήστρωση	ehnorkheestrossee
jazz	τζαζ	dzahz
light music	ελαφρά μουσική	ehlahfrah moosseekee
orchestral music	μουσική ορχήστρας	moosseekee orkheestrahss
pop music	μουσική ποπ	moosseekee pop

Toys   Παιχνίδια

I'd like a toy/ game ...	Θα ήθελα ένα παιχνίδι ...	thah eethehlah ehnah pehkhneedhee
for a boy	για ένα αγόρι	yeeah ehnah ahghorree
for a five-year-old girl	για ένα πεντάχρονο κοριτσάκι	yeeah ehnah pehndah-khronno koreetsahkee
(beach) ball	μια μπάλα (της παραλίας)	meeah bahlah (teess pahrahleeahs)
bucket and spade (pail and shovel)	ένα κουβαδάκι και φτυαράκι	ehnah koovahdahkee keh fteeahrahkee
building blocks (bricks)	ένα παιχνίδι ξυλοκατασκευή	ehnah pehkhneedhee kseelokkahtahskehvee
card game	μια τράπουλα	meeah trahpoolah
chess set	ένα σκάκι	ehnah skahkee
doll	μια κούκλα	meeah kooklah
electronic game	ένα ηλεκτρονικό παιχνίδι	ehnah eelehktronneeko pehkhneedhee
flippers	βατραχοπέδιλα	vahtrahkhopehdheelah
snorkel	ένα αναπνευστήρα	ehnah ahnahpnehfsteerah

Your money: banks—currency

At larger banks there will probably be someone who speaks English, and in most tourist centres you'll find small currency exchange offices — especially during the summer season. Exchange rates shouldn't vary much from office to office, and you'll normally get a slightly better rate for traveller's cheques and Eurocheques than for cash. If possible, change money in a bank rather than a hotel, it's better value for money. Always take your passport and look out for the *change* sign in Latin letters.

Banks are open from Monday to Friday between 8 a.m. and 1 or 2 p.m. However, currency exchange offices within banks may stay open until 7 or 8 in the evening, some on Saturdays and Sundays.

The Greek monetary system is based on the drachma (abbreviated drs. — in Greek Δρχ). There are coins of 1, 2, 5, 10, 20 and 50 drachmas, and bank notes of 50, 100, 500, 1000 and 5000 drachmas.

Where's the nearest bank?	Που είναι η κοντινό-τερη τράπεζα;	poo **ee**neh ee kondeeno-ttehree **trah**pehzah
Where's the nearest currency exchange office?	Που είναι το κοντινότερο γραφείο αλλαγής συναλλάγματος;	poo **ee**neh to kondeeno**tt**ehro ghrah**fee**o ahlah**yeess** seenah**lahgh**mahtoss
What time does the bank open/close?	Τι ώρα ανοίγει/κλείνει η τράπεζα;	tee orrah ahn**ee**yee/ **klee**nee ee **trah**pehzah

At the bank   Στη τράπεζα

I want to change some dollars/pounds.	Θέλω να αλλάξω μερικά δολλάρια/ μερικές Αγγλικές λίρες.	**theh**lo nah ahl**lah**kso mehr**ee**kah dhol**lah**reeah/ mehr**ee**kehss ahnng**glee**kehss **lee**rehss

I want to cash a traveller's cheque.	Θέλω να εξαργυρώσω ένα τράβελερς τσεκ.	thehlo nah ehksahryee-rosso ehnah "traveller's" tsehk
What's the exchange rate?	Ποια είναι η τιμή συναλλάγματος;	peeah eeneh ee teemee seenahlahghmahtoss
How much commission do you charge?	Πόση προμήθεια χρεώνετε;	possee prommeetheeah khrehonnehteh
Can you cash a personal cheque?	Μπορείτε να εξαργυρώσετε ένα προσωπικό τσεκ;	borreeteh nah ehksahryeerossehteh ehnah prossoppeeko tsehk
Can you telex my bank in London?	Μπορείτε να στήλετε ένα τέλεξ στη τράπεζα μου στο Λονδίνο;	borreeteh nah steelehteh ehnah "telex" stee trahpehzah moo sto londheeno
I have a/an/some ...	Έχω ...	ehkho
bank card	μια τραπεζιτική κάρτα	meeah trahpehzeeteekee kahrtah
credit card	μια πιστωτική κάρτα	meeah peestotteekee kahrtah
Eurocheques	Eurocheques	"eurocheques"
introduction from ...	μια σύσταση από ...	meeah seestahssee ahpo
letter of credit	μια πιστωτική επιστολή	meeah peestotteekee ehpeestollee
I'm expecting some money from New York. Has it arrived?	Περιμένω μερικά λεφτά από τη Νέα Υόρκη. Μήπως έχουν φθάση;	pehreemehno mehreekah lehftah ahpo tee nehah eeorkee. meeposs ehkhoon fthahssee
Please give me ... notes (bills) and some small change.	Παρακαλώ δώστε μου ... χαρτονομίσματα και μερικά ψιλά.	pahrahkahlo dhosteh moo. khahrtonnommeezmahtah keh mehreekah pseelah

Deposits—Withdrawals Κατάθεση – Ανάληψη

I want to ...	Θέλω να ...	thehlo nah
open an account	ανοίξω λογαριασμό	ahneekso loghahreeahzmo
withdraw ... drachmas	σηκώσω ... δραχμές	seekosso... dhrahkhmehss
Where should I sign?	Που να υπογράψω;	poo ah eepoghrahpso
I want to deposit this in my account.	Θέλω να καταθέσω αυτό στο λογαριασμό μου.	thehlo nah kahtahthehsso ahfto sto loghahreeahzmo moo

NUMBERS, see page 146

Τράπεζα

Business terms   *Εμπορικές εκφράσεις*

My name is ...	Το όνομα μου είναι ...	to onnommah moo eeneh
Here's my card.	Ορίστε η κάρτα μου.	orreesteh ee kahrtah moo
I have an appointment with ...	Έχω ραντεβού με τον/την ...	ehkho rahndehvoo meh tonn/teen
Can you give me an estimate of the cost?	Μπορείτε να μου δώσετε μια εκτίμηση των εξόδων;	borreeteh nah moo dhossehteh meeah ehkteemeessee tonn ehksodhonn
What's the rate of inflation?	Πόσο ψηλός είναι ο πληθωρισμός;	posso pseeloss eeneh o pleethorreezmoss
Can you provide me with an interpreter/ a secretary?	Μπορείτε να μου βρείτε ένα/μια διερμηνέα/ γραμματέα;	borreeteh nah moo vreeteh ehnah/meeah dhee-ehrmeenehah/ ghrahmahtehah
Where can I make photocopies?	Που μπορώ να κάνω φωτοτυπίες;	poo borro nah kahno fottotteepeeehss

amount	το ποσόν	to possonn
balance	το ισοζύγιο	to eessozeeyeeo
capital	το κεφάλαιο	to kehfahleho
cheque	η επιταγή	ee ehpeetahyee
contract	το συμβόλαιο	to seemvolleho
discount	η έκπτωση	ee ehkptossee
expenses	η δαπάνη	ee dhahpahnee
interest	ο τόκος	o tokkoss
investment	η επένδυση κεφαλαίου	ee ehpehndheessee kehfahleho
invoice	το τιμολόγιο	to teemolloyeeo
loss	η ζημιά	ee zeemeeah
mortgage	η υποθήκη	ee eepotheekee
payment	η πληρωμή	ee pleerommee
percentage	το επί τις εκατόν	to ehpee teess ehkahtonn
profit	το κέρδος	to kehrdhoss
purchase	η αγορά	ee aghorrah
sale	η πώληση	ee polleessee
share	η μετοχή	ee mehtokhee
transfer	η μεταβίβαση	ee mehtahveevahssee
value	η τιμή	ee teemee

At the post office

Post offices handle letters, stamp sales, parcels and money orders, but not telegrams and phone calls. They can be recognised by a sign reading ΕΛ.ΤΑ. Hours vary, but main post offices are usually open from 8 a.m. to 8 p.m., Monday to Friday. But you can also buy stamps at newsstands and souvenir shops — with a 10 per cent surcharge. Post boxes are painted yellow, and if you want to send letters by registered post or parcels to foreign destinations, don't seal them until they have been checked at the post office by an official.

Where's the nearest post office?	Που είναι το κοντι- νότερο ταχυδρομείο;	poo **ee**neh to kondeeno- tehro tahkheedhrom**mee**o
What time does the post office open/ close?	Τι ώρα ανοίγει/ κλείνει το ταχυ- δρομείο;	tee **o**rrah ahn**ee**yee/ **klee**nee to tahkhee- dhrom**mee**o
A stamp for this letter/postcard, please.	Γραμματόσημα για αυτό το γράμμα/ αυτή τη κάρτα, παρακαλώ.	ghrahmah**tos**seemah yee**ah** ahf**to** to **ghrah**mah/ ahf**tee** tee **kahr**tah pahrahkah**lo**
A ...-drachma stamp, please.	Γραμματόσημα των... δραχμών, παρακαλώ.	ghrahmah**tos**seemah tonn... dhrahkh**monn** pahrahkah**lo**
What's the postage for a letter to London?	Πόσο κοστίζει ένα γράμμα για το Λονδίνο;	**pos**so kost**ee**zee **eh**nah **ghrah**mah yee**ah** to lond**hee**no
Where's the letter- box (mailbox)?	Που είναι το γραμ- ματοκιβώτιο;	poo **ee**neh to ghrahmah- tok**kee**vottee**o**
I want to send this parcel.	Θέλω να στείλω αυτό το δέμα.	**theh**lo nah **stee**lo ahf**to** to **dheh**mah
I want to send this by...	Θέλω να στείλω αυτό...	**theh**lo nah **stee**lo ahf**to**
air mail	αεροπορικώς	ahehropporr**ee**koss
express (special delivery)	εξπρές	''express''
registered mail	συστημένο	seesteem**eh**no

At which counter can I cash an international money order?	Σε ποιο γκισέ μπορώ να εξαργυρώσω μια διεθνή ταχυδρομική επιταγή;	seh peeo geesseh borro nah ehksahryeerosso meeah dheeehthnee tahkheedhrommeekee ehpeetahyee
Where's the poste restante (general delivery)?	Που είναι η ποστ-ρεστάντ;	poo eeneh ee post-rehstahnd
Is there any post for me? My name is...	Υπάρχει ταχυδρομείο για μένα; Ονομάζομαι...	eepahrkhee tahkheedhrommeeo yeeah mehnah. onnommahzommeh

ΓΡΑΜΜΑΤΟΣΗΜΑ	STAMPS
ΔΕΜΑΤΑ	PARCELS
ΕΠΙΤΑΓΕΣ	MONEY ORDERS

Telecommunications   *Τηλεπικοινωνίες*

Every town of any size has an office of the Greek Telecommunications Organization OTE and this is where to go to telephone or send telegrams — if, that is, your hotel is too small to be able to cope.

Public telephone booths are scattered around the towns. Blue ones are for local calls only, while orange ones permit direct dialling to other towns in Greece and to countries abroad connected to the international network. You'll find directions for use clearly written in English.

Telegrams   *Τηλεγραφήματα*

I want to send a telegram/telex.	Θέλω να στείλω ένα τηλεγράφημα/τέλεξ.	thehlo nah steelo ehnah teelehghrahfeemah/"telex"
May I have a form, please?	Μου δείνετε ένα έντυπο, παρακαλώ;	moo dheenehteh ehnah ehndeepo pahrahkahlo
How much is it per word?	Πόσο κοστίζει η λέξη;	posso kosteezee ee lehksee
How much will this telex cost?	Πόσο θα κοστίση αυτό το τέλεξ;	posso thah kosteessee ahfto to "telex"

Τηλέφωνο

Telephoning   *Τηλεφωνώ*

Where's the telephone?	Που είναι το τηλέφωνο;	poo **ee**neh to teel**eh**fonno
Where's the nearest telephone booth?	Που είναι ο κοντινότερος τηλεφωνικός θάλαμος;	poo **ee**neh o kondeenotehross teelehfonneek**oss** thahlahmoss
May I use your phone?	Μπορώ να χρησιμοποιήσω το τηλέφωνό σας;	borro nah khreesseemoppee**ee**sso to teel**eh**fonno sahss
Do you have a telephone directory for Athens?	Έχετε ένα τηλεφωνικό κατάλογο της Αθήνας;	**eh**khehteh **eh**nah teelehfonneeko kaht**ah**logho teess aht**ee**nahss
I want to telephone to England.	Θέλω να τηλεφωνήσω στην Αγγλία.	**theh**lo nah teelehfonn**ee**sso steen ahnggleeah
What's the dialling (area) code for ...?	Ποιος είναι ο τηλεφωνικός κωδικός αριθμός για...;	pe**oss ee**neh o teelehfonneek**oss** kodheek**oss** ahreethmoss yeeah
How do I get the international operator?	Ποιον αριθμό πρέπει να πάρω για τις διεθνείς πληροφορίες;	pe**on** ahreethmo preh**pee** nah pahro yeeah teess dheeehtheen**eess** pleerofforr**ee**ehss

Operator   *Χειριστής*

Good morning. I want Patras 123456.	Καλημέρα σας. Θέλω Πάτρα 123456.	kahleemehrah sahss **theh**lo pahtrah 123456
Can you help me get this number?	Μπορείτε να με βοηθήσετε να πάρω αυτό τον αριθμό;	borr**ee**teh nah meh voeethe**esseh**teh nah pahro ahfto tonn ahreethmo
I want to place a personal (person-to-person) call.	Θέλω να τηλεφωνήσω με προσωπική κλήση.	**theh**lo nah teelehfonn**ee**sso meh prossoppeek**ee** kle**essee**
I want to reverse the charges (call collect).	Θέλω μια κλήση πληρωτέα από τον παραλήπτη.	**theh**lo meeah kle**essee** pleerott**eh**ah ahpo ton pahrahl**ee**ptee

Speaking   *Στο τηλέφωνο*

Hello, this is ... speaking.	Παρακαλώ, εδώ ...	pahrahkahlo ehd**ho**

NUMBERS, see page 146

I want to speak to ...	Θέλω να μιλήσω με ...	thehlo nah meeleesso meh
I want extension ...	Θέλω εσωτερικό ...	thehlo ehssottehreeko
Is that ...?	Είναι το ...;	eeneh to
Speak louder/more slowly, please.	Μιλάτε πιο δυνατά/ πιο αργά, παρακαλώ.	meelahteh peeo dheenahtah/peeo ahrghah pahrahkahlo

Bad luck   Κακή τύχη

Would you try again later, please?	Μπορείτε να δοκι- μάσετε πάλι αργότερα, παρακαλώ;	borreeteh nah dhokkee- mahssehteh pahlee ahr- ghottehrah pahrahkahlo
Operator, you gave me the wrong number.	Κύριε/Κυρία, μου δώσατε λάθος αριθμό.	keereeeh/keereeah moo dhossahteh lahthoss ahreethmo
Operator, we were cut off.	Κύριε/Κυρία, μας κόπηκε η γραμμή.	keereeeh/keereeah mahss koppeekeh ee ghrahmee

Not there   Δεν είναι εδώ

When will he/she be back?	Πότε θα επιστρέψει;	potteh thah ehpee- strehpsee
Will you tell him/ her I called? My name is ...	Μπορείτε να του/της πείτε ότι τηλεφώνησα; Το όνομα μου είναι ...	borreeteh nah too/teess peeteh ottee teelehfonn- eessah to onnommah moo eeneh
Would you ask him/ her to call me?	Μπορείτε να του/της πείτε να μου τηλεφωνήση;	borreeteh nah too/ teess peeteh nah moo teelehfonneessee
Would you take a message, please?	Μπορώ να αφήσω μια παραγγελία, παρα- καλώ;	borro nah ahfeesso meeah pahrahnggehleeah pahrahkahlo

Charges   Κόστος

What was the cost of that call?	Πόσο κόστισε αυτό το τηλεφώνημα;	posso kosteesseh ahfto to teeleh- fonneemah
I want to pay for the call.	Θέλω να πληρώσω για το τηλεφώνημα.	thehlo nah pleerosso yeeah to teelehfonneemah

Doctor

Make sure your health insurance policy covers any illness or accident while on holiday. If it doesn't, ask your insurance representative, automobile association or travel agent for details of special health insurance.

General   *Γενικά*

Can you get me a doctor?	Μπορείτε να μου βρήτε ένα ιατρό;	borreeteh nah moo vreeteh ehnah eeahtro
Is there a doctor here?	Υπάρχει εδώ κοντά ένας ιατρός;	eepahrkhee ehdho kondah ehnahss eeahtross
I need a doctor – quickly.	Χρειάζομαι ένα ιατρό γρήγορα.	khreeahzommeh ehnah eeahtro ghreeghorrah
Where can I find a doctor who speaks English?	Που μπορώ να βρω ένα ιατρό που να μιλάει Αγγλικά;	poo borro nah vro ehnah eeahtro poo nah meelahee ahnggleekah
Where's the surgery (doctor's office)?	Που είναι το ιατρείο;	poo eeneh to eeahtreeo
What are the surgery (office) hours?	Ποιες είναι οι ώρες επισκέψεων;	peeehss eeneh ee orrehss ehpeeskehpsehonn
Could the doctor come to see me here?	Θα μπορούσε ο ιατρός να έλθη να με δη εδώ;	thah borroosseh o eeahtross nah ehlthee nah meh dhee ehdho
What time can the doctor come?	Τι ώρα μπορεί να έλθη ο ιατρός;	tee orrah borree nah ehlthee o eeahtross
Can you recommend a/an ...?	Μπορείτε να μου συστήσετε ...	borreeteh nah moo seesteessehteh
general practitioner	ένα παθολόγο/ πρακτικό	ehnah pahthologho/ prahkteeko
children's doctor	ένα παιδίατρο	ehnah pehdheeahtro
eye specialist	ένα οφθαλμίατρο	ehnah ofthahlmeeahtro
gynaecologist	ένα γυναικολόγο	ehnah yeenehkollogho
Can I have an appointment ...?	Μπορώ να κλείσω ραντεβού ...;	borro nah kleesso rahndehvoo
tomorrow	για αύριο	yeeah ahvreeo
as soon as possible	όσο το δυνατό συντομώτερα	osso to dheenahto seendommottehrah

CHEMIST'S, see page 108

Parts of the body *Τα μέρη του σώματος*

arm	το χέρι	to **kheh**ree
back	η πλάτη	ee **plah**tee
bladder	η ουροδόχος κύστη	ee ooro**dho**khoss **kee**stee
bone	το κόκκαλο	to **kok**kahlo
bowel	το έντερο	to **ehn**dehro
breast	το στήθος	to **steet**hoss
chest	ο θώρακας	o **thor**rahkahss
ear	το αυτί	to ahf**tee**
eye	το μάτι	to **mah**tee
eyes	τα μάτια	tah **mah**teeah
face	το πρόσωπο	to **pros**soppo
finger	το δάκτυλο	to **dhahk**teelo
foot	το πόδι	to **po**dhee
genitals	τα γεννητικά όργανα	tah yehneetee**kah** **or**ghahnah
gland	ο αδένας	o ah**dheh**nahss
hand	το χέρι	to **kheh**ree
head	το κεφάλι	to keh**fah**lee
heart	η καρδιά	ee kahr**dhee**ah
jaw	το σαγόνι	to sah**gho**nnee
kidney	το νεφρό	to neh**fro**
knee	το γόνατο	to **gho**nnahto
leg	το πόδι	to **po**dhee
lip	το χείλος	to **khee**loss
liver	το συκώτι	to see**ko**ttee
lung	ο πνεύμονας	o **pnehv**monnahss
mouth	το στόμα	to **stom**mah
muscle	ο μυς	o meess
neck	ο σβέρκος	o **zvehr**koss
nerve	το νεύρο	to **nehv**ro
nervous system	το νευρικό σύστημα	to nehvree**ko** **see**steemah
nose	η μύτη	ee **mee**tee
rib	το πλευρό	to pleh**vro**
shoulder	ο ώμος	o **om**moss
skin	το δέρμα	to **dhehr**mah
spine	η σπονδυλική στήλη	ee spondheelee**kee** **stee**lee
stomach	το στομάχι	to stom**mah**khee
tendon	ο τένοντας	o **teh**nnondahss
thigh	ο μηρός	o meer**oss**
throat	ο λαιμός	o leh**moss**
tongue	η γλώσσα	ee **ghlo**ssah
tonsils	οι αμυγδαλές	ee ahmeeghdhah**lehss**
vein	η φλέβα	ee **fleh**vah

Accident – Injury   Δυστύχημα – Τραυματισμός

There has been an accident.	Έγινε ένα δυστύχημα.	**eh**yeeneh **eh**nah dheest**ee**kheemah
My child has had a fall.	Το παιδί μου έπεσε κάτω.	to peh**dhee** moo **eh**pehsseh **kah**to
He/She has hurt his/ her head.	Αυτός/Αυτή χτύπησε στο κεφάλι του/της.	ah**ftoss**/ah**ftee** **kht**eepeesseh sto keh**fah**lee too/teess
He's/She's un- conscious.	Έχασε τις αισθήσεις του/της.	**eh**khahsseh teess ehsth**ee**seess too/teess
He's/She's bleed- ing (heavily).	Αυτός/Αυτή αιμοραγεί (πάρα πολύ).	ah**ftoss**/ah**ftee** ehmor- rah**yee** (**pah**rah pol**lee**)
He's/She's (seri- ously) injured.	Είναι (σοβαρά) τραυματισμένος/-η.	**ee**neh (sovvah**rah**) trahvmahtee**zmeh**noss/-ee
His/Her arm is broken.	Έσπασε το χέρι του/της.	**eh**spahseh to **kheh**ree too/teess
His/Her ankle is swollen.	Πρήστηκε ο αστράγαλος του/της.	**pree**steekeh o ah**strah**ghahloss too/teess
I've been stung.	Κεντρίστηκα.	kehnd**ree**steekah
I've got something in my eye.	Έχω κάτι στο μάτι μου.	**eh**kho **kah**tee sto **mah**tee moo
I've got a/an ...	Έχω ...	**eh**kho
blister	μια φουσκάλα	meeah foo**skah**lah
boil	ένα σπυρί	**eh**nah spee**ree**
bruise	μια μελανιά	meeah mehlah**nee**ah
burn	ένα έγκαυμα	**eh**nah **ehng**gahvmah
cut	ένα κόψιμο	**eh**nah **kop**seemo
graze	ένα γδάρσιμο	**eh**nah **ghdhahr**seemo
insect bite	ένα τσίμπημα απο έντομο	**eh**nah **tseem**beemah ahpo **ehn**dommo
lump	ένα εξόγκωμα	**eh**nah ehk**song**gommah
rash	ένα εξάνθημα	**eh**nah ehk**sahn**theemah
sting	ένα κέντρισμα	**eh**nah kehnd**reezmah
swelling	ένα πρήξιμο	**eh**nah **preek**seemo
wound	μια πληγή	meeah plee**yee**
Could you have a look at it?	Μπορείτε να το εξετάσετε;	bor**ee**teh nah to ehkseh**tahs**sehteh
I can't move my ...	Δεν μπορώ να κουνή- σω το ... μου.	dhehn bor**ro** nah koon**ee**sso to ... moo

🗨	🗨
Που σας πονάει;	Where does it hurt?
Τι είδους πόνους έχετε;	What kind of pain is it?
υπόκοφους/οξείς/περιοδικούς διαρκείς/που έρχονται και φεύγουν	dull/sharp/throbbing constant/on and off
Είναι ...	It's ...
σπασμένο/στραμπουλιγμένο εξαρθρωμένο/σχισμένο	broken/sprained dislocated/torn
Θέλω να κάνετε μια ακτινο-γραφία.	I want you to have an X-ray.
Θα βάλετε γύψο.	You'll get a plaster.
Είναι μολυσμένο.	It's infected.
Έχετε κάνει τα εμβόλια για τον τέτανο;	Have you been vaccinated against tetanus?
Θα σας δώσω ένα αντισηπτικό/παυσίπονο.	I'll give you an antiseptic/a painkiller.

Illness   *Αρρώστια*

I'm not feeling well.	Δεν αισθάνομαι καλά.	dhehn ehs**thah**nommeh ka**hlah**
I'm ill.	Είμαι άρρωστος.	**ee**meh **ah**rostoss
I feel ...	Αισθάνομαι ...	ehs**thah**nommeh
dizzy	ζαλάδες	zah**lah**dhehss
nauseous	ναυτία	nahf**tee**ah
shivery	ρίγη	**ree**yee
I've got a fever.	Έχω πυρετό.	**eh**kho peere**hto**
My temperature is 38 degrees.	Έχω 38 βαθμούς πυρετό.	**eh**kho 38 vahth**mooss** peere**hto**
I've been vomiting.	Έκανα εμετό	**eh**kahnah ehme**hto**
I'm constipated/I've got diarrhoea.	Είμαι δυσκοίλιος/Έχω διάρροια.	**ee**meh dheeskee**leeoss**/ **eh**kho dheeah**rree**ah
I'm allergic to ...	Είμαι αλλεργικός στο ...	**ee**meh ahlehryee**koss** sto
I'm diabetic.	Είμαι διαβητικός/-ή.	**ee**meh dheeahvee-tee**koss**/-**ee**

I've got (a/an) ...	Έχω ...	ehkho
asthma	άσθμα	ahsthmah
backache	πόνο στη πλάτη	ponno stee plahtee
cold	κρυολόγημα	kreeoloyeemah
cough	βήχα	veekhah
cramps	κράμπες	krahmbehss
earache	πόνο στο αυτί	ponno sto ahftee
hay fever	συνάχι	seenahkhee
headache	πονοκέφαλο	ponnokehfahlo
indigestion	χαλασμένο στομάχι	khahlahzmehno stommahkhee
nosebleed	αιμορραγία στη μύτη	ehmorrahyeeah stee meetee
palpitations	ταχυπαλμία	tahkheepahlmeeah
rheumatism	ρευματισμούς	rehvmahteezmooss
sore throat	λαιμόπονους	lehmopponnoss
stiff neck	στραβολαιμιάσει	strahvollehmeeahssee
stomach ache	πόνο στο στομάχι	ponno sto stommahkhee
sunstroke	ηλίαση	eeleeahssee
I have difficulties breathing.	Έχω δυσκολίες στην αναπνοή.	ehkho dheeskoleeehss steen ahnahpnoee
I have a pain in my chest.	Έχω πόνους στο στήθος μου.	ehkho ponnooss sto steethoss moo
I had a heart attack ... years ago.	Έχω πάθει καρδιακή προσβολή πριν από ... χρόνια.	ehkho pahthee kahrdheeahkee prosvollee preen ahpo ... khronneeah
My blood pressure is too high/too low.	Η πίεση μου είναι πολύ ψηλή/πολύ χαμηλή.	ee peehssee moo eeneh pollee pseelee/pollee khahmeelee

Women's section   Γυναικείο παράρτημα

I have period pains.	Έχω πόνους από τη περίοδο.	ehkho ponnooss ahpo tee pehreeodho
I have a vaginal infection.	Έχω μια φλεγμονή της μήτρας.	ehkho meeah fleghmonnee teess meetrahss
I'm on the pill.	Παίρνω αντισυλληπτικά χάπια.	pehrno ahndeessee- leepteekah khahpeeah
I haven't had my period for 2 months.	Δεν έχω περίοδο εδώ και 2 μήνες.	dhehn ehkho pehreeodho ehdho keh 2 meenehss
I'm (3 months) pregnant.	Είμαι (3 μηνών) έγκυος.	eemeh (3 meenonn) ehnggeeoss

👈	👉
Από πότε αισθάνεστε έτσι;	How long have you been feeling like this?
Είναι η πρώτη φορά που το έχετε αυτό;	Is it the first time you've had this?
Θα σας μετρήσω την θερμοκρασία/πίεση σας.	I'll take your temperature/ blood pressure.
Σηκώστε το μανήκι σας, παρακαλώ.	Roll up your sleeve, please.
Παρακαλώ, γδυθείτε (μέχρι τη μέση).	Please undress (down to the waist).
Παρακαλώ, ξαπλώστε εκεί.	Please lie down over here.
Ανοίξτε το στόμα σας.	Open your mouth.
Αναπνέετε βαθειά.	Breathe deeply.
Βήξτε, παρακαλώ.	Cough, please.
Που έχετε πόνους;	Where do you feel the pain?
Έχετε ...	You've got (a/an) ...
αφροδισιακό νόσημα	venereal disease
γαστρίτιδα	gastritis
γρίππη	flu
ίκτερος	jaundice
ιλαρά	measles
κυστίτιδα	cystitis
πνευμονία	pneumonia
σκωληκοειδίτιδα	appendicitis
τροφική δηλητηρίαση	food poisoning
φλέγμοση από ...	inflammation of ...
(Δεν) Είναι μεταδοτική.	It's (not) contagious.
Θα σας κάνω μια ένεση.	I'll give you an injection.
Θέλω δείγμα από το αίμα/κόπρανα/ούρα σας.	I want a specimen of your blood/stools/urine.
Πρέπει να μείνετε στο κρεββάτι για ... μέρες.	You must stay in bed for ... days.
Θα ήθελα να δείτε ένα ειδικό.	I want you to see a specialist.
Θα ήθελα να πάτε στο νοσοκομείο για μια γενική εξέταση.	I want you to go to the hospital for a general checkup.

Prescription – Treatment Συνταγή – Θεραπεία

This is my usual medicine.	Αυτό είναι το συνηθισμένο φάρμακο μου.	ahfto eeneh to seeneetheezmehno fahrmahko moo
Can you give me a prescription for this?	Μπορείτε να μου δώσετε μια συνταγή για αυτό;	borreeteh nah moo dhossehteh meeah seendahyee yeeah ahfto
Can you prescribe a/an/some ...	Μπορείτε να μου γράψετε ...	borreeteh nah moo ghrahpsehteh
antidepressant	ένα μέσο κατά της μελαγχολίας	ehnah mehsso kahtah teess mehlahnkholleeahss
sleeping pills	μερικά υπνωτικά	mehreekah eepnotteekah
tranquillizer	μερικά ηρεμιστικά	mehreekah eerehmeesteekah
I'm allergic to antibiotics/penicillin.	Είμαι αλλεργικός στα αντιβιοτικά/στη πενικιλλίνη.	eemeh ahlehryeekoss stah ahndeeveeotteekah/stee pehneekeeleenee
Must I swallow them whole?	Πρέπει να τα καταπίνω ολόκληρα;	prehpee nah tah kahtahpeeno olloklleerah

---

☞	☜
Τι θεραπεία κάνετε;	What treatment are you having?
Τι φάρμακα παίρνετε;	What medicine are you taking?
Σαν ένεση ή χάπια;	By injection or orally?
Να παίρνετε... κουταλιές από αυτό το φάρμακο...	Take ... teaspoons of this medicine ...
Να παίρνετε ένα χάπι με ένα ποτήρι νερό...	Take one pill with a glass of water...
κάθε ... ώρες	every ... hours
... φορές την μέρα	... times a day
πριν/μετά από κάθε γεύμα	before/after each meal
το πρωί/το βράδυ	in the morning/at night
εάν αισθάνεστε πόνους	if there is any pain
για ... μέρες	for ... days

Ιατρός

CHEMIST'S, see page 108

Fee *Αμοιβή*

How much do I owe you?	Τι σας οφείλω;	tee sahss offeelo
May I have a receipt for my health insurance?	Μπορώ να έχω μια απόδειξη για την ασφάλεια υγείας;	borro nah ehkho meeah ahpodheeksee yeeah teen ahsfahleeah eeyeeahss
Can I have a medical certificate?	Μπορώ να έχω μια ιατρική βεβαίωση;	borro nah ehkho meeah eeahtreekee vehvehossee
Would you fill in this health insurance form, please?	Μπορείτε να συμπληρώσετε αυτή την ασφαλιστική αίτηση, παρακαλώ;	borreeteh nah seemblee-rossehteh ahftee teen ahsfahleesteekee ehteessee pahrahkahlo

Hospital *Νοσοκομείο*

What are the visiting hours?	Ποιες είναι οι ώρες επισκέψεως;	peeehss eeneh ee orrehss ehpeeskehpsehoss
When can I get up?	Πότε μπορώ να σηκωθώ;	potteh borro nah seekotho
When will the doctor come?	Πότε έρχεται ο γιατός;	potteh ehrkhehteh o yeeahtross
I'm in pain.	Έχω πόνους.	ehkho ponnooss
I can't eat/sleep.	Δεν μπορώ να φάω/κοιμηθώ.	dhehn borro nah faho/keemeetho
Can I have a pain-killer/some sleeping pills?	Μπορώ να έχω ένα παυσίπονο/μερικά υπνωτικά χάπια;	borro nah ehkho ehnah pahvseeponno/mehreekah eepnotteekah khahpeeah
Where is the bell?	Που είναι το κουδούνι;	poo eeneh to koodhoonee

nurse	η νοσοκόμα	ee nossokkommah
patient	ο/η άρρωστος	o/ee ahrostoss
anaesthetic	η νάρκωση	ee nahrkossee
blood transfusion	η μετάγγιση αίματος	ee mehtahnggeessee ehmahtoss
injection	η ένεση	ee ehnehssee
operation	η εγχείρηση	ee ehngkheereessee
bed	το κρεββάτι	to krehvahtee
bedpan	το ουροδοχείο	to oorodhokheeo
thermometer	το θερμόμετρο	to thehrmommehtro

Dentist   Οδοντίατρος

Can you recommend a good dentist?	Μπορείτε να μου συστήσετε ένα καλό οδοντίατρο;	borreeteh nah moo seesteessehteh ehnah kahlo odhondeeahtro
Can I make an (urgent) appointment to see Dr. ...?	Μπορώ να κλείσω ένα (επείγον) ραντεβού για να δω το γιατρό...;	borro nah kleesso ehnah (ehpeeghonn) rahndehvoo yeeah nah dho to yeeahtro
Can't you make it earlier than that?	Μπορείτε να το κάνετε πιο σύντομα;	borreeteh nah to kahnehteh peeo seendommah
I have a broken tooth.	Έχω σπασμένο δόντι.	ehkho spahzmehno dhondee
I have a toothache.	Έχω πονόδοντο.	ehkho ponnodhondo
I have an abscess.	Έχω ένα απόστημα.	ehkho ehnah ahposteemah
This tooth hurts.	Αυτό το δόντι με πονά.	ahfto to dhondee meh ponnah
at the top	στην κορυφή	steen korreefee
at the bottom	στη ρίζα	stee reezah
in the front	εμπρός	ehmbross
at the back	πίσω	peesso
Can you fix it temporarily?	Μπορείτε να το σφραγίσετε προσωρινά;	borreeteh nah to sfrahyeessehteh prossorreenah
I don't want it taken out.	Δεν θέλω να το βγάλετε.	dhehn thehlo nah to vghahlehteh
Could you give me an anaesthetic?	Μπορείτε να μου κάνετε μια αναισθητική ένεση;	borreeteh nah moo kahnehteh meeah ahnehstheeteekee ehnehssee
I've lost a filling.	Έφυγε ένα σφράγισμα.	ehfeeyeh ehnah sfrahyeezmah
The gum is ...	Το ούλο ...	to oolo
very sore	είναι ερεθισμένο	eeneh ehrehtheezmehno
bleeding	αιμορραγεί	ehmorrahyee
I have broken this denture.	Έσπασα αυτή την οδοντοστοιχία.	ehspahssah ahftee teen odhondosteekheeah
Can you repair this denture?	Μπορείτε να επιδιορθώσετε αυτή την οδοντοστοιχία;	borreeteh nah ehpeedheeorthossehteh ahftee teen odhondosteekheeah

Reference section

Where do you come from? *Από που είστε;*

Africa	Αφρική	ahfreekee
Asia	Ασία	ahsseeah
Australia	Αυστραλία	ahfstrahleeah
Europe	Ευρώπη	ehvroppee
North America	Βόρειος Αμερική	vorreeoss ahmehreekee
South America	Νότιος Αμερική	notteeoss ahmehreekee
Albania	Αλβανία	ahlvahneeah
Austria	Αυστρία	ahfstreeah
Belgium	Βέλγιο	vehlyeeo
Bulgaria	Βουλγαρία	voolghahreeah
Canada	Καναδά	kahnahdhah
China	Κίνα	keenah
Cyprus	Κύπρος	keepross
Denmark	Δανία	dhahneeah
England	Αγγλία	ahnggleeah
Finland	Φιλλανδία	feelahndheeah
France	Γαλλία	ghahleeah
Germany	Γερμανία	yehrmahneeah
Great Britain	Μεγάλη Βρεττανία	mehghahlee vrehtahneeah
Greece	Ελλάδα	ehlahdhah
India	Ινδία	eendheeah
Ireland	Ιρλανδία	eerlahndheeah
Israel	Ισραήλ	eesraheel
Italy	Ιταλία	eetahleeah
Japan	Ιαπωνία	eeahponneeah
Luxembourg	Λουξεμβούργο	looksehmvoorgho
Netherlands	Ολλανδία	ollahndheeah
New Zealand	Νέα Ζηλανδία	nehah zeelahndheeah
Norway	Νορβηγία	norveeyeeah
Portugal	Πορτογαλλία	portoghahleeah
Scotland	Σκωτία	skotteeah
South Africa	Νότιος Αφρική	notteeoss ahfreekee
Soviet Union	Σοβιετική Ένωση	sovveeehteekee ehnossee
Spain	Ισπανία	eespahneeah
Sweden	Σουηδία	sooeedheeah
Switzerland	Ελβετία	ehlvehteeah
Turkey	Τουρκία	toorkeeah
United States	Ηνωμένες Πολιτίες	eenommehnehss polleeteeehss
Wales	Ουαλία	ooahleeah
Yugoslavia	Γιουγκοσλαβία	yeeoogoslahveeah

Numbers *Αριθμοί*

0	μηδέν	**meedhehn**
1	ένας, μια, ένα	ehnahss, meeah, **ehnah**
2	δύο	**dheeo**
3	τρία	**treeah**
4	τέσσερα	**tehssehrah**
5	πέντε	**pehndeh**
6	έξι	**ehksee**
7	επτά	**ehptah**
8	οκτώ	**okto**
9	εννιά	**ehneeah**
10	δέκα	**dhehkah**
11	έντεκα	**ehndehkah**
12	δώδεκα	**dhodhehkah**
13	δεκατρία	**dhehkahtreeah**
14	δεκατέσσερα	**dhehkahtehssehrah**
15	δεκαπέντε	**dhehkahpehndeh**
16	δεκαέξι	**dhehkahehksee**
17	δεκαεπτά	**dhehkahehptah**
18	δεκαοκτώ	**dhehkahokto**
19	δεκαεννιά	**dhehkahehneeah**
20	είκοσι	**eekossee**
21	είκοσι ένα	eekossee **ehnah**
22	είκοσι δύο	eekossee **dheeo**
23	είκοσι τρία	eekossee **treeah**
24	είκοσι τέσσερα	eekossee **tehssehrah**
25	είκοσι πέντε	eekossee **pehndeh**
26	είκοσι έξι	eekossee **ehksee**
27	είκοσι επτά	eekossee **ehptah**
28	είκοσι οκτώ	eekossee **okto**
29	είκοσι εννιά	eekossee **ehneeah**
30	τριάντα	**treeahndah**
31	τριάντα ένα	treeahndah **ehnah**
32	τριάντα δύο	treeahndah **dheeo**
33	τριάντα τρία	treeahndah **treeah**
40	σαράντα	**sahrahndah**
41	σαράντα ένα	sahrahndah **ehnah**
42	σαράντα δύο	sahrahndah **dheeo**
43	σαράντα τρία	sahrahndah **treeah**
50	πενήντα	**pehneendah**
51	πενήντα ένα	pehneendah **ehnah**
52	πενήντα δύο	pehneendah **dheeo**
53	πενήντα τρία	pehneendah **treeah**
60	εξήντα	**ehkseendah**
61	εξήντα ένα	ehkseendah **ehnah**

62	εξήντα δύο	eh**kseen**dah **dhee**o
63	εξήντα τρία	eh**kseen**dah **tree**ah
70	εβδομήντα	ehvdho**mmeen**dah
71	εβδομήντα ένα	ehvdho**mmeen**dah **eh**nah
72	εβδομήντα δύο	ehvdho**mmeen**dah **dhee**o
73	εβδομήντα τρία	ehvdho**mmeen**dah **tree**ah
80	ογδόντα	ogh**dhon**dah
81	ογδόντα ένα	ogh**dhon**dah **eh**nah
82	ογδόντα δύο	ogh**dhon**dah **dhee**o
83	ογδόντα τρία	ogh**dhon**dah **tree**ah
90	ενενήντα	ehneh**neen**dah
91	ενενήντα ένα	ehneh**neen**dah **eh**nah
92	ενενήντα δύο	ehneh**neen**dah **dhee**o
93	ενενήντα τρία	ehneh**neen**dah **tree**ah
100	εκατό	eh**kah**to
101	εκατόν ένα	ehkah**tonn eh**nah
102	εκατόν δύο	ehkah**tonn dhee**o
110	εκατόν δέκα	ehkah**tonn dheh**kah
120	εκατόν είκοσι	ehkah**tonn ee**kossee
130	εκατόν τριάντα	ehkah**tonn** tree**ahn**dah
140	εκατόν σαράντα	ehkah**tonn** sah**rahn**dah
150	εκατόν πενήντα	ehkah**tonn** peh**neen**dah
160	εκατόν εξήντα	ehkah**tonn** eh**kseen**dah
170	εκατόν εβδομήντα	ehkah**tonn** ehvdho**meen**dah
180	εκατόν ογδόντα	ehkah**tonn** ogh**dhon**dah
190	εκατόν ενενήτα	ehkah**tonn** ehneh**neen**dah
200	διακόσια	dheeah**koss**eeah
300	τριακόσια	treeah**koss**eeah
400	τετρακόσια	tehtrah**koss**eeah
500	πεντακόσια	pehndah**koss**eeah
600	εξακόσια	ehksah**koss**eeah
700	επτακόσια	ehptah**koss**eeah
800	οκτακόσια	oktah**koss**eeah
900	εννιακόσια	ehneeah**koss**eeah
100	χίλια	**khee**leeah
1100	χίλια εκατό	**khee**leeah ehkah**to**
1200	χίλια διακόσια	**khee**leeah dheeah**koss**eeah
2000	δύο χιλιάδες	**dhee**o kheeleeah**dhehss**
5000	πέντε χιλιάδες	**pehn**deh kheeleeah**dhehss**
10,000	δέκα χιλιάδες	**dheh**kah kheeleeah**dhehss**
50,000	πενήντα χιλιάδες	peh**neen**dah kheeleeah**dhehss**
100,000	εκατό χιλιάδες	ehkah**to** kheeleeah**dhehss**
1,000,000	ένα εκατομμύριο	eh**nah** ehkah**tommee**reeo
1,000,000,000	ένα δισεκατομμύριο	eh**nah** dheessehkah**tommee**reeo

first	πρώτος, πρώτη, πρώτο	prottoss prottee protto
second	δεύτερος, -η, -ο	dhehftehross -ee -o
third	τρίτος, -η, -ο	treetoss -ee -o
fourth	τέταρτος, -η, -ο	tehtahrtoss -ee -o
fifth	πέμπτος, -η, -ο	pehmptoss -ee -o
sixth	έκτος, -η, -ο	ehktoss -ee -o
seventh	έβδομος, -η, -ο	ehvdhommoss -ee -o
eighth	όγδοος, -η, -ο	oghdho-oss -ee -o
ninth	έnατος, -η, -ο	ehnahtoss -ee -o
tenth	δέκατος, -η, -ο	dhehkahtoss -ee -o
once	μια φορά	meeah forrah
twice	δύο φορές	dheeo forrehss
three times	τρεις φορές	treess forrehss
a half/half a ...	μισό/μισό ...	meesso/meesso
half of ...	το μισό του...	to meesso too
half (adj.)	μισός, -ή, -ό	meessoss -ee -o
a quarter	ένα τέταρτο	ehnah tehtahrto
one third	ένα τρίτο	ehnah treeto
a pair of	ένα ζευγάρι	ehnah zehvghahree
a dozen	μία δωδεκάδα	meeah dhodhekahdhah
one per cent	ένα τις εκατό	ehnah teess ehkahto
3.4%	3.4 τις εκατό	3 kommah 4 teess ehkahto
1987	χίλια εννιακόσια ογδόντα επτά	kheeleeah ehneeahkos-seeah oghdhondah ehptah
1992	χίλια εννιακόσια ενενήντα δύο	kheeleeah ehneeahkos-seeah ehnehneendah dhee
2003	δύο χιλιάδες τρία	dheeo kheeleeahdhehss treeah

Year and age *Χρόνια και ηλικία*

year	ο χρόνος	o khronnoss
decade	η δεκαετία	ee dhehkahehteeah
century	ο αιώνας	o ehonnahss
this year	φέτος	fehtoss
last year	πέρσι	pehrsee
next year	ο επόμενος χρόνος	o ehpommehnoss khronnoss
each year	κάθε χρόνο	kahtheh khronno
the 16th century	ο δέκατος έκτος αιώνας	o dhehkahtoss ehktoss ehonnahss
in the 20th century	στον εικοστό αιώνα	stonn eekostonn ehonnah

How old are you?	Πόσο χρονών είστε;	posso khronnonn eesteh
I'm 30 years old.	Είμαι 30 χρονών.	eemeh 30 khronnonn
He/She was born in 1960.	Αυτός/Αυτή γεννήθηκε το χίλια εννιακόσια εξήντα.	ahftoss/ahftee yehneetheekeh to kheeleeah ehneeahkosseeah ehkseendah
What is his/her age?	Πόσο χρονών είναι αυτός/αυτή;	posso khronnonn eeneh ahftoss/ahftee
Children under 16 are not admitted.	Απαγορεύεται η είσοδος κάτω των δεκαέξι χρονών.	ahpahghorrehvehteh ee eessodhoss kahto tonn dhehkahehksee khronnonn

Seasons   *Εποχές*

spring	η άνοιξη	ee ahneeksee
summer	το καλοκαίρι	to kahlokkehree
autumn	το φθινόπωρο	to ftheenopporro
winter	ο χειμώνας	o kheemonnahss
high season	η σαιζόν	ee sehzonn
low season	έξω από την σαιζόν	ehkso ahpo teen sehzonn

Months   *Μήνες*

January	Ιανουάριος	eeahnooahreeoss
February	Φεβρουάριος	fehvrooahreeoss
March	Μάρτιος	mahrteeoss
April	Απρίλιος	ahpreeleeoss
May	Μάιος	maheeoss
June	Ιούνιος	eeooneeoss
July	Ιούλιος	eeooleeoss
August	Αύγουστος	ahvghoostoss
September	Σεπτέμβριος	sehptehmvreeoss
October	Οκτώβριος	oktovreeoss
November	Νοέμβριος	noehmvreeoss
December	Δεκέμβριος	dhehkehmvreeoss

in September	το Σεπτέμβριο	to sehptehmvreeo
since October	από τον Οκτώβριο	ahpo tonn oktovreeo
the beginning of January	οι αρχές του Ιανουαρίου	ee ahrkhehss too eeahnooahreeoo
the middle of February	τα μέσα του Φεβρουαρίου	tah mehssah too fehvrooahreeoo
the end of March	τα τέλη του Μαρτίου	tah tehlee too mahrteeoo

Days and date   Μέρες και ημερομηνίες

What day is it today?	Τι μέρα είναι σήμερα;	tee **mehrah** eeneh **see**mehrah
Sunday	Κυριακή	keereeahkee
Monday	Δευτέρα	dhehftehrah
Tuesday	Τρίτη	treetee
Wednesday	Τετάρτη	tehtahrtee
Thursday	Πέμπτη	pehmptee
Friday	Παρασκευή	pahrahskehvee
Saturday	Σάββατο	sahvahto
It's ...	Είναι ...	eeneh
July 1	πρώτη Ιουλίου	prottee eeooleeoo
March 10	δέκα Μαρτίου	dhehkah mahrteeoo
in the morning	το πρωί	to prooee
during the day	κατά την διάρκεια της μέρας	kahtah teen dheeahrkeeah teess mehrahss
in the afternoon	το απόγευμα	to ahpoyehvmah
in the evening	το βράδυ	to vrahdhee
at night	τη νύκτα	tee neektah
yesterday	χθες	khthehss
today	σήμερα	**see**mehrah
tomorrow	αύριο	ahvreeo
the day after tomorrow	μεθαύριο	mehthahvreeo
the day before	η προηγούμενη μέρα	ee proeeghoomehnee mehrah
the next day	η επόμενη μέρα	ee ehpommehnee mehrah
two days ago	πριν δύο μέρες	preen dheeo mehrehss
in three days' time	σε τρεις μέρες	seh treess mehrehss
last week	η περασμένη βδομάδα	ee pehrahzmehnee vdhommahdhah
next week	η επόμενη βδομάδα	ee ehpommehnee vdhommahdhah
for a fortnight (two weeks)	για δύο βδομάδες	yeeah dheeo vdhomahdhehss
birthday	τα γενέθλια	tah yehnehthleeah
day off	η άδεια	ee ahdheeah
(public) holiday	η αργία	ee ahryeeah
holidays/vacation	οι διακοπές	ee dheeahkoppehss
week	η βδομάδα	ee vdhommahdhah
weekend	το Σαββατοκύριακο	to sahvahtokkeereeahko
working day	η εργάσιμη μέρα	ee ehrghahsseemee mehrah

Public holidays *Δημόσιες αργίες*

Banks, offices and shops are closed on the following days:

Jan. 1	Πρωτοχρονιά	New Year's Day
Jan. 6	Θεοφάνια	Epiphany
March 25	Εικοστή πέμπτη Μαρτίου (Του Ευαγγελισμού)	Greek Independence Day
May 1	Πρωτομαγιά	May Day
Aug. 15	Δεκαπεντάυγουστος (Της Παναγίας)	Assumption Day
Oct. 28	Εικοστή ογδόη Οκτωβρίου (Μέρα του ΟΧΙ)	"No" Day commemorating Greek defiance of Italian ultimatum and invasion of 1940
Dec. 25	Χριστούγεννα	Christmas Day
Dec. 26	Δεύτερη μέρα των Χριστουγέννων	St. Stephen's Day
Movable dates:	Καθαρή Δευτέρα	1st day of Lent: Clean Monday
	Μεγάλη Παρασκευή	Good Friday
	Δευτέρα του Πάσχα	Easter Monday
	Αναλήψεως	Ascension
	Αγίου Πνεύματος	Whit Monday ("Holy Spirit")

Merry Christmas!	Καλά Χριστούγεννα!	kahlah khree**stoo**yehnah
Happy New Year!	Ευτυχισμένος ο Καινούργιος Χρόνος!	ehfteekhee**zmeh**noss o kehnooryeeoss **khron**noss
Happy Easter!	Καλό Πάσχα!	kahlo **pahs**khah
Happy birthday!	Χρόνια Πολλά!	khronneeah pollah
Best wishes!	Χαιρετίσματα!	khehrehteezmahtah
Congratulations!	Συγχαρητήρια!	seengkhahreeteereeah
Good luck/All the best!	Καλή τύχη/Με το καλό!	kahlee teekhee/meh to kahlo
Have a good trip!	Καλό ταξίδι!	kahlo tahkseedhee
Have a good holiday!	Καλές διακοπές!	kahlehss dheeahkoppehss
Best regards from ...	Χαιρετισμούς από ...	khehrehteezmooss ahpo
My regards to ...	Τους χαιρετισμούς μου στον/στην...	tooss khehrehteezmooss moo stonn/steen

What time is it? *Τι ώρα είναι;*

Excuse me. Can you tell me the time?	Με συγχωρείτε. Μπορείτε να μου πείτε τι ώρα είναι;	meh seengkhorreeteh. borreeteh nah moo peeteh tee orrah eeneh
It's ...	Είναι ...	eeneh
five past one	μια και πέντε	meeah keh pehndeh
ten past two	δύο και δέκα	dheeo keh dhehkah
a quarter past three	τρεις και τέταρτο	treess keh tehtahrto
twenty past four	τέσσερις και είκοσι	tehssehreess keh eekossee
twenty-five past five	πέντε και εικοσιπέντε	pehndeh keh eekossee-pehndeh
half past six	έξι και μισή	ehksee keh meessee
twenty-five to seven	επτά παρά εικοσιπέντε	ehptah pahrah eekosseepehndeh
twenty to eight	οκτώ παρά είκοσι	okto pahrah eekossee
a quarter to nine	εννιά παρά τέταρτο	ehneeah pahrah tehtahrto
ten to ten	δέκα παρά δέκα	dhehkah pahrah dhehkah
five to eleven	έντεκα παρά πέντε	ehndehkah pahrah pehndeh
twelve o'clock (noon/midnight)	δώδεκα (το μεσημέρι/τα μεσάνυκτα)	dhodhehkah (to mehsseemehree/tah mehssahneektah)
in the morning	το πρωί	to proee
in the afternoon	το απόγευμα	to ahpoyehvmah
in the evening	το βράδυ	to vrahdhee
The train leaves at ...	Το τραίνο φεύγει...	to trehno fehvyee
13.04 (1.04 p.m.)	στις δεκατρείς και τέσσερα λεπτά	steess dhehkahtreess keh tehssehrah lehptah
0.40 (0.40 a.m.)	στις μια παρά είκοσι το πρωί	steess meeah pahrah eekossee to proee
in five minutes	σε πέντε λεπτά	seh pehndeh lehptah
in a quarter of an hour	σε ένα τέταρτο της ώρας	seh ehnah tehtahrto teess orahss
half an hour ago	πριν μισή ώρα	preen meessee orrah
about two hours	σε δύο ώρες περίπου	seh dheeo orrehss pehreepoo
more than 10 minutes	σε περισσότερο από δέκα λεπτά	seh pehreessottehro ahpo dhehkah lehptah
less than 30 seconds	σε λιγότερο από τριάντα λεπτά	seh leeghottehro ahpo treeahndah lehptah
The clock is fast/ slow.	Το ρολόι πάει μπροστά/ πίσω.	to rolloee pahee brostah/ peesso

Common abbreviations   *Γερικές συντομογραφίες*

Δις.	Δεσποινίς	Miss
Διδα/Δδα.		
δρχ.	δραχμές	drachmas
Ε.Ε.Σ.	Ελληνικός Ερυθρός Σταυρός	Greek Red Cross
Ε.Λ.Π.Α.	Ελληνική Λέσχη Περιηγήσεως και Αυτοκινήτου	Automobile and Touring Club of Greece
ΕΛ.ΤΑ.	Ελληνικά Ταχυδρομεία	Greek Post Office
Ε.Ο.Τ.	Ελληνικός Οργανισμός Τουρισμού	Greek Tourist Organization
Η.Π.Α.	Ηνωμένες Πολιτείες Αμερικής	U.S.A.
Κ., κ., Κος.	Κύριος	Mr.
Κα.	Κυρία	Mrs.
μ.μ.	μετά μεσημβρίας	p.m.
Ο.Σ.Ε.	Οργανισμός Σιδηροδρόμων Ελλάδος	Railway Company of Greece
Ο.Τ.Ε.	Οργανισμός Τηλεπικοινωνιών Ελλάδος	Telecommunications Company of Greece
π.μ.	προ μεσημβρίας	a.m.
Τ.Α.	Τουριστική Αστυνομία	Tourist Police
τηλ.	τηλέφωνο	telephone
Φ.Π.Α.	Φόρος Προστιθεμένης Αξίας	VAT, value-added tax
χλμ.	χιλιόμετρα	kilometres

Signs and notices   *Σήματα*

Αναβατήρας	Lift
Ανδρών	Gentlemen
Ανοικτό	Open
Απαγορεύεται...	... forbidden
Απαγορεύεται η είσοδος	No entrance
Απαγορεύεται το κάπνισμα	No smoking
Γυναικών	Ladies
Είσοδος	Entrance
Είσοδος ελευθέρα	No admission charge
Έξοδος	Exit
Έξοδος κινδύνου	Emergency exit
Κατειλημμένος	Occupied
Κίνδυνος	Danger
Κίνδυνος - Θάνατος	Danger of death
Κλειστό	Closed
Κρατημένο	Reserved
Πληροφορίες	Information
Πρώτες βοήθειες	First aid
Στάσις λεωφορείου	Bus stop

Emergency   Κίνδυνος

Call the police	Καλέστε την αστυνομία	kahlehsteh teen ahsteenoomeeah
Consulate	Προξενείο	proksohnneeo
DANGER	ΚΙΝΔΥΝΟΣ	keendheenoss
Embassy	Πρεσβεία	prehzveeah
FIRE	ΦΩΤΙΑ	foteeah
Gas	Αέριο	ahehreeo
Get a doctor	Καλέστε ένα γιατρό	kahlehsteh ehnah yeeahtro
Go away	Φύγετε	feeyehteh
HELP	ΒΟΗΘΕΙΑ	voeetheeah
Get help quickly	Καλέστε βοήθεια αμέσως	kahlehsteh voeetheeah ahmehssos
I'm ill	Είμαι άρρωστος	eemeh ahrostoss
I'm lost	Έχω χαθεί	eehkho khahtheeh
Leave me alone	Αφήστε με ήσυχο/-η	ahfeesteh meh eesseekho/-ee
LOOK OUT	ΠΡΟΣΟΧΗ	prossokhee
Poison	Δηλητήριο	dheeleeteereeo
POLICE	ΑΣΤΥΝΟΜΙΑ	ahsteenomeeah
Stop that man/woman	Σταματήστε αυτόν τον άνδρα/αυτή την γυναίκα	stahmahteesteh ahftonn tonn ahndhrah/ahftee teen yeenehkah
STOP THIEF	ΣΤΑΜΑΤΗΣΤΕ ΤΟΝ ΚΛΕΦΤΗ	stahmahteesteh tonn klehftee

Lost!   Απολεσθέντα!

Where's the ...?	Που είναι...;	poo eeneh
lost property (lost and found) office	το γραφείο απολεσθέντων	to ghrahfeeo ahpolehsthehndonn
police station	το αστυνομικό τμήμα	to ahsteenommeeko tmeemah
I want to report a theft.	Θέλω να καταγγείλω μια κλοπή.	thehlo nah kahtahnggeelo meeah kloppee
My ... has been stolen.	Εκλάπη το ... μου.	ehklahpee to ... moo
I've lost my ...	Έχασα ... μου.	ehkhahssah ... moo
handbag	την τσάντα	teen tsahndah
passport	το διαβατήριο	to dheeahvahteereeo
wallet	το πορτοφόλι	to portoffollee

CAR ACCIDENTS, see page 78

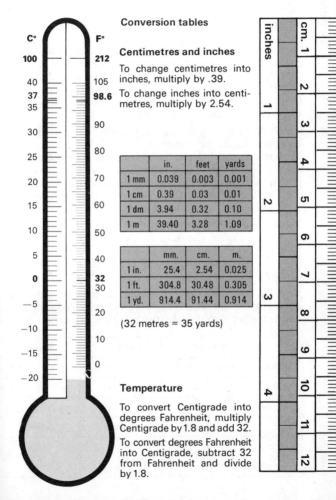

Conversion tables

Centimetres and inches

To change centimetres into inches, multiply by .39.

To change inches into centimetres, multiply by 2.54.

	in.	feet	yards
1 mm	0.039	0.003	0.001
1 cm	0.39	0.03	0.01
1 dm	3.94	0.32	0.10
1 m	39.40	3.28	1.09

	mm.	cm.	m.
1 in.	25.4	2.54	0.025
1 ft.	304.8	30.48	0.305
1 yd.	914.4	91.44	0.914

(32 metres = 35 yards)

Temperature

To convert Centigrade into degrees Fahrenheit, multiply Centigrade by 1.8 and add 32.

To convert degrees Fahrenheit into Centigrade, subtract 32 from Fahrenheit and divide by 1.8.

A very basic grammar

Until recently Greek had evolved comparatively little in the two thousand years which followed Pericles, Plato and Alexander the Great. But there are essentially two forms of modern Greek: the first is a purist – nearly classical – language that's almost never spoken; the second is called Demotike or colloquial. It's the latter we're using in this book.

Those who have studied classical Greek have a great advantage, but should be somewhat cautious on certain details. Modern colloquial Greek differs from the ancient language in the number of cases, verb forms and a more common use of prepositions. Accents indicate the stressed syllable, and in modern Greek only one remains. This is written as a vertical or slightly slanting stroke over the vowel (ά).

Below is the briefest possible outline of some essential features of modern, spoken Greek.

Articles

Nouns in Greek are either masculine, feminine or neuter. They agree with and are classified by the article which precedes them. This is true of both definite (**the**) and indefinite (**a/an**) articles.

	Masculine		**Feminine**		**Neuter**	
Singular	Def.	Indef.	Def.	Indef.	Def.	Indef.
Subject	o	ένας	η	μια	το	ένα
Object	το(ν)	ένα(ν)	τη(ν)	μια(ν)	το	ένα
Possessive	του	ενός	της	μιας	του	ενός
Plural	Definite		Definite		Definite	
Subject	οι		οι		τα	
Object	τους		τις		τα	
Possessive	των		των		των	

Nouns

According to their use in the sentence, Greek nouns change their endings. Since articles and modifying adjectives undergo related changes, the table below shows the declension of three parts of speech. A fourth, the vocative, is rarely encountered, being only used for addressing people.

	Masculine singular (the good man)	**Masculine plural** (the good men)
Subject	ο καλός άνθρωπος	οι καλοί άνθρωποι
Object	τον καλόν άνθρωπο	τους καλούς ανθρώπους
Possessive	του καλού ανθρώπου	των καλών ανθρώπων

	Feminine singular (the good woman)	**Feminine plural** (the good women)
Subject	η καλή γυναίκα	οι καλές γυναίκες
Object	την καλή γυναίκα	τις καλές γυναίκες
Possessive	της καλής γυναίκας	των καλών γυναικών

	Neuter singular (the good child)	**Neuter plural** (the good children)
Subject	το καλό παιδί	τα καλά παιδιά
Object	το καλό παιδί	τα καλά παιδιά
Possessive	του καλού παιδιού	των καλών παιδιών

There are, unfortunately, certain exceptions to the declensions, but the chart below outlines the main rules:

	Masculine			**Feminine**		**Neuter**		
	Singular							
Subject	-ος	-ας	-ης	-η	-α	-ο	-ι	-α
Object	-ο	-α	-η	-η	-α	-ο	-ι	-α
Possessive	-ου	-α	-η	-ης	-ας	-ου	-ιου	-ατος
	Plural							
Subject	-οι	-ες	-ες	-ες		-α	-ια	-ατα
Object	-ους	-ες	-ες	-ες		-α	-ια	-ατα
Possessive	-ων			-ων		-ων	-ων	-ατων

Γραμματική

Adjectives

For declension, see preceding page. The comparative is formed by means of the adverb **πιο** ("more"). The person or thing compared to takes the object case and is preceded by the preposition **από** (our conjunction "than").

Ο Πέτρος είναι πιο πλούσιος από τον Μιχάλη.
Peter is richer than Michael.

The superlative is formed by placing the definite article before the comparative. It's followed by the possessive form.

Ο Πέτρος είναι ο πιο πλούσιος της Αθήνας.
Peter is the richest man in Athens.

A few adjectives have irregular degrees of comparison, like:

| καλός | good | καλύτερος | better | ο καλύτερος | best |
| κακός | bad | χειρότερος | worse | ο χειρότερος | worst |

Personal and possessive pronouns

	Subj.	Dir. obj.	Indir. obj.	Possess.
I, me, my*	εγώ	με	μου	μου
you, your*	(ε)σύ	σε	σου	σου
he, him, his	αυτός	τον	του	του
she, her	αυτή	την	της	της
it, its	αυτό	το	του	του
we, us, our	εμείς	μας		μας
you, your*	εσείς	σας		σας
they, them, their (m.)	αυτοί	τους		⎫
they, them, their (f.)	αυτές	τις		⎬ τους
they, them, their (nt.)	αυτά	τα		⎭

He saw me = Με είδε.
He gave me = Μου έδωσε.

The possessive form of personal pronouns is used as a possessive adjective. It always follows the noun it modifies.

το όνομά μου my name (lit.: the name of me)

---

* There are two forms for "you" in Greek: (ε)σύ is used when talking to relatives, close friends and children; (ε)σείς is the plural and at the same time the polite or formal form.

Demonstratives

"This" (**αυτός**) and "that" (**εκείνος**) preceding a noun are always followed by the article as well.

αυτός ο άνθρωπος — this man
αυτή η γυναίκα — this woman
αυτό το παιδί — this child

Prepositions

Prepositions are followed by the object form. The preposition **σε** ("in", "at", "to") is contracted with the article, e.g., **στον, στην, στο**.

Verbs

Greek verbs may have two different endings: active (ending in **– ω**) and passive (usually ending in **-μαι**). Generally, verbs with active endings express action done **by** the subject, those with passive endings express action done **to** the subject. Unfortunately, there are many exceptions such as **έρχομαι** (I come) which has a passive ending but an active meaning.

Generally, the personal pronoun is not used, since the verb ending indicates the subject.

Within this basic grammar, it's obviously impossible to examine the verb system of Greek, which is very different from English.

But here are the active endings in the present:

	Singular	Plural
1st person	-ω	-με
2nd person	-εις	-τε
3rd person	-ει	-ουν

βλέπω — I see (or: I am seeing)

Passive endings present many irregularities.

In most cases, **negatives** are formed by placing **δεν** before the verb.

> Ο κύριος πεινάει.
> The man is hungry.

> Ο κύριος δεν πεινάει.
> The man isn't hungry.

Questions are simply formed by changing the intonation of your voice. Note the use of the semi-colon in lieu of a question mark.

Auxiliary verbs

Here is the present tense of the two auxiliary verbs **είμαι** (to be) and **έχω** (to have).

I am	είμαι	I have	έχω
you are	είσαι	you have	έχεις
he, she, it is	είναι	he, she, it has	έχει
we are	είμαστε	we have	έχουμε
you are	είστε	you have	έχετε
they are	είναι	they have	έχουν

Note

In Greek, as in many languages, the endings of words sometimes differ according to whether the speaker or the person being spoken to is a man or a woman. We have indicated these cases by offering first the masculine version and then the feminine ending.

I'm American.
(man) **Είμαι Αμερικάνος**
(woman) **Είμαι Αμερικανίδα**
Shown as **Αμερικάνος/-ίδα**

Are you single?
(speaking to a man) **Είστε ελεύθερος**
(to a woman) **Είστε ελεύθερη**
Shown as **ελεύθερος/-η**

Dictionary
and alphabetical index

English—Greek

f féminine   m masculine   nt neuter   pl plural

For adjectives where only the masculine -ος ending is given, the feminine and neuter endings are always -η and -o (see grammar section).

A

a ένας/μια/ένα **eh**nahss/**mee**ah/**eh**nah 156

abbey μοναστήρι nt monnah**stee**ree 81

abbreviation συντομογραφία f seendommoghrah**fee**ah 153

about *(approximately)* περίπου pehr**ee**poo 78, 152

above πάνω pah**no** 15, 63

abscess απόστημα nt ah**pos**teemah 144

absorbent cotton μπαμπάκι nt bahm**bah**kee 109

accept, to δέχομαι **dheh**khommeh 62, 102

accident δυστύχημα nt dhee**stee**kheemah 78, 138

account λογαριασμός m logharreeah**zmoss** 130

ache πόνος m **pon**noss 141

adaptor μετασχηματιστής πρίζας m mehtahskheemahtee**steess** **pree**zahss 119

address διεύθυνση f dhee**ehf**theensee 21, 25, 31, 76, 79, 102

adhesive αυτοκόλητος ahfto**kkol**leetoss 105

admission είσοδος f **ees**sodhoss 82, 89, 153

after μετά meh**tah** 15, 77

afternoon απόγευμα nt ah**po**yehvmah 150, 152

after-shave lotion λοσιόν για μετά το ξύρισμα f losseeonn yeeah mehtah to **ksee**reezmah 110

age ηλικία f eelee**kee**ah 148

ago πριν preen 148, 150

air conditioning κλιματισμός m kleemahtee**zmoss** 23

airmail αεροπορικώς ahehropporree**koss** 132

airplane αεροπλάνο nt ahehro**plah**no 65

airport αεροδρόμιο nt ahehrodhro**mmeo** 16, 21, 65

alarm clock ξυπνητήρι nt kseepnee**tee**ree 121

alcohol αλκοόλ nt ahlko-**ol** 37

alcoholic οινοπνευματώδης/-ης/-ες eenopnehvmah**todheess** 59

allergic αλλεργικός ahlehryee**koss** 140, 142

allow, to επιτρέπω ehpee**treh**po 82

almond αμύγδαλο nt ah**meegh**dhahlo 53, 54

alphabet αλφάβητο nt ahl**fah**veeto 6

alter, to *(garment)* διορθώνω dheeor**thon**no 115

amazing καταπληκτικός kahtahpleek**tee**koss 84

ambulance ασθενοφόρο nt ahstenno**fforro** 79

American Αμερικάνικος ahmehreekah**nee**koss 105, 126

American *(person)* Αμερικάνος/-ίδα m/f ahmehreekah**noss**/-**eed**hah 92, 160

amount τιμή tee**mee** 62; ποσόν nt pos**sonn** 131

anaesthetic νάρκωση f **nahr**kossee 143, 144

analgesic παυσίπονο nt pahf**see**ponno 109

anchovy αντζούγια f ahnd**zoo**yeeah 41, 44

and και keh 15

animal ζώο nt **zo**-o 85

ankle αστράγαλος m ah**strah**ghahloss 138

anorak αδιάβροχο τζάκετ nt ahdhee**ah**vrokho **tzah**keht 116

antibiotic αντιβιοτικό nt ahndeeveeot**tee**ko 142

antiques αντίκες *f/pl* ahndeekehss 83

antique shop κατάστημα για αντίκες *nt* katahsteemah yeeah ahndeekehss 98

antiseptic αντισηπτικός ahndeeseepteekoss 100

any αρκετά ahrkehtah 14

anyone κανείς kahnees 12, 16

anything κάτι kahtee 25, 101

apartment *(flat)* διαμέρισμα *nt* dheeahmehreezmah 22

aperitif απεριτίφ *nt* ahpehreeteef 56

appendicitis σκωληκοειδίτιδα *f* skolleekooeedheeteedhah 141

appetizer ορεκτικό *nt* orrehkteeko 41

apple μήλο *nt* meelo 53, 60, 64, 120

appliance συσκευή *f* seeskehvee 119

appointment ραντεβού *nt* rahndehvoo 30, 131, 136, 144

apricot βερύκοκο *nt* vehreekokko 53

April Απρίλιος *m* ahpreeleeoss 149

archaeology αρχαιολογία *f* ahrkheholloyeeah 83

architect αρχιτέκτονας *m/f* ahrkheetehktonnahss 83

area code υπεραστικός αριθμός *m* eepehrahsteekoss ahreethmoss 134

arm χέρι *nt* khehree 137, 138

arrival άφιξη *f* ahfeeksee 16, 65

arrive, to φθάνω fthahno 65, 69, 130

art τέχνη *f* tehkhnee 83

artery αρτηρία *f* ahrteereeah 137

art gallery γκαλερί τέχνης *f* gahlehree tehkhnees 81, 98

artichoke αγγινάρα *f* ahnggeenahrah 41, 42, 49

artificial τεχνητός tehkhneetoss 124

artist καλλιτέχνης *m* kahleetehkhneess 81, 83

ashtray σταχτοδοχείο *nt* stahktodhokheeo 27

ask, to ερωτώ ehrotto 36, 76

asparagus σπαράγγια *nt/pl* spahrahnggeeah 41, 50

aspirin ασπιρίνη *f* ahspeereenee 109

asthma άσθμα *nt* ahsthmah 140

at στο sto 15

at once αμέσως ahmehssoss 31

aubergine μελιτζάνα *f* mehleedzahnah 49

August Αύγουστος *m* ahvghoostoss 149

aunt θεία *f* theeah 93

automatic αυτόματος ahftommahtoss 20, 122, 124

autumn φθινόπωρο *nt* ftheenopporro 110

awful τρομερός trommehross 84; απαίσιος ahpehsseeoss 94

B

baby μωρό *nt* morro 24, 111

baby food παιδική τροφή *f* pehdheekee troffee 111

babysitter μπέιμπυ σίτερ *f* ''babysitter'' 27

back πλάτη *f* plahtee 137

backache πόνος στην πλάτη *m* ponnoss steen plahtee 140

backgammon τάβλι *nt* tahvlee 127

bacon μπέικον *nt* ''bacon'' 38, 46

bad κακός kahkoss 14

bag τσάντα *f* tsahndah 18, 103

baggage αποσκευές *f/pl* ahposkehvehss 17, 18, 26, 31, 70

baggage cart καροτσάκι αποσκευών *nt* kahrotsahkee ahposkevonn 18, 70

baggage check γραφείο διαφυλάξεως αποσκευών *nt* ghrahfeeo dheeahfeelahksehoss ahposkehvonn 66, 70

baker's αρτοποιείο *nt* ahrtopeeeeo 98

balance *(account)* ισοζύγιο *nt* eessozeeyeeo 131

balcony μπαλκόνι *nt* bahlkonnee 23

ball *(inflated)* μπάλα *f* bahlah 128

ballet μπαλέτο *nt* bahlehto 88

ball-point pen στυλό διαρκείας *nt* steelo dheeahrkeeahss 104

banana μπανάνα *f* bahnahnah 53, 64

Band-Aid λευκοπλάστης *m* lehfkoplahsteess 109

bank *(finance)* τράπεζα *f* trahpehzah 98, 129, 130

banknote χαρτονόμισμα *nt* khahrtonnommeezmah 130

barber's κουρείο *nt* kooreeo 30, 98

basil βασιλικός *m* vahseeleekoss 51

basketball καλαθόσφαιρα *f* kahlahthosfehrah, μπάσκετ *f* ''basket'' 89

bath *(hotel)* μπάνιο *nt* bahneeo 23, 25, 27

bathing cap σκούφια για το μπάνιο *f* skoofeeah yeeah to bahneeo 116 bathing hut καμπίνα f kahmbeenah 91

bathrobe μπουρνούζι nt boornoozee 116

bathroom μπάνιο nt bahneeo 27

bath towel πετσέτα του μπάνιου f pehtsehtah too bahneeoo 27

battery μπαταρία f bahtahreeah 75, 78, 119, 121, 125

be, to είμαι eemeh 11, 160

beach παραλία f pahrahleeah 90

beach ball μπάλα της παραλίας f bahlah teess pahrahleeahss 128

bean φασολάκι nt fahssollahkee 50

beard γένεια nt/pl yehneeah 31

beautiful ωραίος/-α/-ο orrehoss 14, 84

beauty salon ινστιτούτο καλλονής nt eensteetooto kahlonneess 30, 98

bed κρεββάτι nt krehvahtee 24, 141, 143

bed and breakfast δωμάτιο και πρόγευμα nt dhommahteeo keh proyehvmah 24

bedpan ουροδοχείο oorodhokheeo 143

beef βοδινό nt vodheeno 46

beer μπύρα f beerah 56, 64

before (place) πριν preen 15

begin, to αρχίζω ahrkheezo 87

beginning αρχή f ahrkhee 149

behind πίσω από peesso ahpo 15, 77

bell (electric) κουδούνι nt koodhoonee 127, 143

below κάτω kahto 15, 63

belt ζώνη f zonnee 117

bend (road) στροφή f stroffee 79

berth κρεββάτι nt krehvahtee 68, 69, 70

better καλύτερος kahleetehross 14, 25, 101, 113

between ανάμεσα ahnahmehssah 15

bicycle ποδήλατο nt podheelahto 74

big μεγάλος mehghahloss 13, 25

bill λογαριασμός m loghahreeahzmoss 31, 62, 102; (banknote) χαρτονόμισμα nt khartonnommeezmah 130

billion (Am.) δισεκατομμύριο nt dheessehkahtommeereeo 147

binoculars κυάλια nt/pl keeahleeah 123

bird πουλί nt poolee 85

birthday γενέθλια nt/pl yehnehthleeah 150, 151

biscuit (Br.) μπισκότο nt beeskotto 64

bitter πικρός peekross 61

black μαύρος mahvross 38, 53, 60, 105, 113

bladder ουροδόχος κύστη f oorodhokhoss keestee 137

blade ξυραφάκι nt kseerahfahkee 110

blanket κουβέρτα f koovehrtah 27

bleach ξέβαμμα nt ksehvahmah 30

bleed, to αιμορραγώ ehmorrahgho 138, 144

blind ρολό nt rollo 29

blister φουσκάλα f fooskahlah 138

blood αίμα nt ehmah 141

blood pressure πίεση f peeehssee 140, 141

blood transfusion μετάγγιση αίματος f mehtahnggeessee ehmahtoss 143

blouse μπλούζα f bloozah 116

blow-dry στέγνωμα nt stehghnommah 30

blue μπλε bleh 105, 113

blusher ρουζ nt rooz 110

boarding house πανσιόν f pahnseeonn 19, 22

boat βάρκα f vahrkah 73, 74

bobby pin τσιμπιδάκι nt tseembeedhahkee 111

body σώμα nt sommah 137

boil σπυρί nt speeree 138

boiled egg βραστό αυγό nt vrahsto ahvgho 38

bone κόκκαλο nt kokkahlo 137

book βιβλίο nt veevleeo 12, 104

booking office γραφείο κρατήσεως nt ghrahfeeo krahteessehoss 66

bookshop βιβλιοπωλείο nt veevleeoppolleeo 98, 104

boot μπότα f bottah 118

botanical gardens βοτανικός κήπος nt vottahneekoss keeposs 81

botany βοτανική f vottahneekee 83

bottle μπουκάλι nt bookahlee 17, 58, 59

bottle-opener ανοιχτήρι για μπουκάλια nt ahneekhteeree yeeah bookahleeah 106

bowel έντερο nt ehndehro 137

box κουτί nt kootee 120

boxing πυγμαχία f peeghmahkheeah 89

boy αγόρι nt ahghorree 112, 128

boyfriend φίλος m feeloss 93

bra σουτιέν nt sooteeehn 116

bracelet βραχιόλι *nt* vrahkheeollee 121

braces *(suspenders)* τιράντες *f/pl* teerahndehss 116

brake φρένο *nt* frehno 75, 78

brandy κονιάκ *nt* konneeahk 59

bread ψωμί *nt* psommee 36, 38, 64

break, to σπάζω spahzo 123, 138

breakdown βλάβη *f* vlahvee 78

breakdown van ρυμουλκό *nt* reemoolko 78

breakfast πρόγευμα *nt* proyehvmah 24, 34, 38

breast στήθος *nt* steethoss 137

breathe, to αναπνέω ahnahpneho 140, 141

bridge γέφυρα *f* yehfeerah 85

briefs κυλότες *f/pl* keelottehss 116

bring, to φέρνω fehrno 13

British Βρεττανός/-ίδα *m/f* vrehtahnoss/-eedhah 92

broken σπασμένος spahzmehnoss 29, 119, 139, 144

brooch μπρελόκ βραχιόλι *nt* brehlokk vrahkheeollee 121

brother αδελφός *m* ahdhehlfoss 93

brown καφέ kahfeh 113

bruise μελανιά *f* mehlahneeah 138

brush βούρτσα *f* voortsah 111

bubble bath αφρός μπάνιου *m* ahfross bahneeoo 110

bucket κουβάς *m* koovahss 128

buckle εγγράφα ζώνης *f* ehnggrahfah zonneess 117

build, to κτίζω kteezo 83

building κτίριο *nt* kteereeo 81, 83

bulb λάμπα *m* lahmbah 28, 75, 119

burn έγκαυμα *nt* ehnggahvmah 138

burn out, to καίγομαι kehghommeh 28

bus λεωφορείο *nt* lehofforreeo 18, 19, 65, 72, 80

business εμπόριο *nt* ehmborreeo 131

bus stop στάση *f* stahssee 72, 153

busy απασχολημένος ahpahskholleemehnoss 96

but αλλά ahlah 15

butane gas υγραέριο *nt* eeghrahehreeo 32, 106

butcher's κρεοπωλείο *nt* krehoppolleeo 98

butter βούτυρο *nt* vooteero 36, 38, 64, 120

button κουμπί *nt* koombee 29, 117

buy, to αγοράζω aghghorrahzo 67, 82, 104

C

cabbage λάχανο *nt* lahkhahno 49

cabin *(ship)* καμπίνα *f* kahmbeenah 74

cable car εναέριο βαγκόνι *nt* ehnahehreeo vahgonnee 74

café καφενείο *nt* kahfehneeo 33

cake κέικ *nt* "cake" 54, 64; γλυκό *nt* ghleeko 37

calculator υπολογιστική μηχανή *f* eepolloyeesteekee meekhahnee 105

calendar ημερολόγειο *nt* eemehrollo-yeeo 104

call, to *(summon)* καλώ kahlo 78, 79, 154; *(phone)* τηλεφωνώ teelehfonno 135

calm ήσυχος eesseekhoss 90

camera φωτογραφική μηχανή *f* fottoghrahfeekee meekhahnee 124, 125

camera shop φωτογραφείο *nt* fottograhfeeo 98

camp, to κατασκηνώνω kahtah-skeenonno 32

campbed κρεββάτι εκστρατείας *nt* krehvahtee ekstrahteeahss 106

camping κατασκήνωση *f* kahtahskeenossee, κάμπινγκ *nt* "camping" 32, 106

camp site μέρος για κάμπινγκ *nt* mehross yeeah "camping" 32

can *(of peaches)* κονσέρβα *f* konsehrvah 120

can, to *(be able)* μπορώ borro 12

Canadian Καναδός/-έζα *m/f* kahnahdhoss/-ehzah 92

canal κανάλι *nt* kahnahlee 85

cancel, to ακυρώνω ahkeeronno 65

candle κερί *nt* kehree 106

candy καραμέλα *f* kahrahmehlah 54, 126

can opener ανοιχτήρι κονσέρβας *nt* ahneekhteeree konsehrvahss 106

cap κασκέτα *f* kahskehtah 116

capital *(finance)* κεφάλαιο *nt* kehfahleho 131

car αυτοκίνητο *nt* ahftokkeeneeto 19, 20, 26, 32, 75, 76, 78

carafe καράφα *f* kahrahfah 58

carat καράτι *nt* kahrahteeonn 121

caravan τροχόσπιτο *nt* trokhospeeto 32

carbonated αεριούχος/-α/-ο aehreeookhoss 60

carburettor καρμπυρατέρ nt kahrbeerahtehr 78

card κάρτα f kahrtah 130; (playing card) χαρτί nt khahrtee 93

card game τράπουλα f trahpoolah 128

cardigan πλεκτή ζακέττα f plehktee zahkehtah 116

car hire ενοικίαση αυτοκινήτου nt ehneekeeahssee ahftokeeneetoo 19, 20

car park πάρκινγκ nt "parking" 77

car rental ενοικίαση αυτοκινήτου nt ehneekeeahssee ahftokeeneetoo 19, 20

carrot καρόττο nt kahrotto 49

carry, to μεταφέρω mehtahfehro 21

cart καροτσάκι nt kahrotsahkee 18, 70

carton (of cigarettes) κούτα f kootah 17, 126

cartridge (camera) φιλμ κασέττα nt feelm kahssehtah 124

cash, to εξαργυρώνω ehksahryeeronno 129, 133

cash desk ταμείο nt tahmeeo 103, 155

cassette κασέττα f kahssehtah 119, 127

castle πύργος m peerghoss 81

catalogue κατάλογος m kahtahloghoss 82

cathedral μητρόπολη f meetroppollee 81

Catholic καθολικός kahtholleekoss 84

cauliflower κουνουπίδι nt koonoopeedhee 49

caution κίνδυνος m keendheenoss 79, 153, 154

cave σπήλαιο m speeleho 81

cellophane tape σελοτέιπ nt "Sellotape" 104

cemetery νεκροταφείο nt nehkrottahfeeo 81

centimetre εκατοστό nt ehkahtosto 112

centre κέντρο nt kehndro 19, 21, 76

century αιώνας m ehonnahss 148

ceramics κεραμική m kehrahmeekee 83

certificate βεβαίωση m vehvehossee 143

chain (jewellery) αλυσίδα f ahleesseedhah 121

chair καρέκλα f kahrehklah 106

change (money) ψιλά nt/pl pseelah 62, 77, 130

change, to αλλάξω ahlahkso 18, 65, 68, 123, 129

chapel παρεκκλήσι nt pahrehkleessee 81

charcoal κάρβουνα nt/pl kahrvoonah 106

charge τιμή f teemee 20; λογαριασμός m loghahreeahzmoss 28

charge, to κοστίζω kosteezo 32; πληρώνω pleeronno 24

cheap φτηνός fteenoss 14, 24, 25, 101

check τσεκ nt tsehk 130; (restaurant) λογαριασμός m loghahreeahzmoss 62

check to, ελέγχω ehlehngkho 75; (baggage) καταγράφω kahtahghrahfo 70

check out, to αναχωρώ ahnahkhorro 31

checkup (medical) εξέταση f ehksehtahssee 141

cheers! στην υγειά σας steen eeyeeah sahss 56

cheese τυρί nt teeree 40, 43, 52

chef μάγειρας m mahyeerahss 40

chemist's φαρμακείο nt fahrmahkeeo 98, 108

cheque τσεκ nt tsehk 130

cherry κεράσι nt kehrahssee 53

chess σκάκι nt skahkee 93, 128

chest στήθος nt steethoss 140

chewing gum τσίχλα f tseekhlah 126

chicken κοτόπουλο nt kottoppoolo 41, 43, 48, 63

chicory (Br.) ραδίκι nt rahdheekee 49

child παιδί nt pehdhee 24, 61, 82, 138, 149

children's doctor παιδίατρος m pehdheeahtross 136

chips πατάτες τηγανιτές f/pl pahtahtehss teeghahneetehss 40; (Am.) τσιπς (πατατάκια) nt/pl tseeps (pahtahtahkeeah) 64

chocolate σοκολάτα f sokkollahtah 38, 54, 61, 64, 120, 126

choice προτίμηση f protteemeessee 40

chop μπριζόλα f breezollah 46

Christmas Χριστούγεννα nt/pl khreestooyehnah 151

church εκκλησία f ehkleesseeah 81, 84

DICTIONARY

cigar πούρο nt **poo**ro 126
cigarette τσιγάρο nt tseeg**hah**ro 17, 95, 126
cigarette lighter αναπτήρας m ahnahp**tee**rahss 121
cine camera κινηματογραφική μηχανή f keeneemahtoghrahfookee meekhahnee 124
cinema κινηματογράφος m keeneemahtog**hrah**foss 86, 96
city πόλη f **po**llee 81
clam μύδι nt **mee**dhee 44
classical κλασσικός klah**ssee**koss 128
clean καθαρός kahtah**ross** 61
clean, to καθαρίζω kahtah**ree**zo 29, 76
cleansing cream γαλάκτωμα nt ghah**lahk**tommah 110
cliff γκρεμός m greh**moss** 85
clip κλιπς nt kleeps 121
cloakroom γκαρντερόμπα f gahrndeh**rom**bah 87
clock ρολόι nt rol**loee** 121, 152
clog, to βουλώνω voo**lonno** 28
close, to κλείνω **klee**no 11, 82, 108, 132
closed κλειστός klee**stoss** 153
cloth ύφασμα nt ee**fahz**mah 118
clothes ρούχα nt/pl **roo**khah 29, 116
clothes peg μανδαλάκια nt/pl mahndhah**lah**keeah 106
clothing ένδυμα nt **ehn**dheemah 112
cloud σύνεφο nt **see**nehfo 94
coach (bus) λεωφορείο nt leho**fforreeo** 71
coat παλτό nt pahl**to** 116
cod μπακαλιάρος m bahkah**leeah**ross 44
coffee καφές m kah**fehss** 38, 60, 64
coin νόμισμα nt **nom**meezmah 83
cold κρύος **kree**oss 14, 25, 38, 41, 61, 94
cold (illness) κρυολόγημα nt kreeol**lo**yeemah 108, 140
collect call κλήση πληρωτέα από τον παραλήπτη f **klee**ssee pleerot**teh**ah ahpo tonn pahrah**leep**tee 134
colour χρώμα nt **khrom**mah 103, 112, 124
colour chart δειγματολόγιο nt dheeghmahtol**lo**yeeo 30
colour negative έγχρωμο αρνητικό nt **ehng**khrommo ahrnee**tee**ko 124
colour rinse ρενσάζ f reh**nsahz** 30

colour slide έγχρωμο σλάιντ nt **ehng**khrommo "slide" 124
comb χτένα f kh**teh**nah 111
come, to έρχομαι ehrk**hom**meh 36, 59, 92, 94, 136, 143, 145
commission προμήθεια f prommee**theeah** 130
common (frequent) χρήσιμος **khree**sseemoss 153
compact disc δίσκο για πικ-απ λέιζερ nt **dhee**sko yeeah "pick-up laser" 128
compartment διαμέρισμα nt dheeah**meh**reezmah 69
compass πυξίδα f peek**see**dhah 106
complaint παράπονο nt pah**rah**ponno 61
concert συναυλία f seenahv**lee**ah 88
confirm, to επιβεβαιώνω ehpeevev**veh**onno 65
confirmation επιβεβαίωση f ehpeevehveh**ho**ssee 23
congratulations συγχαρητήρια nt/pl seenghkahreeteer**ee**ah 151
connection (train) ανταπόκριση f ahndahpok**ree**ssee 65, 67
constipated δυσκοίλιος/-α/-ο dhees**kee**lleeoss 139
consulate προξενείο nt proksehneeo 154
contact lens φακός επαφής m fah**koss** ehpah**fees** 123
contain, to περιέχω pehreeeh**khko** 37
contagious μεταδοτικός mehtah**dhot**teekoss 141
contraceptive αντισυλληπτικό nt ahndeessee**leep**teeko 109
control έλεγχος nt **ehl**ehngkhoss 16
convent μοναστήρι nt monnah**steer**ee 81
cookie μπισκότο nt bees**kotto** 54, 64
copper χαλκός m khah**lkoss** 122, 12
corduroy βελούδο κοτλέ nt vehloodho **kotleh** 114
cork φελός m **feh**loss 61
corkscrew τιρ-μπουσόν nt teerbooss**onn** 106
corn (Am.) καλαμπόκι nt kahlahm**bok**kee 49
corner γωνία f ghonn**eeah** 21, 36, 7
cost έξοδα nt/pl **ehks**odhah 131
cost, to κοστίζω kos**tee**zo 11, 80, 134
cot παιδικό κρεββάτι nt pehdhee**ko** krehv**vah**tee 24

Λεξικό

cotton βαμβακερό *nt* vamvahkehro
113, 114
cotton wool μπαμπάκι *nt* bahmbahkee
109
cough βήχας *m* veekhahss 108, 140
cough, to βήχω veekho 141
cough drops παστίλλιες για τον βήχα
f/pl pahsteelee-ehss yeeah tonn
veekhah 109
counter γκισέ *nt* geesseh 133
country χώρα *f* khorrah 92
countryside ύπεθρος *f* eepehthross 85
cousin ξάδελφος *m* ksahdhehlfoss,
ξαδέλφη *f* ksahdhehlfee 93
cover charge κουβέρ *nt* koovehr 62
crab καβούρι *nt* kahvooree 41, 44
cracker κράκερ *nt* krahkehr 64
cramp κράμπα *f* krahmbah, 140
cream κρέμα *f* krehmah 60, 110
credit πίστωση *f* peestossee 130
credit card πιστωτική κάρτα *f*
peestotteekee kahrtah 20, 31, 62,
102, 130
crisps τσιπς (πατατάκια) *nt/pl* tseeps
(pahtahtahkeeah) 64
crockery πιατικά *nt/pl* peeahteekah
107
cross σταυρός *m* stahvross 121
crossing *(by sea)* διαδρομή *f*
dheeahdhrommee 74
crossroads σταυροδρόμι *nt*
stahvrodhrommee 77
cruise κρουαζιέρα *f* krooahzeeehrah 74
crystal κρύσταλλο *nt* kreestahlo 122
cucumber αγγούρι *nt* ahnggooree 42,
49
cup φλιτζάνι *nt* fleedzahnee 36, 60,
107
currency exchange office γραφείο
αλλαγής συναλλάγματος *nt*
grahfeeo ahlahyeess
seenahlahghmahtoss 18, 129
current ρεύμα *nt* rehvmah 90
curtain κουρτίνα *f* koorteenah 28
curve *(road)* στροφή *f* stroffee 79
customs τελωνείο *nt* tehlonneeo 16,
102
cut κόψιμο *nt* kopseemo 30, 138
cut, to κόβω kovvo 30
cutlery μαχαιροπήρουνα *nt/pl*
mahkhehroppeeroonah 107, 121
cycling ποδηλασία *f* podheelahsseeah
89
cystitis κυστίτιδα *f* keesteeteedhah
141

D
dairy γαλακτοπωλείο *nt*
ghahlahktoppolleeo 98
dance, to χορεύω khorrehvo 88, 96
danger κίνδυνος *nt* keendheenoss 79,
153, 164
dangerous επικίνδυνος
ehpeekeendheenoss 90
dark σκοτεινός skotteenoss 25, 112;
σκούρος/-α/-ο skooross 101
date ημερομηνία *f* eemehrommee-
neeah 25, 150; (fruit) χουρμάς *m*
khoormahss 53
daughter κόρη *f* korree 93
day μέρα *f* mehrah 16, 20, 24, 32,
80, 150
decaffeinated χωρίς καφεΐνη
khorreess kahfeheenee 60
December Δεκέμβριος *m*
dhehkehmvreeoss 149
decision απόφαση *f* ahpoffahsse 25,
102
deck *(ship)* κατάστρωμα *nt* kahtah-
strommah 74
deck chair πολυθρόνα *f*
polleethronnah 91, 106
declare, to δηλώνω dheelonno 16, 17
delay καθυστέρηση *f*
kahtheestehreessee 68
delicatessen μπακάλικο *nt*
bahkahleeko 98
deliver, to στέλνω stehlno 102
delivery παράδοση *f* pahrahdhossee
102
dentist οδοντίατρος *m/f*
odhondeeahtross 98, 144
denture οδοντοστοιχία *f*
odhondosteekheeah 144
deodorant αποσμητικό *nt*
ahpozmeeteeko 110
department τμήμα *nt* tmeemah 83,
100
department store μεγάλο εμπορικό
κατάστημα *nt* meghahlo
ehmborreeko kahtahsteemah 98
departure αναχώρηση *f*
ahnahkhorreessee 65
deposit *(car hire)* εγγύηση *f*
ehnggeeeessee 20
deposit, to *(bank)* καταθέτω
kahtahthehto 130
dessert επιδόρπιο *nt* ehpeedhorpeeo
37, 40, 54
detour *(traffic)* αλαγή πορείας *f*
ahlahyee porreeahss 79

develop, to εμφανίζω ehmfahneezo 125

diabetic διαβητικός dheeahveeteekoss 37, 140

dialling code υπεραστικός αριθμός m eepehrahsteekoss ahreethmoss 134

diamond διαμάντι nt dheeahmahndee 122

diaper πάννα για μωρά f pahnah yeeah morrah 111

diarrhoea διάρροια f dheeahreeah 139

dictionary λεξικό nt lehkseeko 104

diesel πετρέλαιο nt pehtrehleho 75

diet δίαιτα f dheeehtah 37

difficult δύσκολος dheeskolloss 14

difficulty δυσκολία f dheeskolleeah 28, 102, 140

digital ψηφιακός pseefeeahkoss 122

dining car βαγόνι εστιατόριο nt vahghonee ehsteeahtorreeo 70

dining room τραπεζαρία f trapehzahreeah 27

dinner δείπνος m dheepnoss 34

direct κατευθείαν kahtehftheeahn 65, 68

direct, to δείχνω dheekhno 12

direction κατεύθυνση f kahtehftheensee 76

disabled ανάπηρος m ahnahpeeross 82

discotheque δισκοθήκη f dheeskotheekee 88

disease νόσος f nossoss 142

dish πιάτο nt peeahto 37, 40, 42

dishwashing detergent απολυμαντικό πιάτων nt ahpolleemahndeeko peeahtonn 106

disinfectant απολυμαντικό nt ahpolleemahndeeko 109

dislocate, to εξαρθρώνω ehksahrthronno 139

dissatisfied δυσαρεστημένος dheessahrehsteemehnoss 103

disturb, to ενοχλώ ehnokhlo 155

diversion (traffic) αλλαγή πορείας f ahlayee porreeahss 79

dizziness ζαλάδες f/pl zahlahdhehss 139

doctor ιατρός m/f eeahtross 79, 136, 145

dog σκύλος m skeeloss 155

doll κούκλα f kooklah 127, 128

dollar δολλάριο nt dhollahreeo 18, 102, 129

door πόρτα f portah 26

double διπλός dheeploss 23, 74

double bed διπλό κρεββάτι nt dheeplo krehvahtee 23

double room διπλό δωμάτιο nt dheeplo dhommahteeo 19

down κάτω kahto 15

downtown κέντρο της πόλης nt kehndro teess polleess 81

dozen δωδεκάδα f dhodhehkahdhah 120, 148

drachma δραχμή f drahkhmee 18, 101

dress φόρεμα nt forrehmah 116

drink ποτό nt potto 40, 59, 61, 94

drink, to πίνω peeno 35, 36

drinking water πόσιμο νερό nt posseemo nehro 32, 155

drip, to (tap) στάζω stahzo 28

drive, to οδηγώ odheegho 21, 76

driving licence άδεια οδηγήσεως f ahdheeah odheeyeessehoss 20, 79

drugstore φαρμακείο nt fahrmahkeeo 98, 108

dry ξηρός kseeross 30, 58, 111

dry cleaner's στεγνοκαθαριστήριο nt stehghnokkahthahreesteereeo 29, 98

duck πάπια f pahpeeah 48

dummy κούκλα f kooklah 111

during κατά την διάρκεια kahtah teen dheeahrkeeah 15, 150

duty (customs) φόρος m forross 17

duty-free shop κατάστημα αφορολογήτων nt kahtahsteemah ahforrolloyeetonn 19

dye βαφή f vahfee 30

E

each κάθε kahtheh 125, 142, 148

ear αυτί nt ahftee 137

earache πόνος στο αυτί m ponnoss sto ahftee 140

early νωρίς norreess 14, 31

earring σκουλαρίκι nt skoolahreekee 121

east ανατολή f ahnahtollee 77

Easter Πάσχα nt pahskhah 151

easy εύκολος ehfkolloss 14

eat, to τρώγω trogho 36, 37, 143

eel χέλι nt khehlee 41, 44

egg αυγό nt ahvgho 38, 41, 42, 64

eggplant μελιτζάνα f mehleedzahnah 49

eight οκτώ okto 146

eighteen δεκαοκτώ dhehkahokto 146

eighth όγδοος **oghdho**-oss 148
eighty ογδόντα **oghdhon**dah 146
elastic ελαστικός ehlahstee**koss** 109
Elastoplast λευκοπλάστης *m*
lehfkoplah**steess** 109
electrical ηλεκτρικός eelehk-
tree**koss** 119
electrician ηλεκτρολόγος *m*
eelehktrolloghoss 98
electricity *(current)* ρεύμα *nt* **rehv**-
mah 32
electronic ηλεκτρονικός
eelehktronnee**koss** 125, 128
elevator ασανσέρ *nt* ahssahn**sehr** 27,
100; αναβατήρας *m*
ahnahvah**teer**ahss 100, 153
eleven έντεκα **ehn**dehkah 146
emerald σμαράγδι *nt* smah**rahgh**dhee
122
emergency κίνδυνος *m* **keen**dhee-
noss 154
emergency exit έξοδος κινδύνου *f*
ehksodhoss keen**dhee**noo 27, 99
emery board γυαλόχαρτο για τα νύχια
nt yeeah**lo**khahrto yeeah tah
neekheeah 110
empty άδειος/-α/-ο ah**dhee**oss 14
enamel σμάλτο *nt* **smahl**to 122
end τέλος *nt* **teh**loss 149
endive *(Am.)* ραδίκι *nt* rah**dhee**kee 49
engine *(car)* μηχανή *f* meek**hah**nee 78
English Αγγλικός ahng**glee**koss 126
English *(language)* Αγγλικά *nt/pl*
ahng**glee**kah 11, 16, 80, 104;
(person) Άγγλος/-ίδα *m/f*
ahnggloss/ahng**gleed**hah 92
enjoy oneself, to διασκεδάζω
dheeahskeh**dhah**zo 96
enlarge, to μεγενθύνω mehyehn**theen**o
125
enough αρκετά ahr**keh**tah 14
entrance είσοδος *f* **ees**sodhoss 66,
82, 99, 153
envelope φάκελλος *m* **fahk**ehloss 27,
104
equipment εξάρτηση *f* eh**ksahr**teessee
91
eraser γομολάστιχα *f*
ghommollah**steek**hah 104
escalator κινητή σκάλα *f* keenee**tee**
skahlah 100
estimate εκτίμηση *f* ehk**teem**eessee
131
evening βράδυ *nt* **vrah**dhee 87, 94,
95, 96, 150, 152

evening dress βραδυνό ρούχο *nt*
vrahdhee**no** **rookh**o 88; *(woman)*
βραδυνό φόρεμα *nt* vrahdhee**no**
forrehmah 116
everything τα πάντα tah **pahn**dah 31
examine, to εξετάζω ehkseh**tah**zo 138
exchange, to αλλάζω ah**lah**zo 103
exchange rate τιμή συναλλάγματος *f*
teemee seenah**lahgh**mahtoss 18,
130
excursion εκδρομή *f* ehkdh**rom**mee 80
excuse, to συγχωρώ seeng**khorro** 69,
78, 152
exhaust pipe εξάτμηση *f*
eh**ksahtm**eessee 78
exhibition έκθεση *f* ehk**thess**ee 81
exit έξοδος *f* **ehks**odhoss 66, 79, 99
expect, to περιμένω pehree**meh**no
130
expensive ακριβός ahkree**voss** 14,
19, 24, 101
express εξπρές ''express'' 132
expression έκφραση *f* ehk**frahss**ee
10, 100
expressway αυτοκινητόδρομος *m*
ahftokeeneeto**dhromm**oss 76
extension cord/lead μπαλαντέζα *f*
bahlahn**dehz**ah 119
external εξωτερικός ehksotehree**koss**
109
extra επιπλέον ehpee**pleh**onn 24, 27
eye μάτι *nt* **mah**tee 137
eye drops κολλύριο *nt* ko**lleereeo** 109
eyeliner γραμμή για τα μάτια *f*
ghrah**mee** yeeah tah **mah**teeah
110
eye pencil μολύβι για τα μάτια *nt*
mo**llee**vee yeeah tah **mah**teeah 110
eye shadow σκιά για τα μάτια *f*
skee**ah** yeeah tah **mah**teeah 110
eyesight όρασις *f* **orr**ahsseess 123
eye specialist οφθαλμίατρος *m*
ofthahl**mee**ahtross 136

F

face πρόσωπο *nt* **pross**oppo 137
face pack μάσκα για το πρόσωπο *f*
mahskah yeeah to **pross**oppo 30
face powder πούδρα για το πρόσωπο *f*
poodrah yeeah to **pross**oppo 110
factory εργοστάσιο *nt*
ehrghos**tahss**eeo 81
fair πανηγύρι *nt* pahnee**yee**ree 81
fall *(autumn)* φθινόπωρο *nt*
ftheen**opp**orro 150

family οικογένεια f eekoyehneeah 93

fan ανεμιστήρας m ahnehmeesteerahss 28

fan belt ιμάντας του ανεμιστήρα m eemahndahss too ahnehmee-steerah 75

far μακρυά mahkreeah 100

fare τιμή f teemee 21

farm αγρόκτημα nt aghrokteemah 85

fat (meat) λίπος nt leeposs 37

father πατέρας m pahtehrahss 93

February Φεβρουάριος m fehvrooahreeoss 149

fee (doctor) αμοιβή f ahmeevee 143

feeding bottle πιπερό nt peepehro 111

feel, to (physical state) αισθάνομαι ehsthahnommeh 139, 141

felt τσόχα f tsokhah 114

felt-tip pen μαρκαδόρος m mahrkahdhorross 104

ferry φέρρυ-μπωτ nt "ferry boat" 74

fever πυρετός m peerehtoss 139

few λίγα leeghah 14; μερικά mehreekah 14, 16

field χωράφι nt khorrahfee 85

fifteen δεκαπέντε dhekahpehndeh 146

fifth πέμπτος pehmptoss 148

fifty πενήντα pehneendah 146

fig σύκο nt seeko 53

file (tool) λίμα f leemah 110

fill in, to συμπληρώνω seembleeronno 26, 143

filling (tooth) σφράγισμα nt sfrahyeezmah 144

filling station πρατήριο βενζίνης nt prahteereeo vehnzeeneess 75

film φιλμ nt feelm 86, 124, 125

filter φίλτρο nt feeltro 125, 126

find, to βρήσκω vreesko 11, 84, 100

fine (OK) καλά kahlah 10; εντάξει ehndahksee 25

fine arts καλές τέχνες f/pl kahlehss tehkhnehss 83

finger δάκτυλο nt dhahkteelo 137

finish, to τελειώνω tehleeonno 125

fire φωτιά f fotteeah 154

first πρώτος prottoss 67, 68, 72, 74, 148

first-aid kit φαρμακείο για πρώτες βοήθειες nt fahrmahkeeo yeeah prottehss voeethee-ehss 106

first class πρώτη θέση f prottee thehssee 68

first name όνομα nt onnommah 25

fish ψάρι nt psahree 43, 44

fish, to ψαρεύω psahrehvo 90

fishing ψάρεμα nt psahrehmah 90

fishing tackle εξοπλισμός για ψάρεμα nt ehksopleezmoss yeeah psahrehmah 106

fishmonger's ιχθυοπωλείο nt eekhtheeoppolleeo 98

fit, to ταιριάζω tehreeahzo 115

fitting room δοκιμαστήριο nt dhokkeemahsteereeo 115

five πέντε pehndeh 146

fix, to σφραγίζω sfrahyeezo 75, 144

fizzy (mineral water) αεριούχος/-α/-ο ahehreeookhoss 60

flannel φανέλλα f fahnehlah 114

flash (photography) φλας nt flahss 125

flashlight φακός m fahkoss 106

flat ισιος eessеeoss 118

flat (apartment) διαμέρισμα nt dheeahmehreezmah 22

flea market λαϊκή αγορά f laheekee aghorrah 81

flight πτήση f pteessee 65

flippers βατραχοπέδιλα nt/pl vahtrahkhoppehdheelah 128

floor όροφος m orroffoss 27

florist's ανθοπωλείο nt ahnthoppolleeo 98

flour αλεύρι nt ahlehvree 37

flower λουλούδι nt looloodhee 85

flu γρίππη f ghreepee 141

fluid υγρό nt eeghro 123

fog ομίχλη f ommeekhlee 94

folk music λαϊκή μουσική f laheekee moosseekee 128

food φαγητό nt fahyeeto 37, 61

food poisoning τροφική δηλητηρίαση f troffeekee dheeleetee-reeahssee 141

foot πόδι nt podhee 137

football ποδόσφαιρο nt podhosfehro 89

footpath μονοπάτι nt monnoppahtee 85

for για yeeah 15

forbid, to απαγορεύω ahpahghorrehvo 153

forecast πρόβλεψη f provlehpsee 94

forest δάσος nt dhahssoss 85

forget, to ξεχνώ ksehkhno 61

fork πηρούνι nt peeroonee 36, 61, 107

form (document) έντυπο nt ehndeepo 25, 133

fortnight δύο βδομάδες f/pl **dheeo vdhommahdhess** 150
fortress φρούριο nt **frooreeo** 81
forty σαράντα **sahrahndhah** 146
foundation cream βάση f **vahssee** 110
fountain πηγή f **peeyee** 81
fountain pen πενοφόρος m **pehnofforross** 104
four τέσσερα **tehssehrah** 146
fourteen δεκατέσσερα **dhekahtehsserah** 146
fourth τέταρτος **tehtahrtoss** 148
frame (glasses) σκελετός m **skehlehtoss** 123
free ελεύθερος **ehlehfthehross** 13, 69, 82, 95, 155
french fries πατάτες τηγανιτές f/pl **pahtahtehss teeghahneetehss** 40
fresh φρέσκος/-ια/-o **frehskoss** 53, 61
Friday Παρασκευή f **pahrahskehvee** 150
fried egg τηγανιτό αυγό nt **teeghahneeto ahvgho** 38
friend φίλος m **feeloss** 92, 95
from από **ahpo** 15
front μπροστά **brostah** 75
frost παγετός m **pahyehtoss** 94
fruit φρούτο nt **frooto** 37, 40, 53
fruit cocktail φρουτοσαλάτα f **frootosahlahtah** 53, 54
fruit juice χυμός φρούτων m **kheemoss frootonn** 37, 38, 60
frying pan τηγάνι nt **teeghahnee** 106
full γεμάτος **yehmahtoss** 14
furniture έπιπλα nt/pl **ehpeeplah** 83
furrier's γουναράδικο nt **ghoonahrahdheeko** 98

G

gallery γκαλερί f **gahlehree** 81
game παιχνίδι nt **pehkhneedhee** 128; (food) κυνήγι nt **keeneeyee** 40
garage γκαράζ nt **gahrahz** 26, 78
garden κήπος m **keeposs** 85
garlic σκόρδο nt **skordho** 51
gas αέριο nt **ahehreeo** 154
gasoline βενζίνη f **vehnzeenee** 75, 78
gastritis γαστρίτιδα f **ghahstreeteedhah** 141
gem πολύτιμος λίθος m **polleeteemoss leethoss** 121
general γενικός **yehneekoss** 27, 100
general delivery ποστ-ρεστάντ f **post-rehstahnd** 133

general practitioner παθολόγος m/f **patholloghoss, πρακτικός** m/f **prahkteekoss** 136
genitals γεννητικά όργανα nt/pl **yehneeteekah orghahnah** 137
geology γεωλογία f **yeholloyeeah** 83
get, to (find) βρίσκω **vreesko** 19, 21, 31, 32, 136; (obtain) πέρνω **pehrno** 108, 134
get off, to κατεβαίνω **kahtehvehno** 72
get to, to πηγαίνω **peeyehno** 19
get up, to σηκώνομαι **seekonnommeh** 143
gift (present) δώρο nt **dhorro** 17
gin τζιν nt **tzeen** 59
gin and tonic τζιν και τόνικ nt **tzeen keh tonneek** 59
girdle λαστέξ nt **lahstehks** 116
girl κορίτσι nt **korreetsee** 112, 128
girlfriend φίλη f **feelee** 93, 95
give, to δίνω **dheeno** 13, 123, 126
give way, to (traffic) δίνω πρωτο- πορεία **dheeno prottopporeeah** 79
gland αδένας m **ahdhehnahss** 137
glass ποτήρι nt **potteeree** 36, 58, 59, 61, 142
glasses γυαλιά nt/pl **yeeahleeah** 123
glove γάντι nt **ghahndee** 116
glue κόλλα f **kollah** 105
go, to πηγαίνω **peeyehno** 96, 163
go away, to φεύγω **fehvgho** 154
gold χρυσός m **khreessoss** 121, 122
golden χρυσαφένιος/-ια/ο **khreessafehneeoss** 113
golf γκολφ nt "golf" 90
good καλός **kahloss** 14, 101
goodbye αντίο **ahndeeo** 10
goods εμπορεύματα nt/pl **ehmborrehvmahtah** 16
goose χήνα f **kheenah** 48
gram γραμμάριο nt **ghrahmahreeo** 120
grammar book βιβλίο γραμματικής nt **veevleeo ghrahmahteekeess** 105
grape σταφύλι nt **stahfeelee** 53, 64
grapefruit γκρέιπφρουτ nt "grapefruit" 38, 53, 60
gray γκρίζος **greezoss** 113
graze γδάρσιμο nt **ghdhahrseemo** 138
greasy λιπαρός **leepahross** 30, 111
great (excellent) υπέροχος **eepehrokhoss** 95
Greece Ελλάδα f **ehlahdhah** 145
Greek Ελληνικός **ehleeneekoss** 55, 60, 114

Greek *(language)* Ελληνικά *nt/pl*
ehleeneekah 11

green πράσινος prahsseenoss 113

greengrocer's μανάβικο *nt*
mahnahveeko 98

greeting χαιρετισμός *m*
khehrehteezmoss 10, 151

grey γκρίζος greezoss 113

grocery παντοπωλείο *nt*
pahndoppolleeo 98, 120

ground floor ισόγειον *nt* eessoyeonn
23

group ομάδα *f* ommahdah 82

guide ξεναγός *m/f* ksehnahghoss 80

guidebook τουριστικός οδηγός *m*
tooreesteekoss odheeghoss 82,
104, 105

gum *(teeth)* ούλο *nt* oolo 144

gynaecologist γυναικολόγος *m/f*
yeenehkolloghoss 136

H

hair μαλλιά *nt/pl* mahleeah 30, 111

hairbrush βούρτσα *f* voortsah 111

haircut κούρεμα *nt* koorehmah 30

hairdresser's κομμωτήριο *nt*
kommotteereeo 27, 30, 98

hair dryer στεγνωτήρας μαλλιών *m*
stehghnotteerahss mahleeonn
119

hairgrip τσιμπιδάκι *nt*
tseembeedhahkee 111

hair lotion λοσιόν για μαλλιά *f*
losseeonn yeeah mahleeah 111

hairspray λακ *f* lahk 30

half μισός meessoss 148

half an hour μισή ώρα *f* meessee
orrah 153

half price *(ticket)* μισή τιμή meessee
teemee 68

hall *(large room)* αίθουσα *f* ehthoossah
88

ham ζαμπόν *nt* zahmbonn 38, 41, 42,
46, 64

hammock κούνια *f* kooneeah 106

hand χέρι *nt* khehree 137

handbag τσάντα *f* tsahndah 116,
154

handicrafts χειροτεχνία *f*
kheerottehkhneeah 83

handkerchief μαντήλι *nt* mahndeelee
116

handmade χειροποίητος
kheeroppeeeetoss 113

hanger κρεμάστρα *f* krehmahstrah 27

happy ευτυχισμένος
ehfteekheezmehnoss 151

harbour λιμάνι *nt* leemahnee 74, 81

hard σκληρός skleeross 123

hat καπέλλο *nt* kahpehlo 116

have, to έχω ehkho 160

hayfever συνάχι *nt* seenahkhee 108,
110

hazelnut φουντούκι *nt* foondookee
53

he αυτός ahftoss 158

head κεφάλι kehfahlee 46, 137, 138

headache πονοκέφαλος *m*
ponnokehfahloss 108, 140

headphones ακουστικά *nt/pl*
akhoosteekah 119

head waiter αρχισερβιτόρος *m*
ahrkheessehrveetorross 61

health υγεία *f* eeyeeah 56

health food shop κατάστημα δίαιτας
nt kahtahsteemah dheeehtahss 99

health insurance ασφάλεια υγείας *f*
ahsfahleeah eeyeeahss 143

heart καρδιά *f* kahrdheeah 46, 137

heart attack καρδιακή προσβολή *f*
kahrdheeahkee prosvollee 140

heat, to θερμαίνω thehrmehno 90

heating θέρμανση *f* thehrmahnsee
23

heavy βαρύς/-ιά/-ύ vahreess 14, 101

heel τακούνι *nt* tahkoonee 118

helicopter ελικόπτερο *nt*
ehleekoptehro 74

help βοήθεια *f* voeetheeah 154

help! βοήθεια! voeetheeah 154

help, to βοηθώ voeetho 12, 21, 70,
100, 134; *(oneself)* εξυπηρετώ
ehkseepeerehto 64, 120

her της teess 161

herbs βότανα *nt/pl* vottahnah 51

herb tea τσάι από βότανα *nt* tsahee
ahpo vottahnah 60

here εδώ ehdho 13, 21

high ψηλός pseeloss 140

high season σαιζόν *f* sehzonn 149

high tide παλίρροια *f* pahleerreeah 90

hill λόφος *m* loffoss 85

hire ενοικίαση *f* ehneekeeahssee 20,
74

hire, to νοικιάζω neekeeahzo 19, 20,
74, 90, 91

his του too 158

history ιστορία *f* eestorreeah 83

hitchhike, to κάνω ωτοστόπ kahno
ottostopp 74

DICTIONARY

hole τρύπα f treepah 29

holiday αργία f ahryeeah 150, 151

holidays διακοπές f/pl
dheeahkoppehss 16, 150, 151

honey μέλι nt mehlee 38, 127

horse racing ιπποδρομία f
eepodhrommeeah 89

hospital νοσοκομείο nt
nossokkommeeo 99, 141, 143

hot ζεστός zehstoss 14, 23, 25, 28,
38, 60, 94

hot-water bottle θερμοφόρα f
thermofforrah 27

hotel ξενοδοχείο nt ksehnodhokheeo
19, 21, 22, 26, 80

hour ώρα f orrah 89, 152

house σπίτι nt speetee 83, 85

how πως poss 11

how far πόσο μακρυά posso
mahkreeah 11, 76, 85

how long σε πόσο χρόνο seh posso
khronno 11, 24

how many πόσα possah 11

how much πόσο posso 11, 24

hundred εκατόν ehkahtonn 147

hungry, to be πεινώ peeno 13, 35

hurry (to be in a) είμαι βιαστηκός
eemeh veeahsteekoss 21, 36

hurt, to πονώ ponno 138, 144;
(oneself) χτυπώ khteepo 138

husband σύζυγος m seezeeghoss 93

hydrofoil ιπτάμενο δελφίνι nt
eeptahmehno dhehlfeenee 74

I

I εγώ ehgho 158

ice πάγος m pahghoss 94

ice-cream παγωτό nt pahghotto 54,
64

ice cube παγονιέρα f pahghonneeehrah
27

ill άρρωστος ahrostoss 139, 154

illness αρρώστια f ahrosteeah 139

important σοβαρός sovvahross 13

imported εισαγώμενος
eessahghommehnoss 113

in μέσα mehssah 15

include, to συμπεριλαμβάνω
seembehreelahmvahno 20, 24, 31,
32, 62, 80

indigestion χαλασμένο στομάχι nt
khahlahzmehno stommahkhee
140

inexpensive φθηνός ftheenoss 35,
124

infect, to μολύνω molleeno 139

inflammation φλέγμωση f
fleghmossee 141

inflation πληθωρισμός m
pleethorreezmoss 131

influenza γρίππη ghreepee 141

information πληροφορία f
pleerofforreeah 66, 153

injection ένεση f ehnehssee 141,
142, 143

injure, to τραυματίζω trahvmahteezo
79, 138

injury τραυματισμός m
trahvmahteezmoss 138

ink μελάνι nt mehlahnee 105

inn πανδοχείο nt pahndhokheeo 22

insect bite κέντρισμα nt
kehndreezmah 108

insect repellent εντομοκτόνο nt
ehndommoktono 109

inside μέσα mehssah 15

instead αντί ahndee 37

insurance ασφάλεια f ahsfahleeah 20,
79, 143

interest τόκος m tokkos 131

interested, to be ενδιαφέρομαι
ehndheeahfehrommeh 83, 96

interesting ενδιαφέρον
ehndheeahfehronn 84

international διεθνής/-ής/-ές
dheeehthneess 133, 134

interpreter διερμηνέας m/f
dhee-ehrmeenehahss 131

intersection σταυροδρόμι nt
stahvrodhrommee 77

introduce, to γνωρίζω ghnorreezo
92

introduction σύσταση f seestahssee
92, 130

investment επένδυση κεφαλαίου f
ehpehndheessee kehfahlehoo 131

invitation πρόσκληση f proskleessee
94

invite, to προσκαλώ proskahlo 94

invoice τιμολόγιο f teemolloyeeo
131

iodine ιώδιο nt eeodheeo 109

Irish (person) Ιρλανδός/-έξα m/f
eerlahndhoss/-ehzah 92

iron (laundry) σίδηρο nt seedheero
119

iron, to σιδερώνω seedhehronno 29

its τοο too 158

ivory ελεφαντόδοντο nt
ehlehfahndodhondo 122

Λεξικό

J

jacket ζακέττα f zahkehtah 116
jam μαρμελάδα f mahrmehlahdhah 38, 120
jam, to μπλέκω blehko 28, 125
January Ιανουάριος m eeahnooahreeoss 149
jar κουτί nt kootee 120
jaundice ίκτερος m eektehross 141
jaw σαγόνι nt sahghonnee 137
jazz τζαζ nt dzahz 128
jeans μπλου-τζήν nt bloodzeen 116
jeweller's κοσμηματοπωλείο nt kosmeemahtoppolleeo 99, 121
joint άρθρωση f ahrthrossee 137
journey ταξίδι nt tahkseedhee 71, 151
juice χυμός m kheemoss 38, 60
July Ιούλιος m eeooleeoss 149
June Ιούνιος m eeooneeoss 149

K

kerosene φωτιστικό πετρέλαιο nt fotteesteeko pehtrehleho 106
key κλειδί nt kleedhee 27
kidney νεφρό nt nehfro 137
kilogram κιλό nt keelo 120
kilometre χιλιόμετρο nt kheeleeommehtro 20, 78
kind ευγενικός ehvyehneekoss 95
kind (type) είδος nt eedhoss 46, 53
knee γόνατο nt ghonnahto 137
knife μαχαίρι nt mahkhehree 36, 61, 107
know, to γνωρίζω ghnorreezo 16, 96, 114

L

label ετικέττα f ehteekehtah 105
lace δαντέλλα f dhahndehlah 114
lake λίμνη f leemnee 23, 85
lamb αρνί nt ahrnee 46
lamp λάμπα f lahmbah 29, 106, 119
landscape φύση f feessee 92
lantern φανάρι nt fahnahree 106
large μεγάλος mehghahloss 20, 101, 118, 130
last τελευταίος tehlehftehoss 11, 67, 72, 149
last name επώνυμο nt ehponneemo 25
late αργά ahrghah 14
later αργότερα ahrghottehrah 135
laugh, to γελώ yehlo 95
launderette αυτόματο πλυντήριο nt ahftommahto pleendeereeo 99

laundry (place) πλυντήριο nt pleendeereeo 29, 99
laundry service πλυντήριο nt pleendeereeo 23
laxative καθαρτικό nt kahthahrteeko 109
leather δέρμα nt dhehrmah 114
leave, to αφήνω ahfeeno 26, 70, 154; φεύγω fehvgho 31, 68, 71, 73
left αριστερός ahreestehross 21, 63, 68, 77
left-luggage office γραφείο αποσκευών nt ghrahfeeo ahposkehvonn 66, 70
leg πόδι nt podhee 137
lemon λεμόνι nt lehmonnee 37, 38, 53, 60, 64
lemonade λεμονάδα f lehmonnahdhah 60, 64
lens φακός nt fahkoss 123, 125
lentil φακή f fahkee 43, 50
less λιγότερα leeghottehrah 14
lesson μάθημα nt mahtheemah 91
letter γράμμα nt ghrahmah 28, 132
letter box γραμματοκιβώτιο nt ghrahmahtokkeevotteeo 132
lettuce μαρούλι nt mahroolee 42, 49
library βιβλιοθήκη f veevleeotheekee 81, 99
licence (permit) άδεια f ahdheeah 20, 79
lie down, to ξαπλώνω ksahplonno 141
life belt σωσίβιο nt sosseeveeo 74
life boat ναυαγοσωστική λέμβος f nahvahghossosteekee lehmvoss 74
lifeguard ακτοφύλακας m ahktoffeelahkahss 90
lift ασανσέρ nt ahssahnsehr 27, 100; αναβατήρας m ahnahvahteerahss 100, 153
light φως nt foss 28; (cigarette) φωτιά f fotteeah 95
light ελαφρής/-ιά/-ύ ehlahfreess 14, 54, 101; (colour) ανοιχτός ahneekhtoss 101, 112, 113
lighter αναπτήρας m ahnahpteerahss 126
light meter φωτόμετρο nt fottomehtro 125
lightning αστραπή f ahstrahpee 94
like to αρέσω ahrehsso 25, 61, 92, 96, 102; (want) θέλω thehlo 13, 20, 23, 38
lip χείλος nt kheeloss 137

lipsalve κρέμα για τα χείλια f **kreh**-mah yeeah tah **kheel**eeah 110

lipstick κραγιόν για τα χείλια nt krah-yeeonn yeeah tah **kheel**eeah 110

liqueur λικέρ nt **leekehr** 59

listen, to ακούω ahkooo 128

litre λίτρο nt **lee**tro 58, 75, 120

little (a) λίγα **lee**ghah 14

live, to ζω zo 83

liver συκώτι nt **see**kottee 46, 137

lobster αστακός m ahsta**koss** 44

long μακρύς/-ιά/-ύ mah**kreess** 76, 115, 117

long-sighted πρεσβύωπας m/f prehz**vee**oppahss 123

look, to κοιτάζω kee**tah**zo 100, 123

look for, to ψάχνω **psahk**hno 13

look out! προσοχή! pross**okhee** 154

loose φαρδύς/-ιά/-ύ fahr**dheess** 115

lose, to χάνω **khah**no 13, 123, 154

loss ζημιά f zee**meeah** 131

lost property/lost and found office γραφείο απωλεσθέντων αντικειμένων nt ghrah**fee**o ahpollehst**hehn**donn ahndeekee**meh**nonn 66, 154

lot (a) πολλά **pol**lah 14

lotion λοσιόν f loss**eeonn** 110

loud δυνατός dhee**na**htoss 135

lovely υπέροχος eeper**okh**oss 94

low χαμηλός kha**mee**loss 140

low season έξω από την σαιζόν **ehk**so ahpo teen seh**zonn** 149

low tide άμπωτη f **ahm**bottee 90

lozenge παστίλλια f pah**steel**eeah 109

luck τύχη f **teek**hee 151

luggage αποσκευές f/pl ahposkeh-**vehss** 17, 18, 21, 31, 70

luggage locker τμήμα αποσκευών nt **tmee**mah ahposkeh**vonn** 18, 66, 70

luggage trolley καροτσάκι αποσκευών nt kahrot**sahk**ee ahposkeh**vonn** 18, 70

lump (bump) εξόγκωμα nt ehk**song**gommah 138

lunch γεύμα nt **yehv**mah 34, 35, 80, 94

lung πνεύμονας m **pnehv**monnahss 137

M

magazine περιοδικό nt pehreeo-**dheeko** 105

magnificent μεγαλοπρεπής/-ής/-ές mehghahlopreh**peess** 84

maid καμαριέρα f kahmahree**ehr**ah 26

mail, to ταχυδρομώ tahkheedhrommo 28

mail ταχυδρομείο nt tahkheedhrom**mee**o 28, 133

mailbox γραμματοκιβώτιο nt ghrahmahtokkee**vot**teeo 132

make, to κάνω **kah**no 131

make up, to ετοιμάζω ehtee**mah**zo 28, 108

man άνδρας m **ahn**drahss 115

manager διευθυντής m dhee**ehf**thee**ndeess** 26

manicure μανικιούρ nt mahnee**keeoor** 30

many πολλοί pol**lee** 14

map χάρτης m **khahr**teess 76, 105

March Μάρτιος m **mahr**teeoss 149

market αγορά f ahgho**rrah** 81, 99

marmalade μαρμελάδα πορτοκάλι f mahrmeh**lahd**hah porto**kkahl**ee 38

married παντρεμένος pahndreh**mehn**oss 93

mass (church) λειτουργία f leetoor**yeeah** 84

match σπίρτο nt **speer**to 106, 126; (sport) αγώνας m ah**ghon**nahss 89

match, to (colour) ταιριάζω teh**reeah**zo 112

material (cloth) ύφασμα nt **ee**fahzmah 113

mattress στρώμα nt **strom**mah 106

May Μάιος m **mah**eeoss 149

may (can) μπορώ bo**rro** 12

meadow λιβάδι nt lee**vahd**hee 85

meal γεύμα nt **yehv**mah 24, 62, 142

mean, to σημαίνω see**meh**no 11, 25

measles ιλαρά f eela**hrah** 141

measure, to πέρνω μέτρα **pehr**no **meh**trah 114

meat κρέας nt **kreh**ahss 40, 46, 61

mechanic μηχανικός m meekhah-**neek**oss 78

medical ιατρικός eeah**tree**koss 143

medicine ιατρική f eeah**tree**kee 83; (drug) φάρμακο nt **fahr**mahko 142

meet, to συναντώ seenah**ndo** 96

melon πεπόνι nt peh**ponn**ee 41, 53

mend, to διορθώνω dhee**orth**onno 29, 75

menu μενού nt meh**noo** 36, 37, 40

message παραγγελία f pahrahng**gehl**eeah 28, 135

metre μέτρο nt **meh**tro 112

middle κέντρο nt **kehndro** 68, 87; μέση f **mehsee** 68

midnight μεσάνυκτα nt **mehssahneektah** 152

milk γάλα nt **ghahlah** 38, 60, 64

million εκατομμύριο nt **ehkahtommeereeo** 147

mineral water μεταλλικό νερό nt **mehtahleeko nehro** 60, 64

mint δυόσμος m **dheeozmoss** 51

minute λεπτό nt **lehpto** 21, 152

mirror καθρέφτης m **kahthrehfteess** 115, 123

Miss δεσποινίδα f **dhehspeeneedhah** 10, 153

miss, to λείπω **leepo** 18, 29, 61

mistake λάθος nt **lahthoss** 31, 61, 62, 102

moccasin μοκασίν nt **mokkahsseen** 118

moisturizing cream υδατική κρέμα f **eedhahteekee krehmah** 110

moment στιγμή f **steeghmee** 12

Monday Δευτέρα f **dhehftehrah** 150

money λεφτά nt/pl **lehftah** 130

month μήνας m **meenahss** 16, 149

moon φεγγάρι nt **fehnggahree**, σελήνη f **sehleenee** 94

moped μοτοποδήλατο nt **mottoppodheelahto** 74

more περισσότερα **pehreessottehrah** 14

morning πρωί nt **proee** 150, 152

mortgage υποθήκη f **eepotheekee** 131

mosque τζαμί nt **dzahmee** 84

mosquito net κουνουπιέρα f **koonoopeeehrah** 107

motel μοτέλ nt **motehl** 22

mother μητέρα f **meetehrah** 93

motorbike μοτοσυκλέτα f **mottosseeklehtah** 74

motorboat βάρκα με μηχανή f **vahrkah meh meekahnee** 91

motorway αυτοκινητόδρομος m **ahftokkeeneetodhrommoss** 76

mountain βουνό nt **voono** 23, 85

moustache μουστάκι nt **moostahkee** 31

mouth στόμα nt **stommah** 137

move, to κουνώ **koono** 138

movie φιλμ nt **feelm** 86

movie camera κινηματογραφική μηχανή f **keeneemahtoghrahfeekee meekhahnee** 124

movies κινηματογράφος m **keeneemahtoghrahfoss** 86, 96

Mr. κύριος m **keereeoss** 10, 153

Mrs. κυρία f **keereeah** 10, 153

much πολύ **pollee** 14

mug κύπελλο nt **keepehlo** 107

muscle μυς m **meess** 137

museum μουσείο **moosseeo** 81

mushroom μανιτάρι nt **mahneetahree** 41, 49

music μουσική f **moosseekee** 83, 128

mussel μύδι nt **meedhee** 44

must, to πρέπει **prehpee** 23, 31, 95

mustard μουστάρδα f **moostahrdhah** 51, 64, 120

my μου **moo** 158

N

nail (human) νύχι nt **neekhee** 110

nail brush βούρτσα για τα νύχια f **voortsah yeeah tah neekheeah** 110

nail clippers νυχοκόπτης m **neekhokkopteess** 110

nail file λίμα για τα νύχια f **leemah yeeah tah neekheeah** 110

nail polish βερνίκι για τα νύχια nt **vehrneekee yeeah tah neekheeah** 110

name όνομα nt **onnommah** 23, 25, 35, 79, 92, 131

napkin πετσέτα f **pehtsehtah** 36

nappy πάννα f **pahnah** 111

narrow στενός **stehnoss** 118

nationality εθνικότητα f **ehthneekotteetah** 25, 92

natural φυσικός **feesseekoss** 83

nausea ναυτία f **nahfteeah** 139

near κοντά **kondah** 32

nearby εδώ κοντά **ehdho kondah** 77, 84

nearest κοντινότερος **kondeenottehross** 73, 75, 78

neat (drink) σκέτος **skehtoss** 59

neck σβέρκος m **zvehrkoss** 30, 137

need, to χρειάζομαι **khreeahzomeh** 29, 118, 136

needle βελόνι nt **vehlonnee** 27

negative αρνητικό nt **ahrneeteeko** 125

nephew ανεψιός m **ahnehpseeoss** 93

nerve νεύρο nt **nehvro** 137

nervous νευρικός **nehvreekoss** 137

nervous system νευρικό σύστημα nt **nehvreeko seesteemah** 137

never ποτέ **potteh** 15
new κοινούργιος/-ια/-ο **kehnooryeeoss** 14
newsagent's πρακτορείο nt **prahktorreeo** 99
newspaper εφημερίδα f **ehfeemehreedhah** 104, 105
newsstand περίπτερο nt **pehreeptehro** 19, 66, 99, 104
New Year Καινούργιος Χρόνος m **kehnooryeeoss khronnoss** 151
next επόμενος **ehpommehnoss** 21, 65, 67, 73, 149, 150
next to δίπλα από **dheeplah ahpo** 15, 77
nice (beautiful) ωραίος/-α/-ο **orrehoss** 94
niece ανεψιά f **ahnehpseeah** 93
night νύκτα f **neektah** 10, 150
night-club νυκτερινό κέντρο nt **neektehreeno kehndro** 88
night cream κρέμα νύκτας f **krehmah neektahss** 110
nightdress νυκτικό nt **neekteeko** 116
nine εννιά **ehneeah** 146
nineteen δεκαεννιά **dhehkahehneeah** 146
ninety ενενήντα **ehnehneendah** 147
ninth ένατος **ehnahtoss** 148
no όχι **okhee** 10
noise θόρυβος m **thorreevoss** 25
nonalcoholic μη οινοπνευματώδης/-ης/-ες **mee eenopnehvmahtodheess** 60
nonsmoker μη καπνιστής m **mee kahpneesteess** 36, 69
noodle χιλόπιτα f **kheelopeetah** 43
noon μεσημέρι nt **mehsseemehree** 31, 152
normal κανονικός **kahnonnekoss** 30
north βορράς m **vorrahss** 77
nose μύτη f **meetee** 137
nosebleed αιμορραγία στη μύτη f **eemorrahyeeah stee meetee** 140
nose drops σταγόνες για τη μύτη f/pl **stahghonnehss yeeah tee meetee** 109
not δεν **dhehn** 15, 160
note (banknote) χαρτονόμισμα nt **khartonnommeezmah** 130
notebook τετράδιο nt **tehtrahdheeo** 105
nothing τίποτα **teepottah** 15, 17, 37, 54
notice (sign) σήμα nt **seemah** 153

November Νοέμβριος m **noehmvreeoss** 149
now τώρα **torrah** 15
number αρίθμος m **ahreethmoss** 25, 65, 124, 134, 135, 146
nurse νοσοκόμα f **nossokkommah** 143

O

occupied κατειλημένος **kahteeleemehnoss** 14, 153
October Οκτώβριος m **oktovreeoss** 149
octopus χταπόδι nt **khtahpodhee** 44
office γραφείο nt **ghrahfeeo** 19, 60, 80, 154
oil λάδι nt **lahdhee** 37, 75, 111
oily λιπαρός **leepahross** 30, 111
old παλιός/-ά/ό **pahleeoss** 14; (person) γέρος m **yehross** 14
old town παλιά πόλη f **pahleeah pollee** 81
olive ελιά f **ehleeah** 41
olive oil ελαιόλαδο nt **ehlehollahdho** 127
omelet ομελέττα f **ommehlehtah** 40, 42, 43
on επάνω **ehpahno** 15
once μια φορά **meeah forrah** 148
one ένας/μια/ένα **ehnahss/meeah/ehnah** 146
one-way (ticket) απλό **ahplo** 65, 68
onion κρεμμύδι nt **krehmeedhee** 49
only μόνο **monno** 15, 24, 80
open ανοικτός **ahneektoss** 14, 82, 153
open, to ανοίγω **ahneegho** 11, 17, 108, 130, 132, 141
opera όπερα f **oppehrah** 72, 81, 88
operation εγχείρηση f **ehngkheereessee** 144
operator τηλεφωνητής m **teelehfonneeteess** 134
opposite αντίθετα **ahndeethehtah** 77
optician οπτικός m **opteekoss** 99, 123
or ή **ee** 15
orange πορτοκαλής/-ιά/-ί **portokkahleess** 113
orange πορτοκάλι nt **portokkahlee** 38, 53, 64
orange juice χυμός πορτοκαλιού m **kheemoss portokkahleeoo** 38, 60
orangeade πορτοκαλάδα f **portokkahlahdhah** 60

orchestra ορχήστρα f orkheestrah 88; (seats) πλατεία f plahteeah 87

order (goods, meal) παραγγελεία f pahrahnggehleeah 40, 102

order, to (goods, meal) παραγγέλω pahrahnggehlo 36, 61, 102, 103

oregano ρίγανη f reeghahnee 51

ornithology ορνιθολογία f orneetholloyeeah 83

orthodox ορθόδοξος orthodhoksoss 84

our μας mahss 158

outlet (electric) υποδοχή πρίζας f eepodhokhee preezahss 27

outside έξω ehkso 15, 36

overdone πολύ ψημένος pollee pseemehnoss 61

overtake, to προσπερνώ prospehrno 79

owe, to οφείλω offeelo 143

oyster στρείδι nt streedhee 44

P

pacifier κούκλα f kooklah 111

packet κουτί nt kootee 120, 126

pail κουβάς m koovahss 128

pain πόνος m ponnoss 140, 143

painkiller πασίπονο nt pahfseepono 139, 143

paint, to ζωγραφίζω zoghrahfeezo 83

paintbox κουτί μπογιές nt kootee boyeeehss 105

painter ζωγράφος m zoghrahfoss 83

painting ζωγραφική f zoghrahfeekee 83

pair ζευγάρι nt zehvghahree 116, 118, 148

pajamas πυτζάμα f peedzahmah 117

palace παλάτι nt pahlahtee 81

palpitation ταχυπαλμία f tahkheepahlmeeah 140

panties κυλότες f/pl keelottehss 116

pants (trousers) παντελόνι nt pahndehlonnee 116

panty girdle λαστέξ nt lahstehks 116

panty hose καλτσόν nt kahltsonn 116

paper χαρτί nt khahrtee 105

paperback φτηνό βιβλίο nt fteeno veevleeo 105

paperclip συνδετήρας nt seendhehteerahss 105

paper napkin χαρτοπετσέτα f khahrtoppehtsehtah 105

paraffin (fuel) φωτιστικό πετρέλαιο nt fotteesteeko pehtrehleho 107

parcel δέμα nt dhehmah 132, 133

parents γονείς m/pl ghonneess 93

park πάρκο nt pahrko 81

park, to σταθμεύω stahthmehvo 26, 77

parking στάθμευση f stahthmehfsee 77, 79

parking meter παρκόμετρο nt parkomehtro 77

parliament βουλή f voolee 81

part μέρος nt mehross 137

party (social gathering) πάρτυ nt pahrtee 95

pass (mountain) ορεινή διάβαση f orreenee dheeahvahssee 85

pass, to (car) προσπερνώ prospehrno 79

passport διαβατήριο nt dheeahvahteereeo 16, 17, 25, 26, 124, 154

pasta παστίτσιο nt pahsteetseeo 40

paste (glue) κόλλα f kollah 105

pastry πάστα f pahstah 63, 64

pastry shop ζαχαροπλαστείο nt zahkhahroplahsteeo 99

patch, to (clothes) μπαλώνω bahlonno 29

path μονοπάτι nt monnoppahtee 85

patient άρρωστος/-η m/f ahrostoss/-ee 143

pay, to πληρώνω pleeronno 31, 62, 102, 135

payment πληρωμή f pleerommee 102, 131

pea μπιζέλι nt beezehlee 49

peach ροδάκινο nt rodhahkeeno 53

peak κορυφή f korreefee 85

pear αχλάδι nt ahkhlahdhee 53

pearl μαργαριτάρι nt mahrghahreetahree 122

pedestrian πεζός m/f pehzoss 79

pen στυλό f steelo 105

pencil μολύβι nt molleevee 105

penicillin πενικιλλίνη f pehneekeeleenee 142

penknife σουγιάς m sooyeeahss 107

pensioner συνταξιούχος m/f seendahkseeookhoss 82

people άνθρωποι m/pl ahnthroppee 92

pepper πιπέρι nt peeperee 37, 64

per cent τις εκατόν teess ehkahtonn 148

percentage επί της εκατόν f ehpee teess ehkahtonn 131

per day την μέρα teen mehrah 20, 32, 89

perfume άρωμα *nt* ahrommah 110

perhaps ίσως eessoss 15

per hour την ώρα teen orrah 77, 89

period *(monthly)* περίοδος *f* pehreeodhoss 140

period pains πόνοι της περιόδου *m/pl* ponnee teess pehreeodhoo 140

permanent wave περμανάντ *f* pehrmahnahnd 30

permit άδεια *f* ahdheeah 90

per night την νύκτα teen neektah 24

person άτομο *nt* ahtommo 32

personal προσωπικός prossoppee-koss 17

personal/person-to-person call προσωπική κλήση *f* prossoppeekee kleessee 134

per week την βδομάδα teen vdhommahdhah 20, 24

petrol βενζίνη *f* vehnzeenee 75, 78

pewter κασσίτερος *m* kahsseetehross 122

photo φωτογραφία *f* fottoghrahfeeah 82, 124, 125

photocopy φωτοτυπία *f* fottottee-peeah 131

photographer φωτογράφος *m* fottoghrahfoss 99

photography φωτογραφείο *nt* fottoghrahfeeo 124

phrase φράση *f* frahsee 12

pick up, to *(person)* πέρνω pehrno 96

picnic πικ-νικ *nt* "picnic" 63, 107

picture πίναξ *m* peenahks 83; *(photo)* φωτογραφία *f* fottoghrahfeeah 82

piece κομμάτι *nt* komahtee 120

pigeon περιστέρι *nt* pehreestehree 48

pill χάπι *nt* khahpee 140, 142

pillow μαξιλάρι *nt* mahkseelahree 27

pin καρφίτσα *f* kahrfeetsah 121

pineapple ανανάς *m* ahnahnahss 53

pink ροζ rozz 113

pipe πίπα *f* peepah 126

pipe cleaner καθαριστήρας πίπας *m* kahthahreesteerahss peepahss 126

pipe tobacco καπνός πίπας *m* kahpnoss peepahss 126

pipe tool πανί πίπας *nt* pahnee peepahss 126

place τόπος *m* topposs 25; μέρος *nt* mehross 76

plane αεροπλάνο *nt* ahehroplahno 65

plaster *(cast)* γύψος *m* yeepsoss 139

plastic πλαστικό *nt* plahsteeko 107

plastic bag πλαστική τσάντα *f* plahsteekee tsahndah 107

plate πιάτο *nt* peeahto 36, 61, 107

platform *(station)* αποβάθρα *f* ahpovvahthrah 66, 67, 68, 69

platinum πλατίνα *f* plahteenah 122

play *(theatre)* έργο *nt* ehrgho 86

play, to παίζω pehzo 86, 88, 89, 93

playground γήπεδο *nt* gheepehdho 32

playing cards *(pack)* τράπουλα *f* trahpoolah 105

please παρακαλώ pahrahkahlo 10

plimsolls αθλητικά παπούτσια *nt/pl* ahthleeteekah pahpootseeah 118

plug *(electric)* πρίζα *f* preezah 29, 119

pneumonia πνευμονία *f* pnehvmonneeah 141

poached ποσέ posseh 42, 45

pocket τσέπη *f* tsehpee 117

pocket calculator υπολογιστική μηχανή τσέπης *f* eepolloyeestee-kee meekhahnee tsehpeess 105

point, to *(show)* δείχνω dheekhno 12

poison δηλητήριο *nt* dheeleeteereeo 109, 154

poisoning δηλητηρίαση *f* dheeleeteereeahssee 142

police αστυνομία *f* ahsteenommeeah 78, 154

police station αστυνομικό τμήμα *nt* ahsteenommeko tmeemah 99, 154

pond μικρή λίμνη *f* meekree leemnee 85

pop music μουσική ποπ *f* moossee-kee pop 128

pork χοιρινό *nt* kheereeno 46

port λιμάνι *nt* leemahnee 74

portable φορητός forreetoss 119

porter αχθοφόρος *m* ahkhthofforross 18, 70; *(hotel)* θυραρός *m* theerorross 26

portion μερίδα *f* mehreedhah 37, 54, 61

possible δυνατός dheenahtoss 136

post *(letters)* ταχυδρομείο *nt* tahkheedhrommeeo 28, 133

post, to ταχυδρομώ tahkheedhrommo 28

postage τιμή *f* teemee 132

postage stamp γραμματόσημο *nt* ghrahmahtosseemo 28, 126, 132

postcard καρτ-ποστάλ f kahrt-postahl 105, 126, 132

poste restante ποστ-ρεστάντ f post-rehstahnd 133

post office ταχυδρομείο nt tahkheedhrommeeo 99, 132

potato πατάτα f pahtahtah 40, 49

pothole λακούβα f lahkoovah 79

pottery αγγειοπλαστική f ahnggeeoplahsteekee 83, 127

poultry πουλερικά nt/pl poolehreekah 40, 48

pound (money) Αγγλική λίρα f ahngghleekee leerah 18, 102, 129

powder πούδρα f poodhrah 110, 121

prawn γαρίδα f ghareedhah 41, 44

preference προτίμηση f protteemeessee 101

pregnant έγκυος ehnggeeoss 140

premium (gasoline) σούπερ soopehr 75

prescribe, to γράφω ghrahfo 142

prescription συνταγή f seendahyee 108, 142

present (gift) δώρο nt dhorro 17

press, to (iron) σιδερώνω seedhehronno 29

pressure πίεση f peeehssee 75, 140

pretty όμορφος ommorfoss 84

price τιμή f teemee 68

priest παπάς m pahpahss 84

private ιδιωτικός eedheeotteekoss 23, 80, 91

processing (photo) εμφάνιση f ehmfahneessee 125

profession επάγγελμα nt ehpahnggehlmah 25

profit κέρδος nt kehrdhoss 131

programme πρόγραμμα nt proghrahmah 87

prohibit, to απαγορεύω ahpahghorrehvo 32, 82

Protestant διαμαρτυρόμενος dheeahmahrteerommehnoss 84

provide, to βρίσκω vreesko 131

public holiday δημοσία αργία f dheemosseeah ahryeeah 151

pullover πουλόβερ m poolovvehr 116

purchase αγορά f ahghorrah 131

pure καθαρός kahthahross 114

purple πορφυρός porfeeross 113

put, to βάζω vahzo 24

pyjamas πυτζάμα f peedzahmah 117

Q

quality ποιότητα peeoteetah 103, 113

quantity ποσότητα f possotteetah 14, 103

quarter τέταρτο nt tehtahrto 148

quarter of an hour τέταρτο της ώρας nt tehtahrto teess orrahss 152

quay τα χμπλιμζίας m khahlahzeeahss 122

question ερώτηση f ehrotteessee 11

quick γρήγορος ghreeghorross 14

quickly γρήγορα ghreeghorrah 36, 79, 136

quiet ήσυχος eesseekhoss 23, 25

R

rabbi ραββίνος m rahveenoss 84

rabbit κουνέλι nt koonehlee 48

race course/track ιππόδρομος m eepodhrommoss 90

racket (sport) ρακέτα f rahkehtah 90

radiator (car) ψυγείο nt pseeyeeo 78

radio (set) ράδιο nt rahdheeo 28, 119

railroad/railway station σιδηροδρομικός σταθμός m seedeerodhrommeekoss stathmoss 19, 66

rain, to βρέχω vrehkho 94

raincoat αδιάβροχο nt ahdheeahvrokho 117

raisin σταφίδα f stahfeedhah 53

rangefinder αποστασιόμετρο nt ahpostahsseeommehtro 125

rare (meat) λιγοψημένος leeghopseemehnoss 47

rash εξάνθημα nt ehksahntheemah 138

raspberry βατόμουρο nt vahtommooro 53

rate τιμή teemee f 18, 20, 130

razor ξυριστική μηχανή f kseereesteekee meekhahnee 110

razor blade ξυραφάκι για το ξύρισμα nt kseerahfahkee yeeah to kseereezmah 111

ready έτοιμος ehteemoss 29, 118, 125

real αληθινός ahleetheenoss 121

rear πίσω peesso 75

receipt απόδειξη f ahpodheeksee 103, 143

reception ρεσεψιόν f rehssehpseeonn 23

receptionist υπάλληλος υποδοχής m/f eepahleeloss eepodhokheess, ρεσεπσιονίστ m/f rehssehpseeonneest 26

recommend, to συστήνω seesteeno 22, 35, 36, 41, 49, 136, 144; προτείνω protteeno 80, 86, 88
record *(disc)* δίσκος *m* dheeskoss 128
record player πικ-απ *nt* "pick-up" 119
rectangular μακρόστενος mahkrostehnoss 101
red κόκκινος kokkeenoss 53, 58, 105, 113
reduction έκπτωση *f* ehkptossee 24, 82
refund επιστροφή *f* ehpeestroffee 103
register, to *(luggage)* καταγράφω kahtahghrahfo 70
registered mail συστημένο *nt* seesteemehno 132
registration καταγραφή *f* kahtahgrahfee 25
regular *(petrol)* απλή ahplee 75
religion θρησκεία *f* threeskeeah 83
rent, to *(hire)* νοικιάζω neekeeahzo 19, 20, 74, 90, 91
rental ενοικίαση *f* ehneekeeahssee 20, 74
repair επισκευή *f* ehpeeskehvee 125
repair, to επιδιορθώνω ehpeedheeorthonno 29, 118, 121, 123, 144
repeat, to επαναλαμβάνω ehpahnahlahmvahno 12
report, to *(a theft)* καταγγέλω kahtahnggehlo 154
require, to απαιτώ ahpehto 88
reservation κράτηση *f* krahteessee 19, 23, 65, 68
reservations office γραφείο κρατήσεως *nt* ghrahfeeo krahteessehoss 66
reserve, to κρατώ krahto 19, 23, 35, 36, 87, 153
resinated *(wine)* ρετσινομένος rehtseenommehnoss 58
resinated wine ρετσίνα *f* rehtseenah 58
restaurant εστιατόριο *nt* ehsteeahtorreeo 19, 32, 35, 66
return *(ticket)* μετ'επιστροφής mehtehpeestroffeess 68
return, to *(give back)* επιστρέφω ehpeestrehfo 103
reversed charge call κλήση πληρωτέα από τον παραλήπτη *f* kleessee pleerottehah ahpo tonn pahrahleeptee 134

rheumatism ρευματισμός *m* rehvmahteezmoss 140
rib πλευρό *nt* plehvro 137
rice ρύζι *nt* reezee 40, 49
right δεξιός/-ά/-ό dhehkseeoss 21, 63, 77, 79; *(correct)* σωστός sostoss 14, 69, 76
ring *(on finger)* δακτυλίδι *nt* dhahkteeleedhee 122
river ποταμός *m* pottahmoss 85
road δρόμος *m* dhrommoss 76, 85
road assistance οδική βοήθεια *f* odheekee voeetheeah 78
road map οδηκός χάρτης *m* odheekoss khahrteess 105
road sign σήμα τροχαίας *nt* seemah trokhehahss 79
roast beef ροσμπίφ *nt* rozbeef 46
roasted ψητός pseetoss 47
rock βράχος *m* vrahkhoss 90
roll *(bread)* ψωμάκι *nt* psommahkee 38, 64
room δωμάτιο *nt* dhommahteeo 19, 22, 23, 24, 25, 27, 28; *(space)* μέρος mehross 32
room service σέρβις δωματίου *nt* sehrveess dhommahteeoo 23
rope σχοινί *nt* skheenee 107
rosé ροζέ rozzeh 58
round στρογγυλός stronggeeloss 101
roundtrip *(ticket)* μετ'επιστροφής mehtehpeestroffeess 65, 68
route διαδρομή *f* dheeahdhrommee 85
rowing boat βάρκα με κουπιά *f* vahrkah meh koopeeah 91
royal βασιλικός vahsseeleekoss 81
rubber λάστιχο *nt* lahsteekho 118; *(eraser)* γομολάστιχα *f* ghommollahsteekhah 105
ruby ρουμπίνι *nt* roombeenee 122
rucksack ταξιδιωτικός σάκκος *m* tahkseedheeotteekoss sahkoss 107
ruin ερείπιο *nt* ehreepeeo 81
ruler *(for measuring)* χάρακας *m* khahrahkahss 105
rum ρούμι *nt* roomee 59

S
saddle σέλλα *f* sehlah 46
safe *(not dangerous)* ακίνδυνος ahkeendheenoss 90
safe χρηματοκιβώτιο *nt* khreemahtokkeevotteeo 26

safety pin παραμάνα f pahrahmahnah 111

sailing ιστιοπλοΐα f eesteeoploeeah 89

sailing boat βάρκα με πανί f vahrkah meh pahnee 91

salad σαλάτα f sahlahtah 41, 42, 63

sale πώληση f polleessee 131; *(bargains)* εκπτώσεις f/pl ehkptossess 101

sales tax φόρος m forross 102

salmon σολωμός m sollommoss 41

salt αλάτι nt ahlahtee 37, 64

salty αλμυρός ahlmeeross 61

same ίδιος eedheeoss 118

sand άμμος f ahmoss 90

sandal σάνδαλο nt sahndhahlo 118

sandwich σάντουϊτς nt sahndooeetss 63

sanitary towel/napkin σερβιέττα υγείας f sehrveeehtah eeyeeahss 109

sapphire ζαφείρι nt zahfeeree 122

sardine σαρδέλλα f sahrdhehlah 41, 44

Saturday Σάββατο nt sahvahto 150

sauce σάλτσα f sahltsah 51

saucepan κατσαρόλα f kahtsahrollah 107

saucer πιατάκι nt peeahtahkee 107

sausage λουκάνικο nt lookahneeko 43, 46, 64

scarf κασκόλ nt kahskoll 117

school σχολείο nt skholleeo 79

scissors ψαλίδι nt psahleedhee 107, 110

scooter βέσπα f vehspah 74

Scottish *(person)* Σκωτζέζος/-α m/f skotzehzoss/-ah 92

scrambled egg χτυπητό αυγό khteepeeto ahvgho 38

screwdriver κατσαβίδι nt kahtsahveedhee 107

sculptor γλύπτης m ghleepteess 83

sculpture γλυπτική f ghleepteekee 83

sea θάλασσα f thahlahssah 23, 85, 90

seafood θαλασσινά nt/pl thahlahsseenah 40, 44

season εποχή f ehpokhee 149; *(tourism)* σαιζόν nt sehzonn 149

seasoning καρυκεύματα nt/pl kahreekehvmahtah 37

seat θέση f thehssee 68, 69, 87

second δεύτερος dhehftehross 148

second λεπτό nt lehpto 152

second class δεύτερη θέση f dhehftehree thehssee 68

second-hand μεταχειρισμένος mehtahkheereezmehnoss 104

secretary γραμματέας m/f ghrahmahtehahss 27, 131

see, to βλέπω vlehpo 159

sell, to πολώ pollo 100

send, to στέλνω stehlno 26, 78, 102, 103, 132, 133

sentence πρόταση f prottahssee 12

separately χωριστά khorreestah 62

September Σεπτέμβριος m sehptehmvreeoss 149

serious σοβαρός sovvahross 138

service ποσοστό υπηρεσίας nt possosto eepeerehsseeahss 24; σερβίρισμα nt sehrveereezmah 62; *(religion)* λειτουργία f leetooryeeah 84

serviette πετσέτα f pehtsehtah 36

setting lotion αφρό-λακ m ahfro-lahk 30

seven επτά ehptah 146

seventeen δεκαεπτά dhehkahehptah 146

seventh έβδομος ehvdhommoss 148

seventy εβδομήντα ehvdhommeendah 147

sew, to ράβω rahvo 29

shampoo σαμπουάν nt sahmbooahn 30, 111

shape σχήμα nt skhehmah 103

shape to *(hair)* φορμαρίζω formahreezo 30

share *(finance)* μετοχή f mehtokhee 131

sharp οξύς/-εία/-ύ oksseess 139

shave, to ξυρίζω kseereezo 31

shaver ξυριστική μηχανή f kseereesteekee meekhahnee 27, 119

shaving cream κρέμα ξυρίσματος f krehmah kseereezmahtoss 111

she αυτή ahftee 158

shelf ράφι nt rahfee 120

sherbet γρανίτα f ghrahneetah 54

sherry τσέρι nt tsehree 59

shingle *(on beach)* χαλίκι nt khahleekee 90

ship πλοίο nt pleeo 74

shirt πουκάμισο nt pookahmeesso 117

shivers ρίγος nt reeghoss 139

shoe παπούτσι *nt* pah**poots**ee 118

shoelace κορδόνι υποδημάτων *nt* kordhonnee eepodheemahtonn 118

shoemaker's τσαγκάρης *m* tsahng**gah**reess 99

shoe polish μπογιά *f* boyeeah 118

shoe shop υποδηματοποιείο *nt* eepodheemahtoppeeeeo 99

shop κατάστημα *nt* kahtah**stee**mah 98

shopping ψώνια *nt/pl* psonneeah 97

shopping centre κεντρικά καταστήματα *nt/pl* kehndreekah kahtah**stee**mahta 99

shop window βιτρίνα *f* veetreenah 100, 112

short κοντός kondoss 30, 115

shorts σορτς *nt* sortss 117

short-sighted μύωπας *m/f* meeopahss 123

shoulder ώμος *m* ommoss 137

shovel φτυάρι *nt* fteeahree 128

show παράσταση *f* pahrah**stahss**ee 86, 87

show, to δείχνω dheekhno 12, 76, 100, 101, 103, 119, 124

shower ντους *nt* dooss 23, 32

shrimp γαρίδα *f* ghahreedha 44

shrink, to μαζεύω mahzehvo 29, 114

shut κλειστός kleestoss 14

shutter *(window)* εξώφυλλο *nt* ehksofeelo 29; *(camera)* διάφραγμα *nt* dheeahfrahghmah 125

sick *(ill)* άρρωστος ahrostoss 139, 154

sickness *(illness)* αρρώστια *f* ahrosteeah 139

side πλάγι *nt* plahyee 30

sideboards/burns φαβορίτες *f/pl* fahvorreetehss 31

sightseeing αξιοθέατα *nt/pl* ahkseeothe**hah**tah 80

sightseeing tour περιοδία στα αξιοθέατα *f* pehree**odh**eeah stah ahkseeothe**hah**tah 80

sign *(notice)* σήμα *nt* seemah 77, 79, 153

sign, to υπογράφω eepoghrahfo 26, 130

signature υπογραφή *f* eepoghrah**fee** 25

silk μεταξωτό *nt* mehtahksotto 114

silver *(colour)* ασημένιος/-α/-ο ahsseemehneeoss 113

silver ασήμι *nt* ahss**see**mee 121, 122

silverware ασημικά *nt/pl* ahseemee-kah 122, 127

simple απλός ahploss 124

since από ahpo 15, 149

sing, to τραγουδώ trahghoodho 88

single *(ticket)* απλό ahplo 68, 74

single *(not married)* ελεύθερος/-η *m/f* ehlehfthehross/-ee 93

single room μονό δωμάτιο *nt* monno dhommahteeo 19, 23

sister αδελφή *f* ahdhehlfee 93

sit, to κάθομαι kahthommeh 95

six έξι ehksee 146

sixteen δεκαέξι dhehkahehksee 146

sixth έκτος ehktoss 148

sixty εξήντα ehkseendah 146

size μέγεθος *nt* mehyehthoss 114, 115, 118, 124

skiing χιονοδρομία *f* kheeonnodhrommeeah 89

skin δέρμα *nt* dhehrmah 137

skin-diving υποβρήχιο ψάρεμα *nt* eepovreekheeo psahrehmah 91

skirt φούστα *f* foostah 117

sky ουρανός *m* oorahnoss 94

sleep, to κοιμάμαι keemahmeh 143

sleeping bag σάκος ύπνου *m* sahkoss eepnoo 107

sleeping car βαγκόν-λι *nt* vahgonn lee 68, 69

sleeping pill υπνωτικό χάπι *nt* eepnoteeko khahpee 143

sleeve μανίκι *nt* mahneekee 116

slice φέτα *f* fehtah 120

slide *(photo)* σλάιντ *nt* "slide" 124

slip κομπιναιζόν *nt* kombeenehzonn 117

slipper παντόφλα *f* pahndoflah 118

slow αργός ahrghoss 14

slowly αργά ahrghah 11, 21, 135

small μικρός meekross 14, 20, 25, 37, 54, 101, 118, 130

small change ψιλά *nt/pl* pseelah 130

smoke, to καπνίζω kahpneezo 95

smoked καπνιστός kahpneestoss 41, 45

smoker καπνιστής *m* kahpnee**steess** 69

snack σνακ *nt* "snack" 35, 63

snack bar σνακ μπαρ *nt* "snack bar" 66

snap fastener σούστα *f* soostah 117

sneakers αθλητικά παπούτσια *nt/pl* ahthleeteekah pah**poots**eeah 118

snow χιόνι *nt* kheeonnee 94
snow, to χιονίζω kheeonneezo 94
soap σαπούνι *nt* sahpoonee 27, 111
soccer ποδόσφαιρο *nt* podhosfehro 89
sock κάλτσα *f* kahltsah 117
socket υποδοχή πρίζας *f* eepodhokhee preezahss 27
soft drink αναψυκτικό *nt* ahnahpseekteeko 40, 64
sole σόλα *f* sollah 118; *(fish)* γλώσσα *f* ghlossah 44
some μερικά mehreekah 14
someone κάποιος/-α/ο kahpeeoss 95
something κάτι kahtee 29, 36, 54, 108, 112, 113, 125, 138
somewhere κάπου kahpoo 87
son γιός *m* yeeoss 93
song τραγούδι *nt* trahghoodhee 128
soon σύντομα seendommah 15
sore *(painful)* ερεθισμένος ehrehtheezmehnoss 144
sore throat λαιμόπονος *m* lehmopponnoss 140
sorry *(I'm)* συγνώμη seenghnommee 10, 16
sort *(kind)* είδος *nt* eedhoss 86, 120
soup σούπα *f* soopah 43
souvenir σουβενίρ *nt* soovehneer, ενθύμιο *nt* ehntheemeeo 127
souvenir shop κατάστημα σουβενίρ *nt* kahtahsteemah soovehneer 99
spade, to φτυαράκι *nt* fteeahrahkee 128
spare tyre ρεζέρβα *f* rehzehrvah 75
spark(ing) plug μπουζί *nt* boozee 76
speak, to μιλώ meelo 11, 135
special ειδικός eedheekoss 20, 37
special delivery εξπρές ''express'' 132
specialist ειδικός *m/f* eedheekoss 141
speciality σπεσιαλιτέ *nt* spehsseeahleeteh 40, 59
specimen *(medical)* δείγμα *nt* dheeghmah 141
spell, to συλλαβίζω seelahveezo 12
spend, to ξοδεύω ksodhevo 101
spice μπαχαρικό *nt* bahkhahreeko 51
spinach σπανάκι *nt* spahnahkee 50
spine σπονδυλική στήλη *f* spondheeleekee steelee 137
sponge σφουγγάρι *nt* sfoonggahree 111
spoon κουτάλι *nt* kootahlee 36, 61, 107

sport αθλητισμός *m* ahthleeteezmoss 89
sporting goods shop κατάστημα αθλητικών ειδών *nt* kahtahsteemah ahthleeteekonn eedhonn 99
sprain, to στραμπουλίζω strahmbooleezo 139
spring *(season)* άνοιξη *f* ahneeksee 149; *(water)* πηγή *f* peeyee 85
square τετράγωνος tehtrahghonnoss 101
square *(open space)* πλατεία *f* plahteeah 82
squid καλαμάρι *nt* kahlahmahree 44
stadium στάδιο *nt* stahdheeo 82
stain λεκές *m* lehkehss 29
stamp *(postage)* γραμματόσημο *nt* ghrahmahtosseemo 28, 126, 132
star αστέρι *nt* ahstehree, άστρο *nt* ahstro 94
start, to αρχίζω ahrkheezo 80, 87, 88; *(car)* ξεκινώ ksehkeeno 78
starter *(appetizer)* ορεκτικό *nt* orehkteeko 41
station σταθμός *m* stahthmoss 19, 21, 66, 73
stationer's χαρτοπωλείο *nt* khahrtoppolleeo 99, 104
statue άγαλμα *nt* ahghahlmah 82
stay διαμονή *f* dheeahmonnee 31, 92
stay, to μένω mehno 16, 24, 26, 93
steak μπιφτέκι *nt* beeftehkee 46
steal, to κλέπτω klehpto 154
stiff neck στραβολαίμιαση *f* strahvollehmeeahssee 140
sting κέντρισμα *nt* kehndreezmah 138
sting, to κεντρίζω kehndreezo 138
stitch, to ράβω rahvo 29, 118
stock exchange χρηματιστήριο *nt* khreemahteesteereeo 82
stocking κάλτσα γυναικεία *f* kahltsah yeenehkeeah 117
stomach στομάχι *nt* stommahkhee 137
stomach ache πόνος στο στομάχι *m* ponnoss sto stommahkhee 140
stools κόπρανα *nt/pl* koprahnah 141
stop *(bus)* στάση *f* stahssee 72
stop! σταμάτα! stahmahtah 154
stop, to σταματώ stahmahto 21, 69, 71, 72, 73, 154
store κατάστημα *nt* kahtahsteemah 98
straight *(drink)* σκέτος skehtoss 59

straight ahead ίσια **ee**sseeah 21, 77
strange παράξενος pah**rahk**sehnoss
  84
straw *(drinking)* καλαμάκι *nt*
  kahlah**mah**kee 63
strawberry φράουλα *f* **fr**ahoolah 53
street οδός *f* **o**dhoss 25
street map οδηκός χάρτης *m*
  odhee**koss khar**teess 19, 105
string σπάγγος *m* **spahng**goss 105
student φοιτητής/φοιτήτρια *m/f*
  feetee**teess**/feetee**treeah** 82, 93
study, to σπουδάζω spoo**dhah**zo 93
stuffed γεμιστός yehmee**stoss** 41,
  47
subway *(rail)* Ηλεκτρικός *m*
  eelehk**tree**koss 73
sufficient αρκετός ahrkeh**toss** 67
sugar ζάχαρη *f* **zah**khahree 37, 64
suit κουστούμι *nt* koo**stoo**mee 117;
  (woman) ταγιέρ *nt* tahyee**ehr** 117
suitcase βαλίτσα *f* vah**leet**sah 18
summer καλοκαίρι *nt* kahlo**keh**ree
  149
sun ήλιος *m* **ee**leeoss 94
sunburn ηλιακό έγκαυμα *nt* eeleeah**ko**
  ehng**gah**vmah 108
Sunday Κυριακή *f* keeree**ah**kee 150
sunglasses γυαλιά ήλιου *nt/pl*
  yeeah**lee**ah **ee**leeoo 123
sunshade *(beach)* τέντα για τον ήλιο *f*
  tehndah **yee**ah tonn **ee**leeo 91
sunstroke ηλίαση *f* ee**lee**ahssee 140
sun-tan cream κρέμα για τον ήλιο *f*
  krehmah **yee**ah tonn **ee**leeo 111
sun-tan oil λάδι για τον ήλιο *nt*
  lahdhee **yee**ah tonn **ee**leeo 111
super *(petrol)* σούπερ soo**pehr** 75
supermarket σούπερ μάρκετ *nt*
  ''supermarket'' 99
suppository υπόθετο *nt* ee**po**thehto
  109
surfboard κανώ *nt* kah**no** 91
surname επώνυμο *nt* eh**po**nneemo 25
suspenders *(Am.)* τιράντες *f/pl*
  tee**rah**ndehss 117
swallow, to καταπίνω kahtah**pee**no
  142
sweater πουλόβερ *nt* poo**lovv**ehr 117
sweatshirt φανελάκι σπορ *nt*
  fahneh**lah**kee sporr 117
sweet *(food)* γλυκός ghlee**koss** 55,
  58, 61
sweet *(candy)* καραμέλα *f*
  kahrah**meh**lah 126

sweet corn καλαμπόκι *nt*
  kahlahm**bok**kee 49
sweetener ζαχαρίνη *f* zahkhah**ree**nee
  37
swell, to πρήζω pree**zo** 138
swelling πρήξιμο *nt* **preek**seemo
  138
swim, to κολυμπώ kollee**mbo** 90
swimming κολύμπηση *f*
  ko**lee**mbeessee 89
swimming pool πισίνα *f* pee**ssee**nah
  32, 90
swimming trunks μαγιό *nt* mahyee**o**
  117
swimsuit μαγιό *nt* mahyee**o** 117
switch διακόπτης *m* dhee**ah**kopteess
  29
synagogue συναγωγή *f* seenahgho-
  yee 84
synthetic συνθετικός seenthehtee**koss**
  113
system σύστημα *nt* **see**steemah 137

T

table τραπέζι *nt* trah**peh**zee 36, 107
tablet χάπι *nt* **khah**pee 109
tailor's ραφείο *nt* rah**feeo** 99
take, to παίρνω **pehr**no 18, 25, 63,
  72, 102
talcum powder ταλκ *nt* tahlk 111
tampon τάμπο *nt* **tahm**bo 109
tangerine μανταρίνι *nt*
  mahndah**ree**nee 54
tap *(water)* βρύση *f* **vree**ssee 28
tape recorder κασεττόφωνο *nt*
  kahsseh**toff**onno 119
tart πάστα *f* **pah**stah 54
tax φόρος *m* **for**ross 32, 102
taxi ταξί *nt* tah**ksee** 19, 21, 31
tea τσάι *nt* **tsa**hee 38, 60, 64
team ομάδα *f* o**mah**dhah 89
tear, to σχίζω **skhee**zo 139
teaspoon κουταλάκι *f* kootah**lah**kee
  107, 142
telegram τηλεγράφημα *nt*
  teelehgh**rah**feemah 133
telephone τηλέφωνο *nt* tee**leh**fonno
  28, 78, 79, 134
telephone, to τηλεφωνώ teeleh**fonno**
  134
telephone booth τηλεφωνικός
  θάλαμος *m* teelehfonnee**koss**
  thahlahmoss 134
telephone call τηλεφώνημα *nt*
  teeleh**fonn**eemah 136

telephone directory τηλεφωνικός
κατάλογος *m* teelehfonneekoss
kahtahloghoss 134
telephone number αριθμός τηλεφώνου
m ahreethmoss teelehfonnoo 134,
135
telephoto lens τηλεφακός *m*
teelehfahkoss 125
television *(set)* τηλεόραση *f*
teelehorrahssee 28, 119
telex τέλεξ *nt* "telex" 130, 133
tell, to λέγω lehgho 12, 72, 76, 135,
152
temperature θερμοκρασία *f*
thehrmokrahsseeah 90, 141;
(fever) πυρετός *m* peerehtoss 139
ten δέκα dhehkah 146
tendon τένοντας *m* tehnondahss 137
tennis τέννις *nt* "tennis" 89
tennis court γήπεδο του τέννις *nt*
yeepehdho too "tennis"
tennis racket ρακέτα του τέννις *f*
rahkehtah too "tennis" 90
tent σκηνή *f* skeenee 32, 107
tenth δέκατος dhehkahtoss 148
tent peg πάσσαλος *m* pahssahloss
107
tent pole κοντάρι *nt* kondahree 107
term *(word)* έκφραση *f* ehkfrahssee
131
terrace ταράτσα *f* tahrahtsah 36
tetanus τέτανος *m* tehtahnoss 139
than από ahpo 15
thanks ευχαριστώ ehfkhahreesto 10
that εκείνος ehkeenoss 159
the ο, η, το ο, ee, to 159
theatre θέατρο *nt* thehahtro 82, 86
theft κλοπή *f* kloppee 154
their τους tooss 158
then τότε totteh 15
there εκεί ehkee 13
thermometer θερμόμετρο *nt*
thermommehtro 109, 143
these αυτοί/-ές/-ά ahftee 159
they αυτοί/-ές/-ά ahftee 158
thief κλέφτης *m* klehfteess 154
thigh μηρός *m* meeross 137
thin λεπτός lehptoss 113
think, to *(believe)* νομίζω nommeezo
31, 62
third τρίτος treetoss 148
third τρίτο *nt* treeto 148
thirsty, to be διψώ dheepso 13, 35
thirteen δεκατρία dhehkahtreeah 146
thirty τριάντα treeahndah 146

this αυτός ahftoss 159
those εκείνοι/-αι/-α ehkeenee 159
thousand χίλια kheeleeah 147
thread κλωστή *f* klostee 27
three τρία treeah 146
throat λαιμός *m* lehmoss 137, 140
thr out lozenge παστίλλια για το λαιμό
f pahsteeleeah yeeah to lehmo 109
through δια μέσου dheeah mehssoo
15
thunder βροντή *f* vrondee 94
thunderstorm θύελα *f* theeehlah 94
Thursday Πέμπτη *f* pehmptee 150
ticket εισιτήριο *nt* eesseeteereeo 68,
87, 89
ticket office γραφείο εισιτηρίων *nt*
ghrahfeeo eessseeteereeoonn 67
tide *(high)* παλίρροια *f* pahleereeah
90; *(low)* άμπωτη *f* ahmbottee 90
tie γραβάτα *f* ghrahvahtah 117
tight *(clothes)* στενός stehnoss 115
tights καλτσόν *nt* kahltsonn 117
time *(clock)* ώρα *f* orrah 34, 67, 80,
136, 152; *(occasion)* φορά *f* forrah
142, 148
timetable ωράριο *nt* orrahreeo 67
tin *(can)* κουτί *nt* kootee 120
tinfoil αλλουμινόχαρτο *nt*
ahloomeenokhahrto 107
tin opener ανοιχτήρι κονσέρβας *nt*
ahneekhteeree konsehrvahss 107
tint ελαφριά βαφή *f* ehlahfreeah
vahfee 111
tinted φιμέ feemeh 123
tire λάστιχο *nt* lahsteekho 75, 76
tired κουρασμένος koorahzmehnoss 13
tissue *(handkerchief)* χαρτομάντηλο *nt*
khartommahndeelo 111
to *(direction)* προς pross 158
toast τοστ *nt* tost 38
tobacco καπνός *m* kahpnoss 126
tobacconist's καπνοπωλείο *nt*
kahpnoppolleeo 99, 126
today σήμερα seemehrah 29, 150
toilet *(lavatory)* τουαλέττα *f*
tooahlehtah 23
toilet paper χαρτί υγείας *nt* khahrtee
eeyeeahss 111
toiletry καλλυντικά *nt/pl*
kahleendeekah 110
toilets τουαλέττες *f/pl* tooahlehtehss
32, 37, 67
toilet water ω ντε τουαλλέτ *f* o deh
tooahleht 111
toll διόδια *f* dheeodheeah 79

tomato ντομάτα *f* dommahtah 42, 43, 49

tomato juice χυμός ντομάτας *m* kheemoss dommahtahss 60

tomb τάφος *m* tahfoss 82

tomorrow αύριο ahvreeo 29, 136, 150

tongs τσιμπίδα *f* tseembeedhah 107

tongue γλώσσα *f* ghlossah 46, 137

tonic water τόνικ *nt* tonneek 60

tonight απόψε ahpopseh 86, 87, 96

tonsils αμυγδαλές *m/pl* ahmeeghdhahlehss 137

too πάρα πολύ pahrah pollee 14; *(also)* επίσης ehpeesseess 15

tooth δόντι *nt* dhondee 144

toothache πονόδοντος *m* ponnodhondoss 144

toothbrush οδοντόβουρτσα *f* odhondovoortsah 111, 119

toothpaste οδοντόπαστα *f* odhondopahstah 111

torch *(flashlight)* φακός *m* fahkoss 107

tough *(meat)* σκληρός skleeross 61

tour περιοδεία *f* pehreeodheeah 16, 80

tourist office γραφείο τουρισμού *nt* ghrahfeeo tooreezmoo 19, 80

tow truck ρυμουλκό *nt* reemoolko 78

towards προς pross 15

towel πετσέτα *f* pehtsehtah 111

tower πύργος *m* peerghoss 82

town πόλη *f* pollee 19, 21, 76, 105

town hall δημαρχείο *nt* dheemarkheeo 82

toy παιχνίδι *nt* pehkhneedhee 128

toy shop κατάστημα παιχνιδιών *nt* kahtahsteemah pehkneedheeonn 99

tracksuit φόρμα *f* formah 117

traffic light φανάρι *nt* fahnahree 77

trailer τροχόσπιτο *nt* trokhospeeto 32

train τραίνο *nt* trehno 18, 66, 67, 68, 69, 70, 73, 152

tranquillizer ηρεμιστικό *nt* eerehmeesteeko 142

transfer *(bank)* μεταβίβαση *f* mehtahveevahssee 131

transformer μετασχηματιστής *m* mehtahskheemahteesteess 119

translate, to μεταφράζω mehtahfrahzo 12

transport μεταφορά *f* mehtahforrah 74

travel, to ταξιδεύω tahkseedhehvo 93

travel agency πρακτορείο ταξιδίων *nt* prahktorreeo tahkseedheeonn 99

traveller's cheque τράβελερς τσεκ *nt* trahvehlehrs tsehk 18, 62, 102, 129

travelling bag σακβουαγιάζ *nt* sahkvooahyeeahz 18

travel sickness ναυτία *f* nahfteeah 108

treatment θεραπεία *f* thehrahpeeah 142

tree δέντρο *nt* dhehndro 85

trim, to *(beard)* κόβω kovvo 31

trip ταξίδι *nt* tahkseedhee 71, 151

trolley καροτσάκι *nt* kahrotsahkee 18, 70

trousers παντελόνι *nt* pahndehlonnee 117

trout πέστροφα *f* pehstroffah 44

try, to δοκιμάζω dhokkeemahzo 59, 115, 135

T-shirt τι-σερτ *nt* teessehrt 117

tube σωληνάριο *nt* solleenahreeo 120

Tuesday Τρίτη *f* treetee 150

tuna τόννος *m* tonnoss 41, 44

tunny τόννος *m* tonnoss 41, 44

Turkey Τουρκία *f* toorkeeah 145

turkey γαλοπούλα *f* ghahloppoolah 48

turn, to *(change direction)* στρίβω streevo 21, 77

turquoise τουρκουάζ *nt* toorkooahz 122

tweezers τσιμπίδι για φρύδια *nt* tseembeedhee yeeah freedheeah 111

twelve δώδεκα dhodhehkah 146

twenty είκοσι eekossee 146

twice δύο φορές dheeo forrehss 148

twin beds δύο κρεββάτια *nt/pl* dheeo krehvahteeah 23

two δύο dheeo 146

typewriter γραφομηχανή *f* ghrahfommeekhahnee 21

tyre λάστιχο *nt* lahsteekho 75, 76

U

ugly άσχημος ahskheemoss 14, 84

umbrella ομπρέλα *f* ombrehlah 117

uncle θείος *m* theeoss 93

under κάτω από **kahto ahpo** 15
underdone *(meat)* άψητος **ahpseetoss** 61
underground *(railway)* Ηλεκτρικός *m* **eelehtreekoss** 73
underpants σώβρακο *nt* **şovrahko** 117
undershirt φανέλλα εσώρουχο *f* **fahnehlah ehssorookho** 117
understand, to καταλαβαίνω **kahtahlahvehno** 12, 16
undress, to γδύνομαι **ghdheenommeh** 141
university πανεπιστήμιο *nt* **pahneh-peesteemeeo** 82
unleaded χωρίς μόλυβδο *nt* **khorreess molleevdho** 75
unresinated *(wine)* αρετσίνωτος **ahrehtseenottoss** 58
until μέχρι **mehkhree** 15
up επάνω **ehpahno** 15
upset stomach στομαχική ανωμαλία *f* **stommahkheekee ahnommah-leeah** 108
urgent επείγων/-ουσα/-ον **ehpee-ghonn/-oossah/-onn** 13, 144
urine ούρα *nt* **ooro** 141
use χρήση *f* **khreessee** 17
use, to χρησιμοποιώ **khreesseemoppeeo** 78, 134
useful χρήσιμος **khreesseemoss** 15
usual συνηθισμένος **seeneetheezmehnoss** 142

V

vacant ελεύθερος **ehlehfthehross** 14; άδειος/-α/-ο **ahdheoss** 22
vacation διακοπές *f/pl* **dheeahkoppehss** 150, 151
vaccinate, to εμβολιάζω **ehmvolleeahzo** 139
vacuum flask θερμός *m* **thehrmoss** 107
valley κοιλάδα *f* **keelahdhah** 85
value τιμή *f* **teemee** 131
vanilla βανίλια *f* **vahneeleeah** 54
veal μοσχάρι *nt* **moskhahree** 46
vegetable λαχανικόν *nt* **lahkhahneekonn** 40, 43, 49
vegetable store μανάβικο *nt* **mahnahveeko**
vegetarian χορτοφάγος *m/f* **khortofahghoss** 37
vein φλέβα *f* **flehvah** 137
velvet βελούδο *nt* **vehloodho** 114

venereal disease αφροδισιακό νόσημα *nt* **ahfrodheesseeahko nossseemah** 144
vermouth βερμούτ *nt* **vehrmoot** 59
very πολύ **pollee** 15
vest φανέλλα εσώρουχο *f* **fahnehlah ehssorookho** 117, *(Am.) γιλέκο nt* **yeelehko** 117
video cassette βίντεο-κασέττα *f* **veedeho-kahssehtah** 119, 124
video recorder βίντεο *nt* **veedeho** 119
view θέα *f* **thehah** 23, 25
village χωριό *nt* **khorreeo** 76, 85
vinegar ξύδι *nt* **kseedhee** 37
vineyard αμπέλι *nt* **ahmbehlee** 85
visit, to επισκέπτομαι **ehpeeskehptommeh** 84, 95
vitamins βιταμίνες *f/pl* **veetahmeenehss** 109
vodka βότκα *f* **votkah** 59
volleyball βόλεϋ *nt* **vollehee** 89
vomit, to κάνω εμετό **kahno ehmehto** 139

W

waistcoat γιλέκο *nt* **yeelehko** 117
wait, to περιμένω **pehreemehno** 21, 95, 108
waiter σερβιτόρος *m* **sehrveetorross** 36
waiting room αίθουσα αναμονής *f* **ehthoossah ahnahmonneess** 67
waitress σερβιτόρα *f* **sehrveetorrah** 36
wake up, to ξυπνώ **kseepno** 70
Wales Ουαλία *f* **ooahleeah** 145
walk, to περπατώ **pehrpahto** 74, 85
wall τοίχος *m* **teekhoss** 85
wallet πορτοφόλι *nt* **portoffollee** 154
walnut καρύδι *nt* **kahreedhee** 53
want, to *(wish)* θέλω **thehlo** 13
warm ζεστός **zehstoss** 94
wash, to πλένω **plehno** 29, 114
washbasin νιπτήρας *m* **neepteerahss** 28
washing powder σκόνη πλησίματος *f* **skonnee pleesseemahtoss** 107
watch ρολόι *nt* **rolloee** 121, 122
watchmaker's ωρολογοποιείο *nt* **orrologhoppeeeeo** 99, 121
watchstrap μπρασελέ για ρολόι *nt* **brahssehleh yeeah rolloee** 121
water νερό *nt* **nehro** 23, 28, 32, 38, 75, 90

water flask παγούρι nt pahghooree 107

watermelon καρπούζι nt kahrpoozee 53

waterproof αδιάβροχος ahdheeahvrokoss 122

water-ski θαλάσσιο σκι nt thahlahsseeo "ski" 91

wave κύμα nt keemah 90

way δρόμος m dhrommos 76

we (ε)μείς (eh)meess 158

weather καιρός m kehross 94

weather forecast πρόβλεψη καιρού f provlehpsee kehroo 94

wedding ring βέρα f vehrah 122

Wednesday Τετάρτη f tehtahrtee 150

week βδομάδα f vdhommahdhah 16, 20, 24, 80, 150

weekend Σαββατοκύριακο nt sahvahtokkeereeahko 20, 150

well καλά kahlah 9, 115, 139

well-done (meat) καλοψημένος kahlopseemehnoss 47

west δύσι dheessee 77

what τι tee 11

wheel τροχός m trohkhoss 78

when πότε potteh 11

where που poo 11

which ποιος/ποια/ποιο peeoss/peeah/peeo 11

whisky ουίσκι nt "whisky" 59

white άσπρος ahspross 58, 113

who ποιος peeoss 11

why γιατί yeeahtee 11

wick φιτίλι nt feeteelee 126

wide φαρδύς/-ιά/-ί fahrdheess 118

wide-angle lens ευρυγώνιος φακός m ehvreeghonneeoss fahkoss 125

wife γυναίκα f yeenehkah 93

wig περούκα f pehrookah 111

wind άνεμος m ahnehmoss 94

window παράθυρο nt pahrahtheero 28, 36, 68; (shop) βιτρίνα f veetreenah 100, 112

windscreen/shield παρ-μπριζ nt pahrbreez 122

wine κρασί nt krahssee 40, 57, 58, 61, 64, 127

wine merchant's οινοπωλείο nt eenoppolleeo 99

winter χειμώνας m kheemonnahss 149

viper καθαριστήρας nt kahthahreesteerahss 76

windsurfer γουϊντσέρφερ nt "windsurfer" 91

wish ευχή f ehfkhee 151

with με meh 15

withdraw, to (bank) σηκώνω seekonno 130

without χωρίς khorreess 15

woman γυναίκα f yeenehkah 115

wonderful υπέροχος eepehrokhoss 96

wood (forest) δάσος nt dhahssoss 85

wool μαλλί nt mahlee 114

word λέξη f lehksee 12, 15, 133

work, to (function) λειτουργώ leetoorgho 28; δουλεύω doolehvo 119

worse χειρότερος kheerottehross 14

wound πληγή f pleeyee 138

wrap, to τυλίσσω teeleesso 103

wristwatch ρολόι χεριού nt rolloee khehreeoo 122

write, to γράφω ghrahfo 12, 101

writing paper χαρτί αλληλογραφίας nt kahrtee ahleeloghrahfeeahss 27

wrong λανθασμένος lahnthahzmehnos 14

X
X-ray (photo) ακτινογραφία f ahkteenoghrahfeeah 139

Y
year χρόνος m khronnoss 148

yellow κίτρινος keetreenoss 113

yes ναι neh 10

yesterday χθες khthehss 150

yet ακόμη ahkommee 15, 16, 24

yield, to (traffic) δίνω πρωτοπορεία dheedho prottopporeeah 79

yoghurt γιαούρτι nt yeeahoortee 38, 64

you εσύ ehssee, εσείς ehsseess 158

young νέος/-α/-ο nehoss 14

your σου soo, σας sahss 158

youth hostel ξενώνας νεότητος m ksehnonnahss nehotteetoss 22

Yugoslavia Γιουγκοσλαβία f yeeoonggoslahveeah 145

Z
zero μηδέν meedehn 146

zip(per) φερμουάρ nt fehrmooahr 117

zoo ζωολογικός κήπος m zo-oloyeekoss keeposs 82

zoology ζωολογία f zo-olloyeeah 83

Ελληνικό ευρετήριον